# THE P CR1ME: A STORY OF TRUTH OR FANTASY

BY
PETER HINDLEY
AND
SUSAN GOODSELL

*To Anton
with best wishes
Peter H
6.4.2014*

The contents of this work including, but not limited to, the accuracy of events, people and places depicted, opinions expressed, permission to use previously published material included: and any advice given or actions advocated are solely the responsibility of the authors, who assumes all liability for said work and indemnifies the publisher against any claims stemming from publication of the work.

This is Non-Fictional work. The names, characters, incidents, places, and locations are real and true to fact.

**5 PRINCE PUBLISHING AND BOOKS, LLC**
PO Box 16507
Denver, CO 80216
www.5PrinceBooks.com

Print ISBN 13:978-1-939217-63-9
ISBN 10:1-939217-63-6

The Perfect Crime: A Story of Truth or Fantasy
Peter Hindley and Susan Goodsell
Copyright Peter Hindley and Susan Goodsell
Published by 5 Prince Publishing

Cover Art by Viola Estrella

All rights reserved. No part of this book may be used or reproduced in any manner whatsoever without written permission, except in the case of brief quotations, reviews, and articles. For any other permission please contact 5 Prince Publishing and Books, LLC.

Second Edition/Second Printing May 2013 Printed U.S.A.

5 PRINCE PUBLISHING AND BOOKS, LLC.

# ACKNOWLEDGMENTS

Our profound gratitude goes out to all those, who, with their help and contributions to our true account of my brother, Alan Hindley's, death, and events that led up to that and what has followed as a result, they have all, by their actions, given us the fuel to compile this exposé; an exposé that we feel is in the public's interest to read. Every contributor has, in their way, made it possible to complete our work of recording what happened in this case. But as you read what follows, please bear in mind that this is not an isolated example of what can go wrong; this is happening daily in the United Kingdom.

Firstly I personally must thank my late cousin, Win, for her help with the initial section; her help and encouragement was invaluable when I started this project. Secondly, my thanks goes to Susan, my niece and the daughter of my late brother, Alan; for she has contributed thousands of hours of work, research and thought; not to mention the hundreds of hours of discussions we have had while analysing what has actually occurred. She has become, over time, more and more involved in the writing and editing of this book: Her family must also be thanked for they have been so patient and understanding throughout the long process of creating this edition.

But we need to thank those people from various walks of life who by their actions, no matter whether they have helped or hindered, for they have contributed, without them, there would be no story to tell.

Let's move on to the instigators of the plot; let me start by mentioning those key people, starting with Alan's widow, Wendy Hindley, who is a prime player, if it were not for her desire to ignore her late husband's Last Will and Testament, for whatever reason, and bypass myself and

Susan as the other two named executors, there would not be a tale to tell. The next worthy of a mention is the casual gardener, David Hart, who played his part in so many ways as you will discover as the story develops; and develops it certainly does. Joan Tabram must also have a mention, for she was Alan's mistress and confident in the years before, and up to, the time of his demise. These three were all involved from the start; these are the characters at the birth of the saga.

The list explodes from there and is too great to mention and remain interesting here, but they include many members of what I will call the British Establishment; they include the Devon and Cornwall Constabulary, some of the Kent Constabulary. Numerous British Government Ministers and their minions have given us 'hours of pleasure' (sorry I slipped from the truth) fuel for the book. The solicitors who have been involved in this case and the governing bodies that set the standards of the solicitors: The various other sections of the British Establishment who have proved themselves to be what they are. There have been few honourable people who have helped: Irrespective of the outcome we must thank them all, no matter whom, for their contribution.

Dedicated to Luke and Jake
Alan's two grandsons that he loved
and wished the fruits of his life's toils to benefit

# INTRODUCTION

I started this book 9 years ago in 2002 with the death of my brother, Alan Hindley. I knew at the time things were not running their normal course, but was unsure what exactly was taking place. This was certainly not the first time I had experienced death at close quarters; I had experienced the demise of many close to me; perhaps that is the price of being the youngest of the family.

It was obvious that something unusual was happening, and I felt it was important enough to start recording the events. Writing anything other than business letters was, in fact, foreign to me, although I had needed to record what happened during a long and difficult divorce; that stood me in good stead for what was to come. The writing of what is, firstly, an accurate record of events that happened, secondly, an exposé of how easily the British system can go awry, and once events take that route, how the bureaucracy will stay on the same path for fear of exposing their brethren's inadequacies. The result has given Susan, my niece, and daughter of my late brother, and myself, an incredible voyage of discovery; not one I would want myself or wish for others, but in publishing the tale it may, and I certainly hope it does, ultimately prevent anybody else having a similar experience. Meanwhile, it is important for people to know what can, and does happen; this is an extreme example of what can go wrong, but you should know this it is not an isolated case.

The record of events that surround Alan's death grew and grew as more was disclosed, until it became obvious that the simple notes made at the time became a short story; then that developed into a book.

While working on the first draft of the book I was aided by my late cousin, Win, who would read each chapter as they were finished, and give her suggestions for any changes that would improve or clarify the writing.

Publishing the story happened because Susan and I thought it was in the public's interest to know the truth of what can happen, and did happen, to us: By this time we were fully aware that the British Police and Government could easily prevent such a disclosure being published in the media, especially the press; the establishment would not wish our story to be exposed, as it reveals too much of the way they work. We needed to find a method over which they had no control. It was during one of our telephone discussions that the seed of the idea of using the Internet was born. It must be said that at the time, neither of us knew what we were doing, but as has happened so many times during this journey, we were soon to be given the information and tools for our task. Within days, I had heavily edited the original book in preparation for the web site, and sites were in place ready for the story: Little did we know that those sites would grow, as additions were added, ultimately as developments happened, and be read around the world by hundreds of thousands of people. Readers asked for more, and for a printed book, so we have done that. Susan and I have worked to edit the original book, as parts had become obsolete through events and discoveries, to edit the articles published on the web, and to add new material that had previously been excluded from both.

The result of this amalgamation is what you are about to read. The subject matter is serious; it could not be more so; the story is true and accurate, every effort has been made to make it so; but it is also, hopefully, amusing and entertaining. After all, even in the grimmest of circumstances, humour can, and must be found.

# PREFACE

We have accurately recorded the events near the time of Alan Hindley's death, who was a brother to Peter, and the father of Susan, the two authors of this account, and what followed; they combine, to reveal an intriguing story. Did he die naturally, or was he helped in some way? Has a crime or two taken place? Some may think so. Maybe there is a conspiracy; my lawyer certainly thought so; how far that conspiracy extends is unclear. We are certain that nothing is quite as it should be. Nevertheless this account shows a fascinating view of human nature, English society and the workings of the establishment in the United Kingdom. The story is so bizarre that it could well be fiction, and that is why I have added "A story of truth or fantasy" to the title. What is frightening is that it is all **absolutely true.**

The normal formalities that follow a death were not adhered to after Alan's demise: Why the mandatory procedures were bypassed may not be evident, but during the course of our nine year account they certainly do become evident.

Why did his wife act as she did, and who aided her? These and so many other questions will become apparent.

In this case, what is certain now is that the will and wishes of the deceased, Alan Edward Hindley of Paignton, Devon, has not been adhered to, and the UK law and establishment did nothing to aid its rectification: The laws relating to Wills are fatally flawed, and the government is fully aware of that. As named executors we have been denied the right to execute his wishes. You may think this is not possible, but it is, and it has proved to be absolutely legal.

His wife, Wendy, acted as sole executor of her husband's Last Will and Testament without the other two named executors, and we reveal how simple it is to do just that. Why she felt this was necessary will ultimately be disclosed. You will learn how the solemn duty of executing a will can be mal administered in a totally legal way, and without fear of retribution.

We have experienced many twists and turns along our path of discovery, and these have been reflected in both the different styles, and structure of the book. Our journey has taken us to numerous office doors, and has led us into the heart of the halls of government, where events have made it very apparent that what we were witnessing was true injustice, and unchecked corruption within the United Kingdom. It is for this reason that we felt it necessary to pen our story, to be able to share our account with you and all our other readers, who have been reading an abridged account on the Internet since May 2008; it is very much in the public's interest to be aware of what can go wrong, and does go very wrong daily.

We have been told that Alan died in his home during the evening of 14th March 2002, in more than one place, and all on the same night, the last time anything vaguely like this happened was two thousand years ago (please forgive the last statement, it is not meant to offend); but first a little background information about the family.

# CHAPTER 1

The year was 2002 and it all started with a telephone call. My brother, Alan, had telephoned to ask me if I could get a copy of the family tree. That would sound ordinary enough to most people, but that particular request from my older brother could not be further from a normal occurrence, it instantly rang major alarm bells for me. To understand my acute concern at this request you need to know something of his background.

Alan was born just before Christmas of 1937 and therefore was nearly 10 years my senior. We were the only two children of older parents. Each of our parents was one of 10 siblings, as were their parents. Well, there was no television and little birth control if we go back to their era.

We had both known hard times. Alan was brought up through the Second World War, and me; I came during the baby boom that followed the great upheaval. Both of us experienced the hardships of rationing, and of having little money. Dad worked at Woolwich Arsenal on munitions, not a highly paid job, and he also lost some of those precious resources by betting on the horses. Mum made a calling out of being ill, although, she did work once I was old enough to be left, initially as a domestic cleaner, and gradually worked her way up via several jobs, until she became a clerical assistant in the civil service. As for me, I was a weedy, sickly child with asthma, medically drugged as a result, for my first 15 years or so.

Amongst our many Aunts and Uncles there was acute rivalry, constantly they crossed swords, and it was, for some, an all out war. I was always aware of the bickering and the feuding that lasted until they expelled their last breaths.

Thinking of my first memories, I recall the last time I saw my Grandmother, who lived with my Aunt Doll and Uncle Dick at Southbourne; I was sent there for virtually all holidays as a child. This scraggy little urchin was sent alone on the train with a carriage label tied to my school jacket lapel. The railway guard would set me off the train at the right station until I grew old enough to manage unaided. My change of clothes would have already been sent in a cardboard shoebox by post.

I think I must have had psychic abilities from a very early age because I can recall, (I must have been about eight years old at the time) it was the end of one holiday as I was leaving to return home. Gran was standing by the kitchen door, waving goodbye, and as I looked back for the final wave, I simply knew it would be the last time I would ever see her. My intuition proved to be correct, for within a few days I was told she had passed away peacefully in her sleep. That was my first recollection of any paranormal abilities.

Returning to those fore mentioned family feuds, some of them were induced by those that I call the vultures in the family, those who grabbed all they could at every opportunity, especially when there had been a death, and the picking plentiful, they were there to be found. After one of my grandparents passed away; an Aunt and Uncle who were wealthy enough, at that time, to have a car, loaded it with spoils before the funeral so their departure, after the ceremony, would not be delayed.

I was too young to be fully aware of what was really happening at the time, but the story was related to me occasionally over the years that followed. Alan, of course being older, was able to witness this, and so much more, first hand. All this grabbing made him resolve to have no part of anything of the sort. He hated anything to do with the politics of Wills and other people's belongings.

Because of his exposure to the bickering in his earlier years, Alan had decided that he would have nothing to do with the extended family, and that is how he lived his life; he had made no contact, or shown interest in any relations outside the immediate family. Once Alan became of an age whereby he was fully independent, he severed contact with all, except the closest, and he showed total lack of interest in family matters, which continued until that phone conversation requesting the family tree.

To give a more recent example of Alan's attitude to family matters, I resumed contact with Cousin Malcolm, after a 30-year break that I had instigated when I tried to talk with Alan about Malcolm, he ignored me, and it took me several attempts before I finally made Alan discuss the reunion. This is why I was so alarmed by his request. I think it is important to establish Malcolm's relationship with Alan and myself. We are cousins, but try if you will to get to grips with his little family anomaly; Malcolm's relationship to us is slightly unusual, his mother's brother was our father, and his father's sister was our mother. Do not feel embarrassed if it takes the use of a pencil and paper to fully comprehend the relationship.

It was Malcolm who held the family Bible and the family tree, which his father had researched and revised. It was here where I went to request a copy for Alan. Unfortunately, because of Malcolm's domestic chaos at the time, there was a delay. There followed several phone conversations when I told Alan that I was trying to get a copy of the family tree for him. Regrettably the tree was not in my possession until the weekend after his funeral.

I was taken aback as the last conversation my brother and I had was somewhat strained, I felt as if I had annoyed Alan, although on reflection, that could not have been the case. Perhaps his attitude was more akin to the distancing that people, who are about to die, do to their close loved ones.

The next phone call I received was from Devon, where Alan lived, it came from David Hart, who told me that my brother had died. You will learn more of that in the fullness of time.

With Alan's request for the family tree and the last, almost aggressive conversation I had with him, my brother's death was not altogether unexpected. What followed after certainly was.

# CHAPTER 2

Taking a step back, I think it is important to go to those years before I was on the scene.

There were many stories repeated in the family about 'that' brother of mine.

Before his school days he was a lively child with spirit; a child who enjoyed making mischief, and was good at it.

He was healthy and intelligent; winning prizes, mainly books, at school as I remember, and Mother told me that there were some prizes that were withheld from Alan to enable other pupils to benefit. Although in recent years he told me that his achievements were poor, as was the school. Nevertheless, I can remember some of those volumes at home, and the dedications written on the flyleaf by the school.

One of the few stories about Alan's time at school relates to an unusual way of earning pocket money, he would buy and sell comics for the odd penny, but that was not the source of income that comes to mind here. The talent he used to gain that little extra was one we also laughed about in later years.

'Find the Lady' is the game he used. A card trick whereby three playing cards, one being a queen, were rearranged rapidly, face down, and then the punter, or in this case, a classmate, would try to identify which was the queen, and place a bet on the selection.

Sounds harmless enough, but for Alan, he found he had an advantage over his friends, he could see through the card and identify the lady. He earned quite well with this until mother discovered what he was actually doing, and forbade the use of this talent, and, to cement the message to desist, gave him a clip round the ear.

That ended Alan's dealings with the paranormal for many years.

Our grandparents must have seen a lot of him, or they certainly must have felt they had. Granddad was on the receiving end of many practical jokes. I do not know how Alan did it, but there was an occasion when he managed to tie Granddad to the cold water tank in his loft; another when he locked him in the chicken run at the bottom of his garden in Woolwich, and, the one prank that appealed to me most of all, was when Alan tied Granddad's shoelaces to the chair when he was sleeping. Then, from the other side of the room Alan cried out for granddad to follow him quickly; Granddad woke from his nap; he sprung to his feet, and fell apex over base as a result of being tethered to the chair. This may have lead to Granddad's downfall, but I would expect Alan might have had another spanking.

Gran did not escape the pranks. One day she had Alan help her shuck the peas, and when they had finished, he asked her whether they were all done; on her confirmation of the finished task, he up ended the contents of the colander, sending the peas in all directions across the floor.

Air guns were also useful to my brother, at best for target practice with pellets. Beetroot was used as a projectile on one occasion, when he dappled an Aunt's bed sheets that were drying on her washing line. He must have been a very popular child.

The best pranks came much later as far as I was concerned.

As I mentioned earlier, Dad worked with munitions, and sometimes, inadvertently, brought live bullets home. These he left in the shed and Alan would empty the explosive onto the ground, or elsewhere, and ignite it; the odd bang or rumble was not that unusual. Bullets sometimes flew.

Let me set the scene; the shed was made of pre-cast concrete, as was the council house we lived in at the time. Not pretty by today's standards, but very functional and well planned. The shed formed part of a block containing an outside toilet and coal bunker, a corrugated asbestos roof covered the lot, and extended beyond the coal shed to form a shelter from the elements. Well, on one particular day Alan surpassed himself, he must have been saving the bullets for a while, and I do not know how he did it, but I remember clearly what happened. He had been in the shed for a while and was quiet, dangerously quiet. Always, throughout his life, being quiet was a warning that something was about to happen. He emerged from the shed and closed the door behind himself. He had a smile on his face (another sign of trouble to come) and a chuckle slipped almost unnoticed from his lips; there followed a powerful thud! The entire length of the roof, about twenty-foot in length, lifted into the air, just a few inches, then settled back onto the walls that formally supported it. Smoke emanated from the grooves, not a lot, it was like a grey sigh from the corrugations in the roof. The neighbour, whose similar utility block was attached to ours, and whose roof also lifted, said nothing.

Strangely enough, nothing was said by anyone as I recall, but we joked about it.

His hatred of the establishment will also become clear, and there will be anecdotes along the way to illustrate how he would do anything to buck (or something that sounds similar) the system whenever he could.

The two years with the Royal Engineers doing his National Service was hell for him, and not too pleasant for those in command I suspect. This was still obligatory and was not uneventful. Part of his time was spent in Germany doing aerial photography. It is quite probable that this was spy photography, as he was certainly debriefed severely on his final trip home, which did not please him.

As he did not want this army duty imposed by the state, he made them very aware of his existence. He had his room cleaned and his bed was made; this he achieved by telling them that the dust aggravated his breathing condition, something at that time he did not have, but he was able to imitate after observing my symptoms.

He overstayed his leave one weekend, and as a result phoned a dentist friend to see whether he could help. On the phone the dentist said he could do nothing, but it was not long before he arrived at home, whisked Alan to his surgery and removed a wisdom tooth or two, stitching the hole to accent the extent of the damage. The extraction prevented the charge of absent without leave, and when he was back in Germany, the dentist told him that he must have had a rough time with the extraction while removing the stitches. I would love to have seen Alan's reaction at such a comment. I doubt whether he even blinked.

Alan was a first class freelance photographer before he was enlisted, and had a thriving business doing all types of work, including weddings that were at that time, before cameras became generally affordable and easy to use, very lucrative. As a child, I can remember going back to one reception in North Woolwich with the proofs to get the orders, not that I did any of this as I was too young, but the folks had to do something with me. The bride's name was Blossom, and I can recall that this was the first Blossom I had met, and certainly at over 300 pounds the biggest bloom.

There were also photographs for the press and commercial work. Home was never dull, as there was a constant flow of people, his associates and friends.

To aid Alan's work, I lost my bedroom; it was converted into a professional darkroom, complete with all the equipment and chemicals needed at that time for processing black and white photographs. Colour printing, as we know it today, was not available; it was done by manually tinting a black and white print that had the colours written onto it with a pencil. Someone would set to work with a paintbrush to give the photograph a pale hint of colour.

The bathroom was frequently commandeered as well, to rinse the chemicals from the photographs before they were finally dried. This was interesting for me, as you never knew what images you would find in the large enamel tray laying in the bath. It could be a famous actress, semi-clad, a motor race at Brands Hatch with cars spinning off the track, or a bottle of 100 Aspirins enlarged to stand 2 foot tall, even a flattering picture of Blossom.

Victor Blackman, who was originally Alan's math teacher at school, and later, became a friend, left teaching to work on the Daily Express as a photographer, and these two got themselves into many scrapes, especially if they could get that special picture to sell to the papers. For a very modest example: Vic would, during their visits to Brands Hatch for motor racing, position himself at the most dangerous corner to be able to get the most spectacular shots of a car spinning or crashing out of control, heading straight towards him. In fact there was an award-winning photograph at the time with Vic clearly fleeing from the path of a racing car which had left the track.

It was not unusual for the police to arrive at home to ask how these two would be able to get to the scene of a motor accident, or other incidents, before the police. The lads always had an answer ready, although with hindsight, I doubt whether they were believed. Perhaps someone may have been listening to the police radio. No doubt there were many other tales to tell, but they did not tell the little brother much.

While the darkroom was operational I had to share Alan's bedroom. That for the most part was fine, but there was the odd occasion when my older brother had been drinking, not always modestly. I would sometimes be woken by, well whatever you would expect from a big brother who had one or two too many sherbets; use your own imagination.

He also would talk loudly in his sleep that worried me in case I did the same to reveal some dark secret: strange, as I was a sweet little boy who had none. That's the worst of being so innocent and perfect!!

Alan made it his ambition to retire at 40.

His photography business also went; partially as a result of the advent of cheap cameras being used by people to take their own wedding snaps. Colour photography may also have had its influence. As I found out in later years, Alan was colour blind.

Once he finished his enforced stint in the army, his life changed direction. He married and had two children.

Alan's first marriage ended with a very ugly divorce, in which both partners used whatever they could as ammunition against the other. During some of this period, I was working with my brother, and for two years, observed the situation.

Both he and his wife Marion were forceful personalities, and the legal battle for a settlement and access to the children must have left all involved parties scarred.

Marion endeavoured to stop Alan from having access to his daughters; the legal fight resulted in the courts granting him 2 hours a month supervised access to his children, within the Maidstone area. Watching his anguish during the week before, and the weeks that followed each visit with his children was terrible. I suspect that Marion may have told the girls bad things about their father, as they sometimes reacted badly when they saw him. The overall effect of this arrangement on his health became very obvious. I can clearly recall the conversation I had with my brother, when I reluctantly advised him to stop these monthly visits in order to lessen the damage to the girls and himself. I told him that I felt sure the children, who were quite young at this time, would, once they obtain their independence, seek out their father and build a good relationship.

Susan was the older of the two daughters of my brother from his first marriage; she has inherited her spirit from both strong-minded parents; quite tall, slim, dark haired and a hint of olive skin from her mother's Italian forebears.

About fifteen years passed before Susan was to seek out her father. Unannounced, Susan knocked on Alan's door early one morning in Devon, and it was answered by Wendy, who told her that Alan was still in bed and to call back later when Alan, who was not a morning person, was about. You can picture the turmoil that ensued once the door was closed; after all it had been many years that Susan and Alan had any contact.

It was David, Susan's boyfriend at that time, who had encouraged Susan to seek out her father and joined her on her pilgrimage. He was an ordinary lad, but underneath his almost rough exterior hid a very genuine soul, who had himself been a victim of family problems. Once Susan and her father had re-established contact, they kept in touch and the strength of their relationship increased and flourished.

Sadly, that was not to be the case with her younger sister Tina, who, as a result of Susan's actions, made contact with Alan. Although I have not seen Tina since she was a babe in arms, I recall how she seemed tranquil and less spirited than her sister. I have spoken to her only once on the phone since she became an adult.

Tina's renewed relationship with her father was to be short-lived. Alan had encouraged her to return to studying, and offered to accommodate her if she were to take her tuition in Devon. All was going well until one day I had a phone call from my older brother, he was in quite a state, and he was asking my advice. This exchange may be an ordinary event in most families, but not for us. Alan had been independent for as long as I can remember; he just did not ask anybody what to do. This was a very rare occurrence.

The phone call went something like this:

"Hello Peter, Can you help? I have just had Tina here; she was going to move in while she studied down here. But she turned up with her boyfriend and I have turned them away. He was a very much older man; he looks like a pensioner. She wanted him to move in as well; I knew nothing of this. Do you think I have done the right thing?" He sounded vexed, angry and confused.

My swiftly considered reply was "It is your house and you can do exactly as you wish." Having an evil sense of humour I could see the funny side of the situation, but this was not the time to laugh. Alan was earnestly asking for help. I continued, "If I had been put in your situation I would have done the same."

It transpires that Tina's partner was many years her senior, and had run off, if run is the right expression, with Tina. Abandoning his wife; he took with him their life savings, a sum that Alan thought was little more than housekeeping money. This came to light when Alan was contacted by the old boy's son, who was angry with Alan for encouraging this new relationship; the son complained because there was no money available to feed 'the old lady.'

Tina did complete her studies elsewhere and has a good job as a result; she also has two children by this partner.

To quote another person who knew the difference in the ages of the couple: "I wonder who helped him sire the children?"

Susan had also been foolish, she had, with her friends in Clapham where she was living at the time, been dabbling in the occult. This started quite innocently by experimenting with the Ouija board. On the several occasions throughout my life that I tried it, it all sounded harmless enough, but I fear that there is a darker side to this. I would actively discourage anyone from trying it.

This brief account is based on what Alan told me. Initially they were fascinated by the Ouija board, but that was to change as the compulsion to use it increased. Then strange things started to happen; for example faces would appear in mirrors, misfortunes would be foretold and come to pass. On one particular evening the group were due to meet for another session on the board, but a couple decided not to go. Strangely enough, at the allotted time, all these friends met, even those who had decided against going. That may not seem that unusual, but in reality; the reluctant folk had arrived without the passage of time and in their Ford Capri. Not that unusual normally, but consider if you will, the car was in the process of being repaired and had no cylinder head to the engine; it's engine could not work in that condition. Consequentially a problem was created; they had to subsequently get the unpowered vehicle back from whence it came.

It was as these paranormal happenings were getting out of hand that Susan contacted her father for advise and help; she had already been to the church and been told it was her imagination that was at work and to go away.

Alan started talking to his friends in Devon and he found help. It transpired that, unknown to him; many of his companions were practising as spiritualists, or involved in the paranormal arts. They did not take Susan's plight lightly, and Alan turned to them for solace. John, a powerful medium whose path I was later to cross, was amongst those who came to Alan's aid.

This strange series of events became the trigger that sparked Alan's investigations into paranormal phenomena.

Alan was someone whose logic or way of thinking was not conventional. This became very apparent to me during the two years working with him at his frozen meat business. For me it was an education, to closely observe someone whose approach to business and life was so unorthodox. It is very difficult to think of an example that would illustrate his reality, but it may become obvious as this story unfolds.

He tried several avenues to earn money, which ultimately resulted in him butchering, turning carcasses into frozen meat products, and shrink-wrapped what he sold too many grocery shops across the south east. He had worked for a while selling frozen meat products from a van to village shops; when he realised he was earning too much money for the boss, he set up on his own. This business flourished for several years. By the time Alan's fortieth birthday neared, he had established himself in a corner shop in a village not far from Maidstone. The premises had room enough for the processing of the meat, and the freezers for storage. A small fleet of vans distributed the pre-packed chops, joints, sausages, beef burgers etc. that was produced throughout Kent and south-east London.

The business had expanded to include several frozen food shops, these proved for the large part, unprofitable. Some managers and staff were less than honest, fiddling in some cases, more than the shops were taking in sales, until their exploits were exposed and they were ousted.

Alan sold his business as his fortieth year approached, but I fear he did not benefit as greatly as he might as it was during a period of a sharp financial recession. Nevertheless, Alan and his second wife, Wendy, decided to take their cabin cruiser from the river Medway in Kent through the canals of France into the Mediterranean. The preparation of the boat for the journey took several months, but once completed they were on their way to warmer climates. They had many adventures en route.

They returned to England for Christmas leaving the boat in Malta, it had been taken out of the water and placed on chocks on the quayside. Unfortunately a ferocious storm struck over the New Year that wrenched the boat from her supports, seriously damaging the keels. Alan was not reassured by the methods used locally to reinstate the keels, and he feared that if they came adrift at any time at sea, the boat would fill with water and sink. He disposed of her.

It was then that Wendy and Alan decided that Devon would be the place for them to live; Alan loved the rolling countryside, green fields and coastline.

Alan and Wendy had been living in Devon for a while, and they had also been living in yet another place that they were converting into flats. This one was a substantial end of terrace house built around the turn of the twentieth century. Red bricks faced the external wall of this typical property for the area. The layout, as I remember, was as you would have expected, an entrance hall and two main reception rooms, were on the ground floor, the front room having a two bend bay window, and a back extension for the kitchen and services. On the floor above were the bedrooms, a bathroom and separate WC. The landing had a small steep staircase to the roof space above, which may have had other rooms, but I can only presume, as I never went up to see.

I was married at this time and my wife, Brenda, and I had been invited to stay for a long weekend. The conversion was still unfinished, there was obviously no building rubble about at this stage, but the furnishings were, shall we say, incomplete and sparse. This did not worry us as we had come to see my brother and his wife, not the house. They were living on the ground floor in the flat that they had created and we were given the run of the flat on the floor above.

There is little more I can recall about this place except for our first night there. It was an ordinary night, nothing memorable. What had happened that day was nothing unusual. Probably just motoring down to the West Country and sitting, chatting with our hosts, catching up on the news until exhaustion took over, we fell into bed and slept. Brenda and I were settled for the night.

I felt Brenda's sharp elbow digging repeatedly into my ribs in her effort to wake me.

She said "Peter, the door keeps banging. Can you stop it?"

I listened for a while, and yes, the door was banging; it was not stormy or windy, there was nothing obvious to cause the door to move. Bleary eyed I groped around the room and spied Brenda's handbag. The term handbag is a loose description; it was more a suitcase that held all but the kitchen sink. That will do nicely, I thought, so I placed it against the door to hold it shut and returned, content, to my slumber.

That is what I thought anyway. Once again I was aroused from my much-needed beauty sleep by those prodding elbows, and the complaint that the door was banging again. The handbag had not resolved the problem; nevertheless, I tried again to move it into a better position to stop the noise before resuming that badly needed therapy, sleep.

Guess what? I was wakened yet again and again. This was becoming boring. Finally I summoned up those precious brain resources in the early hours to beat the banging. It was not a windy night and I could not be bothered to have some simple spectre interrupting my night. This time the handbag was wedged between the doorframe, and the door and a chair lodged on the other side. That kit bag would not be moved easily by anything; after all, I had risked a rupture by lifting it. Mission accomplished I returned to bed knowing that I would have no more interruptions. I was out as my head hit the pillow. Peace at last.

Next morning I was confronted by a very agitated partner, she had not been able to sleep. After the door had been wedged and I had returned to my slumber, she had heard a long "Whoosh" noise followed by the feeling of something brushing across her face. From then she had buried her face beneath the sheets, worried and wide-awake until breakfast time.

It was over breakfast that we were told that Alan could not sleep on that floor, or for that matter, he would feel very uncomfortable if he had to go to the cupboard under the stairs that lead to the attic area, it was deadly cold.

Wendy had not escaped either as she told us how the toilet door would fly open at any time. It may not be the best selling feature for the flat, but it could be useful if you are in the WC and having a problem.

This was our first and last night staying at this house. Brenda would not stay another night in that house; we left that day.

Various properties were bought, renovated and sold over time by Alan and Wendy; one such place was the workshop in Cecil Road. This was an old building with daub and wattle walls, basically cow dung and straw, very uneven and thick. This building had, over the centuries, many owners, and at times been several cottages that were thatched. Two large fireplaces were in place when it was bought, but one collapsed during renovation.

At the time of its acquisition the building consisted of two open floors used as a workshop, with a small courtyard at the rear, and to the rear of the adjacent cottages, there was another area which was covered with a rambling, corrugated roof, large enough to garage several cars.

This roof was unsightly and in poor repair, but it took a fight with the local council to get the needed permission to remove it. They pleaded in court that the removal of the roof would have a detrimental effect on the local areas' solids and voids. Alan won his case and the roof was dismantled and eventually replaced with a small house and car parking spaces. The main building was extended and converted into a house; 50 Cecil Road was where they lived for years.

It was on another visit with my wife to see my brother when he lived on Cecil Road that I was to meet some of his psychic friends; my first real exposure to those who study and practice the arts.

Alan and Wendy had invited some of their friends. There were at least eight of us, but there was plenty of room for us to distribute ourselves. The living room is large, almost a double cube in shape, with a low beamed ceiling; at one end the local stone fireplace almost fills the wall and there is an ancient wooden beam spanning the wide opening for the hearth, the walls were thick and uneven. This part of the house dated back many hundreds of years and Alan had once shown me the original deeds, written on vellum. They were amused that these fragile documents revealed that the house was once owned by a Jasper Carrot, not the comedian that we know today, this was a very old Carrot from another century.

There were always lots of paranormal activity here with entities treating the place like they owned it; at times it could be as busy as Piccadilly Circus. None were hostile; one would, nightly, rattle the biscuits in the tin Alan kept by his bed. Perfectly natural for that house and the present owners find the spirits very reassuring, they would not like to be without their visitors.

Once we were introduced we all sat around talking. I can recall a short man that they called 'Jetlag John.' He gained the nickname as follows: John was on a flight and he was not happy. He did not like flying and this was a turbulent trip. Being a spiritualist he called on his guide for help. This spirited spirit had a sense of humour, for John said "I am not happy here; get me out of this plane." Being a loyal aid the spirit did just that and immediately John felt himself outside the plane, but he felt worse! He had been deposited on the wing and could hear little above the laughter of his guide. "OK get me inside." John ordered his companion and that request was granted. The rest of the journey passed smoothly and he felt quite comfortable for the remainder of the journey; but this is an indication of what may happen if you wish for something. John asked to be outside the aircraft and that is exactly what he got. I did not think Jetlag John was a very powerful medium, although he is called in to exorcise poltergeists and the like from peoples' homes, and has even been broadcast on television.

This evening he was with his wife and another couple, John and Mary. This John was an architect by profession. He stood elegantly tall and took control of the intercourse. Various disciplines were explained and tried. Healing was one Mary undertook. I was anxious with this as I have a slipped disk, to use an incorrect but understandable term, in my neck. I had seen her manipulate others before she practised on me; it takes little to trigger pain in my neck, but complied with their wishes to help and measured my length on the carpet while being worked on. I was not going to be the killjoy of the evening.

John continued to act as master of ceremonies and gave us instructions on how to fold paper money in a certain way in order to attract wealth. I tried his technique, but felt so uncomfortable about it that I stopped my car on the journey home the next day, to straighten my notes. He also gave Brenda affirmations, including a strange one, that she or her twin sister had a particular personal grooming preference; I only know which twin did not, and as I did not wish to risk getting my face slapped, I did not ask the other. John gave Brenda a task to perform that night. Before you get excited the task did not relate to his earlier disclosure.

He had unearthed that Brenda had already undergone an out of body experience when she was going through some crisis years before. I was to get a book and take it to the bedroom, it was to be one she did not know, and open it at any page, I opted to open it to page 186, and then I place it on the top of the wardrobe. Brenda was not to see the page, but she was instructed to think about what was on the page as she went to sleep, and in the morning give me the page number and describe the layout.

The morning arrived and I retrieved the open book from its perch, on top of the wardrobe and asked the questions. The reply from Brenda was: "It is page 86 and there is print on the whole of the left page, and on the right the print covers the top half."

Would you believe the layout was correct as the right hand page formed the end of a chapter, and as I looked to the bottom of the page I saw in black and white the number '186'. This was a remarkable result that is not likely to be explained by coincidence. Had she had an out of body experience and done a little astral travelling through the night?

Thinking of astral travel, I recall during the evening while talking with John, across the room, I was quite relaxed and at ease when I felt myself snap back into my body. I was not aware that I had left it, but from that moment I had the strangest awareness that John and I had been involved in some form of mental battle. It was like no other experience I have had before. Neither of us made a comment, but I remember his look. From then on I felt I had an insight into his real powers and was unsure of his direction. He was powerful.

John introduced me to the phenomena of auras. He explained that these energy forces surround us all, they can be seen by some people either as a grey haze, or others are able to see them in colour and can indicate a person's health. This evening he demonstrated how virtually anybody could feel an aura that surrounds a head. We all joined in and gently tried to locate the auras of our group. It was easy and fascinating to compare the differences. It was during this that John told me that mine was very large and he felt that I could, with such an asset, try anything in the paranormal disciplines. Perhaps it was after his assessment that he induced, as a test, our astral joust?

Although the finished house had a great atmosphere, and many friendly ghosts and spirits passing through, there was no end of problems. The lawyers, who dealt with the conveyancing at the time of purchase, overlooked the lack of easements for gas, electricity, water, etc., on the deed. So although all the amenities were in place and working, the neighbours, whose land had to be crossed for access to these basic services, tried to stop them being used. The feuds continued for years with some of the neighbours, in fact, until the house was sold. The legal repercussions also lasted many years, and Alan headed a campaign to gain satisfaction from the lawyers for their initial oversight, and later, those other lawyers who did not pursue the matter of negligence properly. I have seen the pile of letters, and heard of several court cases in various towns that resulted. In conclusion, a final, out of court settlement for negligence enabled Alan to buy Shorton Cottage, his pride and joy, his final home.

I clearly remember his mid week phone call to me. He had been quiet for a while so I was ready for something, ready for anything. "Hello Peter, can you come down to Devon at the weekend and talk me out of buying a house I have just seen?" As this was a very rare request for help from my older brother, I agreed immediately.

On arrival in Paignton that weekend, Brenda and I were whisked away to view Shorton Cottage, the house by this time was his, the sale had been completed in those few days. My task was not to talk him out of the purchase, it was to advise on the refurbishment, and be involved with the interior designing.

Cottage in the title is a little misleading as the house is a quite sizeable mock Tudor edifice. Set in grounds consisting of several lawns and flower beds; a croquet lawn, which floods readily as the stream that runs through the gardens overflows with each very heavy downpour; a paddock, copse and a vegetable cultivation area. The house had been unoccupied for some time, but the lawns had been regularly mowed, that helped to make them feel alive. Sadly the building had not had any attention for quite some time, and in serious need of tender loving care. Probably an understatement, on reflection, the house needed complete refurbishment.

One memory etched in our minds was of one of the first visits to the cottage. I was with Wendy, Alan, and my wife Brenda. We had been walking alongside the house discussing plans for Wendy and Alan's new home and Brenda said, out of the blue, "I obviously married the wrong brother!" There was a deadly silence following the comment. Alan said nothing at the time, but I was to discover during my divorce that he never forgave her.

It was a long time before I fully appreciated how much that comment revealed the way Brenda thought.

With the previous house, Cecil Road, Alan had walked me round the converted shell at a little slower than normal walking pace. We went from room to room at a speed similar to that which you would use if you were initially viewing a property with a mind to purchase. With his shorthand notebook in his hand, Alan took notes on my sketch ideas for the colours to be used in each room. I thought nothing of it, but my horror came on my next visit to Devon when he took me to the house again to demonstrate that all the schemes that I had suggested had been executed. He was pleased and fortunately the schemes all worked, but I would have been much happier had I worked as I normally do. It takes time to consider everything when putting together a total environment.

With this later project at Shorton Cottage, I was determined it needed to be done with more consideration and set about asking the normal questions I needed for the working brief: Alan and Wendy's likes and dislikes, how the rooms were to be used, and so on. The questions must have seemed endless and been a bit of a shock to them, but without the answers it is difficult to create the right environment for them. It was during these sessions of probing that I discovered the extent of Alan's colour blindness. About ten percent of males suffer with the condition to some extent, commonly the blues and greens are where the problem lies for those with the condition, but in Alan's case he had a difficulty across the spectrum, seeing only the strong, fully saturated colours, no tints or shades. So wherever possible I tried to use the shades of colour that he could see. Fortunately the rooms are large, but natural light was greatly reduced in places by three very wide verandas outside, and some of the walls are very thick. The quality of the natural daylight in the West Country reacts well with bright colours; they do not look brash or cheap if used constructively. So we set to putting together a plan of attack. It was fun working on the transformation.

The oldest part of the house started like Cecil Road, centuries ago with thick walls and was then thatched. During the nineteen thirties it had wings added for the owners and their staff. So in plan it has changed from a long straight cottage built into the hillside at one end, to what it is now, with the added wings, an almost 'H' shape.

When we started the project there were 6 bedrooms, if you include the two in the servant's quarters, this was reduced to 5 bedrooms by converting one bedroom in the original part of the house into a dressing room for the main guest suite. An additional bathroom and WC were added to the servant's landing to service the two end bedrooms, and so the layout was tweaked for the new occupiers.

The project was large, and the quantities of materials needed were considerable, but in fact there was very little wastage with the refurbishment. Building rubble was utilised as hardcore for the collapsing floor of the main dining room. I found when making the curtains that there were only the odd scraps of material left over. This was just as well as the refurbishment budget was quite tight, or it might have been my brother that was tight, possibly both.

The house seems to have its own energy force and determination. I can recall the first visits there, and the feeling of energy that the grounds had; it almost had the effect of charging my batteries. Later as the work progressed, the house came to life itself, but if things were not done right, they would go very wrong.

The main sitting room was one such example. Alan wanted to paint the walls with blue emulsion, I had, in honesty, advised against this, as the colour would do nothing to enhance the room or the views of the garden. Nevertheless he set to it, and papered the walls with a relief paper and applied the emulsion in the blue of his choice. The paper bubbled extensively, and on a trip to see them, it was agreed, with regret, that the only solution was to remove all the paper and start again. I agreed to help with the hanging of the paper and painting, once the blistered wall covering had been removed.

On the next visit we set to and the project was soon completed without any problems, but the colour used was quite different and remained to form the background for the furnishing of the room.

All this time I was going through an extremely ugly divorce and spent time with Wendy and Alan for relief from the tensions. How I recall at the end of each visit I would be asked to come again. They would say, "Next time you come down have a rest. There will be no jobs for you to do." Reality proved that was false. Like 'tomorrow', it never happens.

For therapy, I took on the job of making the curtains. Not a small task. To illustrate the scale of the project, I used several hundred meters of curtain lining. Like elsewhere, the amount of wastage of cloth, like building materials, was minimal. Many of the curtains were made from samples and remnants I had accumulated during my time in the furnishing trade, but some rooms used very large quantities and we had to seek those elsewhere.

The main sitting room was one of these cases and I was asked to seek out an appropriate cloth. The room was quite large with windows on three walls and would need about 100 metres of fabric.

Having scoured the shops in the area for something suitable, I presented Wendy and Alan with a tiny cutting of printed cotton that was readily available. My description to them was accurate, if not flattering. "The colours are vile, I do not like blue and orange together, it is a bad copy of a traditional print, which is badly drawn and printed, but the scale is right. It will look great when made up; let us go to the shop tomorrow morning and see it in the piece." I told them: Once a salesman always a salesman.

Next morning we invaded the shop and I threw, sorry draped, yards of the selected cloth on the floor and they bought it. I returned home days later with the rolls of fabric and set about making those much admired drapes.

The hanging alone of these and the other curtains in the house took me a week to complete.

# CHAPTER 3

I was a sickly child with very little meat on my bones. My early years were not the greatest, because of the asthma and the medication used at that time. A teacher described asthma sufferers, to me, as being virtually invalids who had little scope for physical activities. Now of course, the condition is better managed, and those with the infliction live almost normal lives.

The drugs I had to take had unpleasant side effects. The ephedrine was fine to take by day as it would keep you awake for about three hours, but after that it induced sleep that was hard to fight. The other drug aminophylline would do the reverse, deep sleep for a while, then it was hard not to stop partying, so I took that at night; this latter medication caused one incident that brings a smile to my face.

It was for me a normal night, waking about three in the morning and going for a pee, as small boys do, but this night was slightly different. Drugged and drowsy as normal, I got myself out of bed; went to the cloakroom and stood in front of the WC with my little golden flow linking me to the sewers of the world. I was feeling obviously bored and very weary.

The next thing I can recall is seeing stars very clearly; they were everywhere I looked. Not through the small frosted glass window, you could see nothing through that; the stars were in my head. Next morning when I awoke in my bed, there was a lump on my forehead where I had knocked myself out and been found by my parents at the other end of the landing, having fallen asleep mid flow.

These drugs also affected my work at school. Looking at life through a drugged haze during your childhood has to have repercussions. I missed much school, and was not altogether there for a lot more time, but still managed to do reasonably well. I was not below average and not that much above it either. Secondary School was not really enjoyable for me until the sixth form when the students were treated as individuals by the teachers, and allowed to discipline themselves and the way you approached your studies.

Things were not all bad with school itself; it suited me well in many ways. Being part of the post war baby boom, when schools had to be built to accommodate the inflated numbers of pupils, I was sent to one such new school. Customised as one of the new comprehensive types, although I have seen many variations on the comprehensive system, those have not been that good, this one worked well. We were streamed according to our academic capabilities in various subjects and mixed for tutorial groups, basically what you would call registration. This enabled us to develop our skills with classmates of similar potential; we were not held back by slower learners. In the tutorials we mixed with all grades to learn our social skills. The tutor group had a mix of some of the brightest students, to those with learning difficulties, and some who had quite serious handicaps, which has proved for me, an asset later in the grown up world.

Thinking back to my school days, being a new large school, the teachers differed greatly; they were as diverse in talent and capabilities as were their pupils. I found French interesting for the first few years, being lucky in the teacher's lottery, and then to reverse my fortune and progress, the class was taken over by a Miss Parkes.

On the teacher stakes, she was the short straw who we all dreaded having. Miss Parkes was an interesting creature who had problems controlling herself and had no chance with a class. When agitated, which was most of the time; her arms would bend at the elbows and flap erratically by her side, while her thumbs would be rubbing the palms of her hands that her fingers encircled. In extreme moments, the feet would be stamped, and as her coordination was not the best, she would often step out of her shoes, which in empathy or sympathy would roll onto their sides. With such distractions, it was hardly surprising that my mastery of the language of the country I have grown to love so much, suffered. I would move to France tomorrow if I could; you would not see my rear for dust.

Physics in the first year was unconventional. Mr. Barr took the class. He had been a space scientist working at Woomera and our exercise books were soon filled with useful illustrations on how to make a jet engine, and even better, an atomic bomb; not the normal stink bombs for our class!

One young art master paired me with a classmate to carve a totem pole from a log we collected on a trip to the local woods. This was the first time we had worked together and we just jelled, our sense of humour harmonised; it was one of those rare gleeful times. For many weeks we chipped away at the log, laughing so much that it was amazing the job was ever finished, or that we did not do some damage as we laughed, out of control for the most part. The day of assessment of the finished sculpture came, and we were enthusiastically praised for the way we had used the colouring and grain to such advantage, and worked so hard. Guess what our reaction was? Yes, as you would expect to laugh, as far as we were concerned, we had just had a good time.

This teacher was, in fact, very astute as I later discovered. He entered me into the "O" level art exam. The class I was in had three pupils who were very good, their drawing and cartooning was extremely good, their use of pen and brush and colour was outstanding and I was not one of those talented people. As for me, I became an ogre when handling a brush, something inside me would react so badly, although I do not know why. This was spotted, and I was given work in mediums with little or no contact with the dreaded brush. The closest I came was with a portrait in pen and wash of a classmate. I was pleased with the finished likeness that was used for the exam, but the sitter appeared to have aged by about forty years, her cheeks had sagged a little too much, and the lines around the eyes were over-emphasised. She looked more like her mother or grandmother, assuming that they had a tough life!

The obligatory still life was executed using a plastic cow gum spreader to apply the poster paint to the paper. The main piece submitted was the only piece of pottery that survived the firing in the kiln complete; this tall pot, I was told, went on exhibition at the examining board's headquarters, but I did not like school enough to return to collect it once I had left. Why this exam yielded the top grade still puzzles me.

All was not bad with the school, the facilities and ranges of subject were great, and overall the standards were high; if you wanted to flourish you would be encouraged. The teachers were not all like Miss Parkes, a lot were very good.

In the midst of this organised chaos of the going through the education system and adolescence, two things occurred to change my life.

One transition followed a severe asthma attack when the dreadful adrenaline had to be injected. This would ease the breathing difficulties immediately, but create quite a shock to the nervous system. One moment you would be fighting to breathe, and the next everything was near normal.

Additionally the use of inhalers was introduced about this time. Their side effects were considerably less than the previous tablets and capsules, although if on the rare occasions I resort to the use of an inhaler now, just one puff is enough to make my hands shake for a week.

I was packed off to Farnborough Hospital "to go cold turkey, dry out" from the asthma drugs, and to learn how to control my breathing. This worked well. Having had so many years away from orthodox medication I would avoid their use wherever possible. My body does not always react as it should. Local anaesthetics are a nightmare as they seldom work. A trip to the dentist results in multiple injections that do little to kill the pain, but the chemicals stay in my body for days. One minor procedure to remove a wart from my hand, I recall, took all my will power to remain still; I felt everything as the surgeon dug into my palm with his implement, the injections caused the normal deadening sensations but did not mask any pain.

The other major change started with a trip to a local dance class with two friends. It was a new school teaching Ballroom and Latin American dances. My parents encouraged me to go, in the hopes that I could cope with this form of exercise and that it would ease the breathing problems. Both proved successful, and a new talent was unearthed as a bonus. I could dance. In fact, now I realise that my sense of rhythm is very unusual for a white person, and think of myself as an 'albino wog'; maybe not politically correct, but accurate. The Latin beats get right into my being, and I move parts of my body in a way that would get you arrested under other circumstances if music were not being played.

One day at a class, George, an elderly dancer asked me what I thought about when I was dancing, this shocked me, and it was not something I had considered. When I started to reflect, the answer was simple. I think of nothing. My conscious mind is turned off, and if I am aware of anything it is the holes in the music. Sounds crazy, but it is the only way I can describe how I feel.

Within months I had taken my first medal, a junior bronze, and entered the first national competition, coming in fifth. Throughout the many years of competing that followed, I only ever was placed fifth, second or first, never anything else.

One open competition that I was cajoled into was an elimination event. All grades entered and I was dancing with someone that I had seldom danced with before, I believe it was the Cha Cha Cha, not my favourite of the Latin American rhythms. As the competition was of no real importance to us, and we were not in any way rehearsed, we danced the basic steps that we would use for a bronze or silver medal, nothing fancy or complicated, and we just enjoyed the dancing, there was nothing to lose. We laughed. We laughed more and more as we watched the other dancers putting great effort into their performance, straining to impress the judges who were eliminating couples by tapping them on the shoulder, until all were gone except us. We were relaxed and enjoying the music, keeping the dancing simple. A very valuable lesson was learned that day that I shall never forget and the trophy is the only one that I have on display. It is there to remind me, 'Do whatever you do well and keep it simple.' Build on sound foundations only.

During another competition held at Hammersmith Palais, I was partnering with various medallists in their events. I went into a leg drop, sinking to the ground on the left leg while pointing the right leg behind. The fabric of my trousers failed, and they were split from the waistband to breakfast time. Nothing could be done to conceal the rip so obvious to all the judges and a couple of thousand spectators. All I could do was to continue with the Paso Doble we were dancing. Keeping the aggressive expression on my face was difficult, but essential, as I was supposed to be portraying a bullfighter. The girl in this dance is the cape not the bull (normally). Knowing that immediately once this round was finished I would have no time to repair the damage to my outfit before returning to the competition floor with the next candidate, I resigned myself to the knowledge that my underwear, which was now obviously on view to all, was clean and paid for. At least one of the male adjudicators, whose sexual inclination was, shall we say, unorthodox, would have noticed my partially exposed underwear and probably given an extra mark to my partner. Some say it pays to advertise. It is an ill wind…

*****

As a child I had seen the practice of divining on television; the sight of a person with a 'Y' shaped willow branch walking, and waiting for it to twitch into life over a watercourse was not unfamiliar on the early black and white television programs.

I thought little about it until one day Alan started to tell me that it actually works. The practice is not restricted to locating water below ground; virtually anything can be sought. Some practised people are even employed by large companies to locate oil deposits or other minerals. That is on the large scale, but the technique can be scaled down and used to find the answers to questions.

A small pendulum, a simple weighted object suspended on a few inches of thread or a chain, can be used for divining. The method is simple, hold the pendulum and ask a question which would have a 'Yes' answer, and gently set the weight into a circular motion and let it settle into its own pattern of movement, it could be left to right or sideways. Then when you are getting a constant result try asking something that would yield the answer 'No.' Set the pendulum in motion again exactly as before and note how the direction of natural swing differs from before. Try it until you are at ease and you have, with little effort started divining. It can be used to answer questions, locate hidden objects or even finding locations on maps, but that is not what I am going to tell you today.

Guess what? Alan's explanation of divining led to the inevitable challenge. "Go on Peter, try it."

It does not matter where we were, but it was in the open air and we initially tried to locate water using twigs, but that proved a complete waste of time. Nothing happened using that medium, so somebody had the bright idea of trying rods. To be more accurate; wire coat hangers; this was to be like something you would expect to see on the Blue Peter children's television program. But we did not use sticky back plastic. We crudely reshaped two wire coat hangers onto an 'L' shape; one end about the width of my hand, the other longer.

I was given these two pieces of hi tech engineering implements, I held the shorter length of wire in each hand with the longer arms pointing parallel and forward. Feeling a bit crazy I started to walk forward, mentally seeking water in the earth below. I am not sure who was more surprised when suddenly those bits of metal came to life; without any warning they rotated rapidly in my hands, each veered away from the other until they were no longer parallel, they were pointing in opposite directions. I had not done it. It felt something like the pull of a very strong magnet, forcing them to their new alignment. But I recall something else in the sensations running through my hands. Those two inanimate objects had taken on energy of their own, and they were generating it. They felt alive.

Slightly shaken by this I stopped playing; the point had been made.

When I was in my mid-teens, my father died, and odd things started to happen.

Dad was absolutely petrified of anything electrical, and what followed his demise was a series of events related to virtually all the domestic electrical appliances in the house, not that there were a great number that you would expect to find in today's home. The vacuum cleaner stopped working, and within an hour or so someone arrived who was able to repair it. As I mentioned earlier, money was short at this time and we were not in a position to get on the phone, if we had one that is, and organise a repair or replacement; nevertheless someone arrived who undertook the job. When it was returned to us, it was in working order except for one small thing; the front wheel had to be re installed, which I did. This does not sound that unusual, but this was no different to any other electrical repair at that time; always someone arrived without being summoned, and always something remained incomplete with the repair. As with the vacuum, the front wheel needed to be screwed into place, and in the case of the iron, a small nut and bolt on the heal plate was needed, and so it went on…

One Sunday evening we were having tea in the dining room; Mum, Aunt Ethel and I all heard the front door key being turned in the lock; someone walked down the hall and opened the cupboard under the stairs. We looked at each other in surprise, and then after exchanging a few words decided to go and investigate, only to find nothing. On reflection, the hall cupboard held the electricity meter, so we just assumed that Dad had been back to check that as well.

About this time we dabbled occasionally with what is known as an Ouija board, or in our case, bits of paper with the letters of the alphabet arranged in a circle with an inverted glass in the middle. The Ouija board is not something I would recommend to anyone, or use now, out of choice. It does not work too well for me now, and of course, it can create all sorts of problems if it runs out of control. There are interesting stories of the few times when I have tried it.

A school chum was at home once when we tried this, asking just a few questions and watching the glass glide from letter to letter, spelling out the response. Howard asked about a holiday he was about to take and where he would be staying. The reply gave a different hotel name to the one he expected, so he asked for confirmation; again he was told that he would not be going to the booked place, so he naturally asked why? The glass then flew around the letters and spelt out 'the devil'. With such an answer we immediately stopped this pastime, and were a little dismayed, when we found out the next day, that the holiday arrangements had been changed, as the hotel that had been booked, had burnt down.

Later at Alan's home another Ouija session took place, this time his first wife Marion, Mum and I took part; Alan stayed out of the house, this parlour game was not for him, or maybe he feared another clip round the ear from Mum. He just kept mowing the lawn. It turned out to be an ordinary session, where I was told that I should talk to my brother for advise because I would not be going to college as I had planned, and that I would get only 2 GCE 'O' levels of those that I was awaiting results. This turned out to be true.

Having taken the professional exams before my twenty-fifth birthday and achieved a highly commended grade in

Latin American; I qualified to take part in the annual scholarship. I was the runner up. All those who were eligible were asked to write a short essay about the TV program 'Come Dancing'; an interesting exercise for somebody who had never seen it, I was always out dancing when it was broadcast. Nevertheless, my comments flowed onto the paper, and extended the subject matter into criticising the Ballroom dresses fashionable at the time. These confections had a skirt made with fifty yards of net that looked like a great cone, extending horizontally from the waist. Difficult for the girls to move in as the weight and bulk had to be almost thrown as they moved. For me, they were in constant risk of being ripped apart as I danced. The problem stems from me being slightly knock-kneed. Imagine if you will, dancing close to this mass of net that would force its' way wherever it could, and in my case because of the close proximity of my partner, between the legs. Fine, until, while dancing, I had to bring those legs together. My knees would clamp, vicelike, to any stray lurking net between those limbs of mine and would not move. Fine as long as my partner stayed still, but in the real world… She would move and I could sense the skirt being remodelled between my legs by those knees that were just that bit too close to each other; feeling cloth ripping on many occasions and imagining the trail of newly made rags being dropped around the ballroom floor. This was not the image we had been trained to portray.

It was three years later when one of the scholarship board members, Doris Lavelle, visited the dance school to examine medallists. I was introduced to her and she then reminded me of that fateful essay written for the board of examiners. She had remembered my composition and told me it was the only one to be honest. Boy was I embarrassed, especially as it was from her, the partner of

Monsieur Pierre, who introduced the Latin American dances that we knew at that time to this country.

They were good years dancing. Tough as my teacher was, she was fair and could extract the best from me. Dancing remained fun and taught me so much, not only about dance, but also people, who can be fascinating with their individual stories to tell. It taught me the technique of turning off my conscious mind to get the best from life, the best experiences, and the best answers to any questions.

It was twenty years of learning that I would not have missed for the world.

As a result of my limited school exam results I started work. For the first three years I undertook an apprenticeship at one of the country's leading furnishers, in Bromley, and embarked on the studies for a furnishing diploma at the College for the Distributive Trades, in Charing Cross Road, London. A very busy time as I was also heavily involved in dancing, entering competitions and taking medals.

Once I had qualified in furnishing, I got a job with another specialist furnisher. They were to promote me to buyer of the carpet department. They later added the soft furnishing department to my responsibilities, and I added a wife and her two children from her former marriage. Life was not boring.

Earlier I told you how I did not practice psychic activities; that is not strictly true because there is one skill I have developed while working as a representative for the furnishing fabric manufacturer. My job involved calling on numerous architects and interior designers in the South of England. If you can imagine a northern boundary line starting with the river Thames, continuing westward to Bristol, and then add Wales. That was the area I had to cover. Naturally I was not able to call on all the clients as frequently as I would have liked, in reality, some would be seen just once a year to show them the new ranges of fabrics. Not all these practices were in the towns or cities where, with the use of maps, they could be swiftly located; many were in isolated converted farm buildings or houses, miles from populated areas.

Quite by chance I developed a method to find my way about. I recall that after I had called on a practice once and was, following a lengthy break, calling again, I would hold the customer record card, which had details of the name and address, in my hand as an aide-memoire while I was driving and seeking my destination. It was not long before I became aware that the hairs on the back of my neck would stand on end and I would feel uncomfortable if I were heading away from my client; alternatively, if my course were correct I would feel at ease.

This simple technique saved me hours of driving, and as a result, I used it constantly. Without any preconception I started using these record cards to help me locate unknown places. Naturally I would refer to maps for the general location, but when I was within a few miles, the client's record card would be taken into my hand and I would start to concentrate on the address. Remarkably, this method worked, do not ask me how, I have no idea, but it helped tremendously.

It did however cause me some embarrassment on one occasion. I had phoned a designer whose work included creating schemes for various super luxury hotels around the globe. It was to be my first meeting and I made a phone call to her to arrange a convenient appointment. She gave me her address and having completed our business I placed the telephone receiver on its cradle. My immediate reaction was 'Shit, I should have asked for directions.' The address that I had been given was simply a house name, village, and county somewhere in the London hinterland; nothing familiar, not even a street name or similar.

Rather than make a second contact with my client, I decided to simply leave home a little earlier than normal and give myself additional time. I could, if all else failed, use my record card. On the allotted day I motored round the M25 motorway heading for the nearest major town. From there I started to meander along the winding lanes in the stockbroker belt. As I drove throughout the countryside I could see the occasional large residence, farms and even a small racecourse, I even after a while spotted a sign naming the village I sought. According to the sign I was in the right place, but I found no difference here, there was no village centre, church or pub. I could find neither telephone box nor a pedestrian in order to seek directions. There was no alternative, but to try the card trick.

With the card in my hand I drove along lanes, turning left or right as I fancied. There was not the luxury of a sign post or street name at junctions, no indicators to tell me where I was. I had driven many miles when I passed one junction and I spotted the gateposts at the entrance of two detached houses and decided to stop the car across the entrance of the second to give myself a break. I had no idea where I was at this point, but felt quite at ease. Seated in the car I looked at the house name displayed on the nameplate by the entrance of the closest house. The name was not the one I was looking for so it was clear that this was not to be the end of my journey. I looked back along the lane a few yards to the entrance of the house I had just passed. The house name matched that before me on the card. Unbelievably I had now travelled some 60 miles or more to an area that I had never been before, without any detailed maps, and made my first stop some 10 yards from my destination.

All I had to do then was back the car a few yards up the lane, turn it into the drive, and park it before the house of the designer. We had a very pleasant morning discussing the fabrics and various interior design projects she was involved with. Before I left though, I was taken aback by one question. She asked, "How did you find me? I realised once we had finished our telephone conversation that I had not given you any direction. Only last week the rep from (she then mentioned one of the largest fabric companies) came here, and even with the detailed directions I had given him, he could not find me. He had great problems."

This was going to be embarrassing, if I tell the truth she will think I am off my trolley. But what could I say; there was no alternative that came to mind. I told the truth by giving her a brief account of my journey. Whether she believed me or not I have no idea, but I know how I actually arrived early for our appointment and just yards from her gate.

Let us go back in time to give you more background to my story.

When I was about to marry, my intended wife came as a package with two children from her first marriage. We were going to buy a house, but like most young people there were a lot of things we needed, and her entourage lengthened that list of needs. In the midst of all our preparations for our life together, it was suggested that we make a list of what we required and then cross each item off as they were achieved. It was, when looking at it, long! I estimated that even with a tail wind we would be working through the itinerary for at least a couple of years. As the months passed we diligently deleted, one by one, all our acquisitions from the list, and to our surprise, the task was completed within six months.

*****

I find that I readily accept many disabilities as normal, to an extent that, on occasions, not being aware of abnormalities has proved amusing.

I was in the process of buying a new house with my wife Brenda. The builders were quoting for additional fences and landscaping work but as most people, I asked a local man to estimate as well. On the morning following the site visit of the landscaper, I was chatting to the builders' foreman and he asked me whether the one armed man who had been talking to me the evening before was going to get the garden work. My reply was yes, but insisted that the person he had seen me with had a complete set of limbs. Later I found out the foreman was right.

The local fellow did this heavy garden work very well, and I can recall on many occasions looking in admiration at the way he could handle a builder's shovel with his single arm. It was far more natural and easy than anything I can achieve with the use of both arms. He did other work for us.

A year or two later I met up with the foreman again, this time it was at the barbers in the next village. He told me that the following day he was going into the hospital for plastic surgery. "What on earth for?" I asked

He grabbed a large handful of flesh that hung below his chin and swung it to and fro, saying, "To remove this."

I had not registered the deformity that hung from his face; I had seen only the same person who supervised the building of my house. His physical irregularity obviously was of no importance.

Today, when dealing with people, I still rely on my gut reaction or instinct, and have found to my cost that if I do anything else, things go very wrong. Especially if there is any work to be done.

I was on holiday in France with my wife and a couple of friends many years later.

This couple had heard of the Ouija and were anxious to try it, so we set it up. They were keen to have proof of life after death and to see whether this technique works. Initially nothing happened so I excused myself, at this time this technique seldom worked for me, and I went to lie on the sofa at the other end of the room to relax. The other three continued for quite some time, and they were quite easy about whatever was happening until they seemed to have someone odd giving them answers; that is when I was called back to the table. From the few questions asked, I gathered this was a spirit of a person who had died violently, unexpectedly, and he was confused, trapped between worlds. I had a picture appear in my mind's eye of a group of people amongst clouds, they were silhouetted against the light. On telling this person to look towards the people and light, then go towards it. The glass stopped moving on the table with the last instruction. I found out after we returned home from the trip that this had been a typical example of the rescue of a soul. Being selfish, it would have been very interesting to have extended the interrogation before sending him on his journey; it would have been nice to find out more about this person.

I was married for almost twenty years before my wife went on her campaign to muster for herself all she could.

I had been left an inheritance by a dear uncle; it was enough to almost clear a sizeable mortgage we had at the time. For several years I was nagged by Brenda to use this money to pay off the loan. Although I did not wish to do it; for a quiet life, I eventually gave in and did the deed. I cleared the mortgage and would you believe; it was not long after that Brenda started the divorce proceedings.

A long and painful battle followed, I would not agree with the divorce until the allegation that I had hired an assassin to terminate her life, and other lies were removed from the documents. If only I had known a hit man and taken up her idea, I would have suffered far less and it would have been much, much cheaper than the price I paid for her to use the legal system.

Her tactics managed to take from me everything that was mine for a while, that is all except the clothes I stood up in, my faithful old car and camera. It took more than a year before I was able to regain some of what should be mine, but some has been lost to her. Remarkably Deputy District Judge Calvin of the Dartford County Court awarded her my mother's engagement ring. This, along with other injustices I experienced at the time, shattered my belief in the British legal system. It has proved to me that it certainly has nothing to do with justice.

Now, as the divorce is at its worst and Brenda has managed to deprive me of everything that is mine and familiar to me. All I have access to from my old life is my name, an ageing car that I initially slept in, a camera, and the clothes I have on my back. My self-respect remained intact. For a while a very good friend took me into his home until I was able to establish myself in a rented one-bedroom flat until my former home was sold.

How many years it took me to understand that Brenda and her family believe that the world owes them everything; and that is how they lead their lives, just taking, as if it is their right. Nevertheless, I am now much better off and happier without them in my life; they acted like parasites and like all parasites, almost killed their host.

Once she had exhausted her influences over me, I was able to start to build a new life for myself. It was time to re-learn how to do all sorts of things. It was not just the cooking, the groundwork for that started years before we married, or the drudgery of housework; no, one of the toughest tasks was to dispel the guilt I felt if I spent money on anything other than necessities.

It was here that I recalled that first list compiled at the start of my marriage, and I compiled another. This 'Wish list' was far more important to me; it will be the framework of my 'new start in life.' I considered each entry with great care, knowing that it is not simply a matter of what you ask for, but how the request is compiled, that might alter the outcome. The list was completed using the newly acquired second hand computer, and once I had satisfied that it was complete, placed the list in a drawer.

A few months passed before that list resurfaced, I had forgotten about it. My eyes scanned the single page and I mentally crossed off the achievements, one by one. The outcome, to my satisfaction and amazement, was that in such a short time, I had a near total completion of my objectives.

I am not going to bore you with the details of my list, but I did not ask only for material things, they are not everything. I will mention a couple of things that you may find interesting. One item included on the list was a CD player, I was a dancer and naturally love music, the clarity of the sound is important, but this piece of equipment eluded me while I was married. As I looked at the list a smile grew on my face because I had not gotten one of these, I had, by then, become the owner of several. Quite often in this life it is all or nothing.

Help was not far away in the form of my homeopath, Tony, who had been helping me since Brenda had embarked on her mission of destruction.

Always professional, Tony is a gentle soul with a relaxed demeanour, so laid back that he is almost horizontal. The aura that surrounds him, almost certainly, has resulted from him practising meditation and Yoga. At each consultation I have had with him, he has clothed himself in comfortable, casual, but stylishly understated apparel, carefully co-ordinated in hues of earthy colours, always cotton or other natural fibres. His naturally silver streaked hair is combed forward in Romanesque fashion. There is nothing synthetic about him or his clothes.

How readily I recall his reaction to my confession, during a consultation, that I had spent £100.00 at an auction on a complete set of bone china crockery. I had tried to justify the expenditure to myself by calculating that, had I bought it new, the cost would have been four times greater, but he simply said, "Jolly good."

My car was a large 5-door hatch back with a large trunk, it was old and the mileage was considerable, but it remained very reliable. Dropping the rear seats forward gave a large flat area, ideal for transporting all types of artefacts. If ever I voiced my wish to change the motor to Alan, which I did frequently, my brother would present a torrent of reasons why I should not act on my wish. He would point out that whichever model chosen might not be quite so 'Trego friendly' and a sports coupe would be completely impractical. That was a complete no-no.

The 'Trego' he referred to, was Trego Mills, which is a large warehouse complex that they often used; when I went with them they would load my car to capacity at least.

One such occasion involved collecting some heavy hardwood doors to be installed in the cottage. Alan took his Jaguar and managed to carry only two doors, the balance and greater number were loaded into my hatchback. The weight was considerable, suspension was being thoroughly tested, and brakes had to be used with caution. Because of their length the doors rested on top of the front seats; this stack of mahogany was brushing my left ear. The journey was taken extremely cautiously, sharp braking and steep hills were justifiably avoided.

I was bribed to take my car to go on another trip to the 'Big T', as we called Trego Mills. A plate of pasta from the fast food outlet at the complex was proffered. Like a fool I accepted. I knew that large oriental carpet squares were included on the shopping list of my hosts. All went well as we started the spending spree. They started to ask if each item could be accommodated in my car. Yes, was my response to the three large carpet squares, if they were rolled. Yes, lengths of copper pipe, then the free-standing towel rail, and so they went on; the large coffee table would also fit if the packaging was jettisoned and the legs removed.

Lunchtime came; it was time to relax with the promised pasta dish in the courtyard. Quietly munching away at the promised feast (I use the term loosely). It was time to reflect on how the car was to be loaded with the morning's booty. The coffee table inverted to go in first, then the rolled carpets and so on. Mentally I was happy planning the best use of the trunk space when a small oversight came into my mind; my passengers had been omitted from the calculations.

As we were many miles from their home, my error had to be confronted and they were told of my miscalculation. I did actually get them back, but at a cost to their comfort; Wendy sat in the front passenger seat, pushed well forward, holding the end of the copper pipe. Alan was lying in a very strangely contorted position; within the framework of the inverted table while hanging onto, I hate to think what.

Once back at the cottage, it did not take too long to get him straight, after first extracting him from his place of incarceration. Nothing was missing.

My faithful old motor was a very reliable hatchback that I drove for over 220,000 miles before the engine failed and it had to be replaced. On the list I had entered a wish for a certain saloon car or sports car, even mentioning a new car. The latter was like Oliver asking for more in the Dickens's novel, but there was no harm in it. Well, in the lapsed time I had earned well on the renovation of the house I had bought, and had other good fortune, so when the old faithful machine came to a halt, I bought a car, I had to, and quickly, for without it I could not work. Can you believe it was a sports car and it was new? A machine I continue to enjoy.

That was the start of my re-establishing myself, and from that humble beginning, I flourished, building up to the purchase of my little coupe, a Celica, or as I sometimes say, 'my silly car.'

It may be that in some way this wish list had some part in my change of fortune. I had compiled it when things were at their bleakest, and my life has changed for the better since. I have experienced some difficult times since it was compiled, but I still feel optimistic for the future. My life is due to continue to improve, with setbacks and frustrations, but overall it will improve.

Perhaps I should look again to making a wish list.

Following the much-delayed sale of the former marital home, my ex wife tried to have everything, and for a while she managed it. It took many lawyers' letters, and two visits to the courts to get her out of the house and reclaim some of what was mine.

Mick came to my rescue when looking for my first real dwelling. He was a young, enthusiastic and friendly estate agent who understood my needs. Time was then of the highest priority, I needed to quickly buy a house that I could refurbish, and, when the time was right, sell it at a profit; somewhere to live, with room for my goods and chattels. As a furnisher, I could see the potential for change and possible profit in the house that Mick found for me.

The house that I settled on was in the middle of one of the Medway towns. Certainly not an area I would have chosen as ideal, but my funds were extremely limited following the financial drain of the divorce proceedings instigated by Brenda, and the way she had used the legal system in the pursuance of her avaricious goals. Although this house was not in the best part of town, to use a well used expression, I found myself surrounded by some very nice people, the neighbours were friendly and I still have contact with some of them.

It was built in the early years of the last century as part of a terrace, with rooms on three floors, the basement being virtually at street level at the front. Over time only this and the adjoining house remained. The interior was a mess. For example, the living room had walls painted in sunshine yellow gloss, topped with a pillar-box red and grass green gingham frieze; the ornamental ceiling rose was picked out in yellow and green. A dark blue patterned carpet covered the floor and a hotchpotch of cupboards crowned the cacophony of crud that assaulted your eyes. I could fully understand why the previous owners had been trying to sell the house for a considerable time. There were cupboards and wardrobes in most rooms; the main bedroom on the top floor had a mirrored wardrobe some three or four feet deep, with what looked like a maze of shelves within. This structure took quite some time to dismantle. The kitchen was like the rest of the house, revolting, and as you might expect, it was filthy. Apart from the proportions of the rooms, and the view across the river to Rochester with its Cathedral and Castle, this was a house from hell.

It took several months to re-wire, install a new kitchen and bathroom, have carpets fitted and redecorate.

After the initial viewing of this house and whilst awaiting acceptance of my offer to buy it; I went for one of those frequent trips to Devon, where I spent an interesting afternoon in a soft furnishing fabric bargain shop. This turned out to be a different experience for Melvin, who worked there. During the session it became apparent to him that I had taken no measurements and the house was not as yet mine. He would be asked how many metres were on the various rolls of curtain fabrics I selected; frequently he would stop measuring, to tell me the quantity he had reached and ask how much I would need. The reply was "Keep going, how much is on the roll?" At those prices I bought what was on the roll. What he did not fully realise was the fact that years earlier, I had been a furnishing buyer, and had some idea of the quantities needed, and how the cloths would be used if all went according to plan with the purchase of the house. If there were too much it would not be a problem because the extra fabric would be used to increase the amount of fullness to enhance the draping qualities. Alternatively if this house fell through there would be another.

That afternoon concluded with me coming away with a generous mixture of good fabrics, some ready-made curtains, rails and bed linen; almost enough to furnish the three bedroom house, and it was at a good price and, most important, we had some laughs along the way.

Melvin had another shock, when on my birthday I called into the shop with Wendy for a few odds and ends, and proceeded to drink red wine, that we just happened to have in our bags, from the heavy mugs that were normally used for tea by the staff. Our business was done and we all felt better for it.

What made me move earlier than anticipated from Cuxton Road was the way the Medway Council, Valuation Office and Councillors dealt, rather, did not deal, with the problem of the council tax, which I inherited with the property. On taking possession I advised the council of my sole occupancy.

I had bought this 3 storey semi-detached house with the limited funds left following my divorce. It was near the centre of Strood, with a main road at the front, and a full sized train set that carried commuters to London at the bottom of the garden. Inside, the layout was typical of those built about 1900, two main rooms on each level and a back extension for the kitchen and bathroom. This place was just what I needed at the time, a place to put my goods and chattels, and myself. This was where I planned to settle for a while to lick my wounds and plan what I was to do with my new life. I could see the potential of this house, and I knew I would enjoy the challenge of putting new life into it, and when I was ready to move on, there was potential to make a profit.

It was structurally quite sound, although in considerable need of tender loving care. Whoever had owned it before had unorthodox taste in interior design, that is a diplomatic description for what was a visual disaster; but beneath all the cranky, cluttered crud were hidden rooms of pleasant proportions.

I had been there a few weeks and the transformation was well underway. I returned from work, a trying session of 'door knocking', which is what I call the market research interviewing what I do to pay the bills, to find two unsealed envelopes waiting on the doormat in the hall. They contained notices advising me that the bailiffs had called while I was out that day, about the non-payment of Council Tax.

My immediate reaction was to contact the Medway Council to enquire why they had acted as they had; the telephone conversation with the council officers was interesting! We exchanged the normal pleasantries. I had previously advised them that I had moved into the property as a single occupant, nevertheless, they had instructed the bailiffs to recover the outstanding Council Tax debt accrued by the previous owners from the house. When I pointed out that I was not used to visits from bailiffs, nor was I going to accustom myself to such treatment, I have always paid my dues, especially when it is the result of other people's actions. They apologised.

There had been two envelopes left by the bailiffs, one referred to number 38, the house I had bought, and the second set of documents used 38b as the address, so I asked what should be done with it as I had no knowledge of such a place.

The council worker informed me that this referred to the two rooms of my basement, and that these were rated separately. This was all news to me and had not been disclosed by the previous owner in the enquiries or the searches with the borough, before completion of the sale. As the only person living in the house I was expected to pay two lots of council tax for the one house, and according to this bunch of bureaucrats I had bought two dwellings.

Naturally I was having none of this. Consequently I explained my situation in words of one syllable. The council could not grasp the fact that I was living alone, in a house that I had purchased as a single dwelling, and that only one Council Tax payment would ever be paid to them while I was living there.

From that moment on life at number 38 became, shall we say, interesting.

What followed over the next 18 months were a series of negotiations with various officials, including the Valuation Office and Councillors. Medway Council even took me to court twice before the matter was settled.

Michael, a local lawyer, took on the task of representing me for the first court hearing, and he continued with his endeavour to restore the rating to one unit for a further year, without result.

Just weeks before contracts were due to be exchanged on the sale of the house, I took back the task. Full battle mode was engaged and all stops were removed. If there were to be casualties it would be unfortunate, the only thing that mattered to me was the end result; yes, legally paying one set of Council tax for one three story house. Pure determination and bloody-mindedness on my part was how the corrected Council Tax banding was put in place for Michael to be able to proceed with the conveyancing, just days before the house was sold.

The sorry saga did not end there, as the council even sent an official to question a neighbour about the occupant of the basement of the house following the reclassification, and unbelievably, even had the audacity to demand money for their court proceedings.

In fact it was their stupidity that induced my putting the house on the market, to rid myself of the problem.

The protracted fight to get the house rated as one property benefited no one. This was yet another public relations failure by petty officials. The councils are, in my experience, generally large organisations full of small people who frequently fail to honour their obligations. Bless them. I have, as a result of dealing with large bodies, little respect for the establishment.

At an early age I was taught that respect has to be earned; it is not a right.

Since my divorce I have refurbished two houses for profit, to try to recoup some of the losses.

The second house was on the outskirts of Strood, it had a much better outlook. It is slightly elevated and I can look over some of the surrounding house roofs to the farmland and woods beyond, and in the far distance, the Thames Estuary. This place was, as before, in need of refurbishment; it was a 3 bedroom semi-detached house built during the 1960's with a layout that you would anticipate seeing in a similar property built during the 1930's. A shallow porch leads into a compact hall with its staircase leading to the first floor, and doors in the hall open into the through reception room and little kitchen. On the first floor are the two double bedrooms above the living room, a box bedroom over the hall and the bathroom has the kitchen below it. All in all, a very efficient and economic layout, but it is quite small, certainly smaller than the house I was leaving. There would not be enough room to house all my furniture, but that was not the priority. My intention was to renovate and move on, as I had before.

The previous owners had done little to update the house save for adding a small conservatory to the rear of the kitchen.

As a condition in the deeds, the extension needed building permission from the original builder, but it was not available at the time of the purchase. In substitute, an indemnity would need to be purchased and verbally it had been agreed that the vendors and myself would share the cost. Subsequently in the purchase turmoil this did not happen, and it was to be left to me alone to meet the bill.

Naturally I was not happy about this so I sought out the builder and obtained the needed letter of consent without cost; that letter is now lodged at Michael's office with the property deeds.

With this house, the task ahead was to transform the interior and to create the illusion that it appears bigger than it is. Techniques that I had learned years before would be employed to the full, and the rules of design would be used, bent, and broken to achieve the desired effect; the before and after photographs are a testament to the transformation.

Using the computer I drew a plan of the rooms before taking possession. The object of this exercise was to enable me to use the furniture that I had, to the best advantage. Anything surplus could be stored. Moving day would be slightly easier too as a result of this planning because everything had an allocated location.

Renovating this home I experienced great problems trying to find tradesmen to carry out the work. The house was structurally sound but needed to be modernised. This project involved re-wiring, new windows, installing a new kitchen and bathroom then decorating throughout, nothing too major. But could I find anyone to do the work, not this time. I was about to move in and still was without anyone to start the transformation.

As I mentioned before, in order to pay the bills I do market research interviewing, that horrid 'door knocking'. One day whilst doing this wretched work I was interviewing an electrician; normally I would have not mentioned my need for such a fellow whilst working, but as the need was becoming acute I strayed from the norm. My gut reaction about this man was good, I enquired if he did domestic rewiring. He did not, but he knew a man who did; a colleague.

What a find Mike turned out to be. He arrived to inspect the job on time, his assessment of what was needed was realistic, although his price caused me to do what most builders do when they view a job to increase their costs, take a sharp intake of breath that almost whistles through the teeth. Instinctive reaction was good that day so at the eleventh hour the much-needed electrician was found. Weeks later when Mike and his mate arrived to carry out the work as arranged, they worked to the schedule and were so very clean as they progressed in their task. They were happy in their toils, took pride in their work, asking only for a ready access to PG Tip tea, that was not a problem to supply. His name stays in my address book ready for the next project.

That is not so for the installer of the fence here. Introduced by a friendly builder, who had worked on the previous house, this 'bod' arrived telling me that I was lucky to have him do the work, as he was about to do something else. Oh, how I wish he had. I was uneasy with him at first sight, that old instinct thing that works so well for me, and this occasion proved no exception. His erection was to use a biblical phrase 'built on shaky foundations' and what went on top matched. Now parts of the fence are less than vertical and when the winds are strong the structure becomes a mobile, swaying in the wind. You can guess who will not be invited back, and did not qualify to be included in my Christmas card list.

# CHAPTER 4

Alan was always asking me to try different paranormal techniques when I was with him. He would say to me, "Peter can you try this?" or similar. One evening we were chatting in the sitting room at Cecil Road. He told me that he had bought his daughter a ring and he wanted to know whether she still had it.

"How would I know?" was my reply. I had not seen Susan for some time and I was completely unaware of this gift before Alan had mentioned it.

That did not satisfy my brother and he asked me to try and find an answer telepathically; not something I would have ever considered; nevertheless I was game. He instructed me to try and turn off my conscious mind and ask the question, seek the keepsake. As I sat calmly before the fireplace looking into the stones I was surprised to see a large image of a gold sovereign some four feet in diameter, with St George and the dragon on the face and mounted on a simple gold ring. It was a semi-transparent image hanging in space before me, and although I could still see through the ring, the image remained clearly defined and did not vary or waver in any way.

Somewhat taken aback by this phenomenon, I told Alan what was before my eyes, the grossly enlarged sovereign ring. He then started to ask all the design details of what I could see. Bit by bit I delivered the answers he sought. Eventually the questioning stopped and I turned to look at my inquisitor. His face bore a contented grin as he told me that my description was a match, and he was satisfied that Susan had kept the piece of jewellery. Alan was happy and I was baffled.

I have since seen that actual ring in the flesh.

Are you ready for something completely off the wall?

Once again I am staying with my brother at the cottage. The weather had not been the greatest. The sky was a solid expanse of uninterrupted grey. There was not a single break in the clouds, not even a tiny glimpse of blue could be seen anywhere between the horizons. We had been leisurely walking in the grounds of the cottage, just walking and talking. We were on the lawn flanked by the gravel drive between the house and the stream when Alan turned to me, looked up, and said, "Can you punch a hole in those clouds?"

"Don't be daft!" I replied.

"Go on, give it a try, give it a go." Alan started to egg me into action.

Well, I had become quite accustomed to Alan's unconventional practices, and I was doing nothing in particular so there was nothing to lose. I have been exposed to all sorts of paranormal activities so why should this be any different.

Once again I switched on my subconscious mind and tried to concentrate on the crazy challenge. What a hopeless pastime this was going to be. With conviction I concentrated on that seamless blanket of greyness in the sky, willing it to part to reveal the azure that it concealed. I could feel the start of a headache as I looked up to the heavens, and I began to think that this was not fun, when we saw a break in the clouds and the blue sky beyond was revealed. This may not have been a huge area of sky and it did not last long, but we had a flash.

Alan seemed pleased and was joking about the glimpse of blue. A coincidence this may have been, but I was grateful. It gave me the excuse to stop playing, my head was hurting by now and I had more than enough. I wanted to file the episode in the back of my mind and forget it. Alan still wanted to play, but enough is enough.

We resumed our leisurely ambling through the gardens.

*****

Several years later, I was at a gathering of Alan's friends. This to be the last party with my brother, but I was not to know that at the time. His guests were arriving and spreading themselves through the various reception rooms. I was, as I recall, in the dining room when Andrew the artist came in to say hello.

Andrew had been encouraged to develop his psychic skills and with Alan's guidance had unearthed his talent for healing. They frequently worked together to improve Andrew's skills.

Enthusiastically Andrew greeted me and within seconds he said, "Alan has been telling me that you have punched a hole in the clouds."

My heart sunk. I was bowled over by this and did not quite know how to react. Was this my brother having fun and trying to put me into a difficult situation? He liked such pranks. Or was Alan being genuine? I had no idea after all; Andrew was being initiated into psychic meditation and healing by my brother. These are not subjects to be taken lightly.

My mind was racing, trying to fathom how I should deal with this story. Do I dismiss the incident as a bit of nonsense? What if I treat the request seriously?

On balance I decided to simply tell the story as you have just read it. If this were a jape I would be playing along, or if it were genuine interest, I was just telling it as it was.

I relayed my account of the walk in the garden on that cloudy day, without embellishment. Andrew listened attentively; he did not show any sign of being involved in a hoax, there was not a glint in the eyes or a hint of a smile. All the time I mentally reflected how I wanted to thank Alan for putting me in such a difficult predicament. Thanking him is not completely accurate; I wanted to give him a brotherly slap.

Story told, we rejoined the party. Words with my brother would have to wait, for it was now time to enjoy the company and take a certain amount of falling down water; I had earned it.

*****

I am a great believer in our ability to do anything, we are only limited by ourselves, or what we think we are capable of achieving.

This next technique I have seldom utilised since my years on the road as a company representative, and I had forgotten about it until my niece, Susan, reminded me when she telephoned me recently to discuss what we should do regarding those wretched dealings with her deceased father's estate. It took no time at all to deal with that and we went on to chat about other topics.

We were talking about this and that when she said "That thing with parking you told me about works."

"What thing?" puzzled I asked.

"You know; finding a parking space." Susan responded.

"Sorry?" I was still unable to place what she was talking about.

"You know, you told me how you would book a parking place when you were travelling. It works for me." she explained. "I have tried it and it worked."

That is when the penny dropped. I understood what Susan was telling me.

Let me explain. You have heard how I would travel the South of England for the fabric manufacturer. I had to give a presentation of the new ranges to each client when I visited them. The collections I had to show were not modest; each cloth had a sample in excess of a metre long, and was accompanied by a swatch to show all the other colour ways. In total there was enough cloth to tightly fill two suitcases, two very heavy suitcases. I needed to find a place to deposit my car as close as possible to my destination, no matter whether it was a practice out in the sticks (a Kentish term for the country) or in the centre of a town with the obligatory parking restrictions. Carrying those heavy, fully loaded bags was not my idea of fun. As I drove the car I would mentally think about the parking space I would need. You could say I would be psychically booking my parking spot. And it normally worked. It may seem extraordinary, but I did find that there would normally be a space waiting for me. Occasionally there would be no parking space readily available. Then I would drive around the block, and within one lap of the immediate area, I would normally see a car pull away from the curb and leave; I would be able to slip my car into the newly vacated parking spot. It made no difference whether I was in London or Bristol, the method seemed to work and I seldom had to lug those heavy suitcases more than a few yards.

Thinking about parking and something quite different, here is a story that my brother told me.

He had taken his big old Jaguar car into Paignton at the height of the holiday season, and was trying to find somewhere to park. He was passing the Post Office in the centre of the town when someone left their parking space, and he positioned his Jag in front of the space in readiness to reverse into it, when a fellow in a Ford Sierra drove towards the space. To say Alan was not pleased by this may be an understatement, but who would be? Parking spaces were at a premium, so he got out of his car to advise the interloper not to proceed with his intention of high jacking the parking space. The fellow ignored Alan's request and drove forward. With that Alan called across to the two traffic wardens and said, "You had better be a witness to this." He returned to his seat behind the wheel and put his car into reverse gear, lowered his foot onto the accelerator pedal and released the clutch. The rear bumper of the Jaguar swiftly sunk deeply into the bodywork of the interloper's Sierra saloon. This was going to be expensive parking for somebody, but Alan was not worried, as he said later, "My car was paid for, it means nothing to me. I can afford any repairs."

With that thought in his mind Alan drove away, taking with him part of the wing of the Sierra. Alan's bumper had removed it. His Jaguar was unharmed and nothing more was heard about the incident. Alan did not return to the town centre for a while!

*****

At eleven o'clock on the fateful evening when David phoned to tell me that Alan had died. I calmly reacted by saying; "Oh God! It's started; it is going to be like a pack of cards."

"What do you mean?" he asked as if he had been rattled by my reaction.

"I knew this was about to happen, I have been waiting for it." David also had no way of knowing that I have been very worried about the welfare of several people who are very close to me. They were the tumbling cards that I was expecting to start a chain reaction. Nor was he aware of the recent conversations with my brother that had concerned me, nobody was aware.

"Please tell Wendy that I am so very sorry and I will be down, I will throw a few bits in a bag and leave in about half an hour." I said.

"Peter can you tell Susan that her father has died?" he asked.

"Of course, leave that to me."

"I will stay here with Wendy until you arrive." David told me as we ended our conversation.

Within minutes I was talking to Peter, Susan's partner, and he wanted to be the person to tell her of her loss.

My mind was racing now with what had to be done before leaving, and what I needed to take with me. The work I was committed to do would need to be attended too. Clothes for a few days were thrown into a bag and, just in case, clothes suitable for the funeral if the situation did not permit my return earlier. In the spare bedroom were cigarettes that I had promised Wendy, with a set of curtains that I had made for their laundry room; these, with my luggage, were thrown into the trunk of my car. Susan phoned me to say she would follow tomorrow after she had organised things for her boys.

Time flew as I made my preparations, and the thirty minutes had melted away when I received another phone call from David. There was uncertainty in his voice as he said, "There is no need to come down as everything is in hand."

"It is alright, I am still dashing about, but I shall be leaving about midnight and will be with you by five o'clock." I did not want to give them any worry should I encounter any delays on the road to Devon, so this allowed plenty of time. "Susan has been told and will follow tomorrow."

"No need to rush as my wife and I will be here all night."

"Thank you David, I will see you later," and with that I continued my preparations.

# CHAPTER 5

Having travelled there many times I was familiar with most of the roads. It was a particularly black night, with no light from the moon or stars, and from time to time the rain threw itself heavily against the windscreen. This was not going to be a pleasant drive. So I quickly made myself comfortable behind the wheel of my little coupe; a competent machine that responded instantly to my needs, and stayed anchored to the road. It was not many miles before I joined the M25 motorway to bypass London, and join the main A303 road to the west winding mainly through the undulating countryside.

The amount of traffic was becoming less the further I got from London, and the hours passed so I diverted from my normal route, taking a chance that the narrow main road to Honiton would have little to cause delay. This road, although an arterial route, is little more than a winding lane with few opportunities to pass any lorry or farm vehicle that lay ahead before the start of the Honiton bypass, and Exeter that lay beyond. As it was nearing 3am I decided that hold ups were unlikely, and only one dangerous left-hand bend lay ahead and it was well known to me.

As I sped on those meandering roads through the countryside and sleeping villages on that black night, I passed through heavy rain many times. The powerful headlights tried without success to penetrate the fog and low clouds that obscured what lay ahead, adding to the hazards. I switched on the automatic pilot in my brain, using the power of the subconscious to respond to any hazards that may lie ahead. Trusting in positive forces, and knowing the little Toyota Celica coupe could be relied upon to cope with whatever was asked of it. Strange, feeling so assured, that the journey would be completed, uneventful and in safety although the road ahead was not always visible, but remained under those rapidly rotating wheels on that filthy night.

Leaving behind the winding road just before Honiton, where the tarmac widens to a dual carriageway and my speed increased until the intersection of the M5 near Exeter. Here speed limits of 40 mph catches the unwary travellers, the area has a cluster of speed cameras to bolster the income of the authorities. Joining the motorway, heading to the west, it was not long before the start of the climb up Telegraph Hill, only to find myself once again driving in and out of clouds on that Big Dipper of a route that leads to Torbay, the home of my only brother.

Having dropped down the narrow, tree lined Shorton Road, I stopped to swing open the five bar gate, the entrance to his cottage. I inched the car forward and closed the gate behind me. There were no signs of activity in the house, or any greeting from the hyperactive black and white Dalmatian, Bruce, who had full run of the grounds; the dog that would have escaped to explore the area beyond had I not closed that gate before driving over the well worn gravel drive leading to the front of the cottage.

The journey down to Devon and my brother's house on the night of his death took less than 4 hours, but time took on another dimension.

I was not altogether surprised to find Wendy, Alan's widow, in the main kitchen even at 4 am; this was the only room in the rambling house she would use to smoke.

But to find her with David and Jacqueline sitting on those basically uncomfortable wooden chairs after the events of the night and at that hour did not seem logical. They looked as if they had been established there for hours with their cigarettes, alcohol and jovial conversation. No sign of a tear, almost a party atmosphere filled the room;

there was no indication of shock or grief. Why did they not use the study or living room, it would have been more comfortable?

Once I had unloaded the car of luggage I joined the party in the kitchen, another chair was found and we sat chatting and drinking for an hour or two until it was time for some sleep in the guest suite; it had been a long and tiring day.

Having mounted the shallow staircase, I was on the landing approaching the bedroom door when I found that David had followed me up the stairs. He asked me to inspect the carpet in my brothers bedroom for stains; stains that occurred there, and on the stair carpet as a result of Alan's death. He was concerned that no blemish was visible in the bedroom, as it was the intention of Wendy to have Susan, Alan's daughter, use this bedroom when she arrived from Chatham later that day; to have her sleep in the room where her father died the previous night. Wendy had Alan's body removed from the house before my arrival. The cottage is, in reality, a large rambling house with five bedrooms and with only three members of the family due to be staying, it seemed unnecessary to have Alan's daughter put into his room so soon when others were readily available. I voiced my abhorrence of the intention to use that room so soon to David, even offered to use Alan's bedroom myself, and he cautioned me to say nothing to Wendy or Susan.

Being uneasy with the events of that night; I lied to David. I said that I could see no visible stain. Having worked in furnishing and was a carpet buyer years earlier, the treated stain on the plain oatmeal carpet, just a short distance from the shower room door, was obvious to me. I could recall no trace of a stain on the stair carpet that I had climbed minutes before.

Exhausted by the day, it was time to fall into bed, only stopping to remove shoes and trousers for what would be a short sleep. This part of the house is seldom used so the heating is normally kept to a minimum, and although it had been increased for my visit, I knew that from past experience, the fabric of the building would remain cold for days. Over the years I have been through numerous crises and seen many deaths. I have learned how to manage with very little sleep when events such as this occur.

Waking with a start to find it was noon; I had slept for an unprecedented 6 hours. Being a light sleeper I was amazed to have slept so long, especially with so much activity happening in the rooms immediately beneath. A quick wash and I joined the hive of activity on the floor below. David had established himself at the dining table in the hall, using it as his office, he had been busy with the arrangements, and phoning people to advise them of the news, and provisional arrangements for the funeral on the following Friday. Again David told me, as he had last night that Alan had given him his instructions for this eventuality, during the recent weeks, and he was executing them. I was to hear this from David several times before I was to leave.

Wendy was standing in the kitchen with her friend, Irene, who was telling of her love of my brother, and how he had helped her and been such a good friend, but I could have verbally butchered her when she said: 'Alan was a Shit in business.' I was fully aware of the repercussions resulting from her dubious dealings. How she backed out of the purchase of Alan's previous house on the day when contracts were due to exchange. Why Alan had anything to do with this woman I shall never know, he would not normally have had any further contact with people who are not honourable in their transactions. Not being the brightest spark in the barrel, Irene had obviously forgotten that I was staying with Alan and Wendy when she had done her dirty deed. Her last comment was in extremely bad taste, and voiced at the most inappropriate time. Being in someone else's home I kept silent, how I would have loved to have reminded her of her actions, but decided to bite my tongue, resisting the temptation while I certainly thought a lot. But Irene was to continue to show her true colours by asking whether Wendy was going to sell Alan's car, he had not been dead one day, nevertheless, Irene lost no time in asking for first refusal; she did not have the decency to wait until after the funeral. The vultures are always there to pick over the bones, and Irene was not prepared to wait for Alan's body to cool.

Alan loathed Irene's husband for practising pilfering on a grand scale from his employer. I was told of this, and how his loft and shed were filled with these acquired items. I know how Alan could not tolerate this type of theft.

It was not long before it was made very clear that there was nothing for me to do; I was not needed. My previous experience with family losses stood for nothing. So I watched and listened; making mental notes of the events being played out in front of my eyes. I waited for the cremation to take place, and the time when I could, with decency, return home. It was to be a very long and eventful week.

A couple of tasks were later requested, but more of those later, for now I watched and waited.

During my previous two visits to Devon, Alan and Wendy had been discussing how to smarten up the cloakroom. In addition to the WC and wash basin, it was home to the family washing machine, so when the house was first decorated, little care was taken in its' appearance. Now they felt it was time to make some improvements.

They were vexed by the unsightly fixtures and plastering, but to remedy all of these would have involved major alterations, and frankly, the usage of this little room did not warrant the great upheaval. I suggested that if a coloured paint were to be employed in a certain way the majority of the faults would be camouflaged, and the room's apparent proportions improved.

Alan, since my last visit, had done as I had advised, and the techniques employed worked well. I had also been busy making new curtains to compliment the changes; these I had thrown into my car trunk before leaving home. With haste, I hung the curtains at the windows because I was eager to get out of the room as quickly as possible. For the first time I felt uneasy there. Was it the colour that Wendy had chosen that felt so wrong? It was red, a slightly paler tint of the colour of blood.

Hurriedly I hung the new curtains and fled the bloody cell.

The centre of activity was the main kitchen with a steady flow of visitors, but I was uneasy with Wendy's persistent requests from all comers to get her cheap cigarettes if they were going abroad. I had bought some to add to those that she already had; making her grand total well in excess of 1,000. I am the first to admit that life must go on, but her constant need to get her hands on cheap fags was sickening at a time like this.

Having nothing constructive to do with my time except observe enables me to reassess the events that bought me to Devon.

I puzzled over the phone conversations with my brother a month earlier, when he asked whether I knew the location of the family tree, and his request to have sight of it. This request being so out of character triggered so many emotions within me, and numerous questions that still remain unanswered. What was the catalyst that started his inquiry? Why was it so important to see the tree? What was it that he needed to know, or have confirmed? Whatever the reason, it was certainly extremely important to him.

What was it that had caused Alan to be off hand when we last spoke on the telephone; his tone was curt and distancing, as if he was annoyed, but I knew of nothing that I had done to induce such a reaction? Was this a precursor of things to come? Did he have a prior knowledge of what was afoot, and was he giving me an indication? My gut reaction told me that this was so at the time. I have no reason to doubt those same instincts that have proved to be so reliable for the last fifty years or so. Why should they falter now?

Thinking now of the phone call on the night of Alan's death from David. Why had David made the second call just half an hour after, when he told me that all was in hand; I need not hurry down? Had my earlier comment, when I had told him that I knew something was going to happen and I said everything would tumble like a pack of cards. Could that comment have induced some anxiety? What was going on in Devon? These people are into matters spiritual, and I know they believe my psychic talents are greater than they are. I have not sought to develop clairvoyance as they have. Did they think that I was somehow aware of something beyond my ken? If they did why should my presence be a threat?

I have no reason to doubt that my brother had started to prepare for a new life separate from Wendy. If Wendy got wind of this, as I think she had, she would feel very vulnerable and know that she would have to do something very drastic to protect her interests. She would also know that her reaction to the new situation would need to be very, very swift; she had an extremely small window of opportunity, if indeed she was not too late. As an alcoholic, her judgement and reaction would be completely unpredictable. Her motive to rid herself of her husband could not be greater than at the time of Alan's death. Alternatively if my brother's death was a natural one, it must be said that it could not have come at a more fortuitous time for her.

*****

David lives within a mile of my brother, with his latest wife and her children. While recovering from a hip operation he has been working part time, clearing the hedgerows and orchard over recent months at the cottage, so I was not unduly surprised by his presence this evening. He is a robustly built 50 something year old with an outgoing personality who has had several businesses.

Alan and Wendy initially got to know David when they were looking for properties, and he had an estate agency in town. Until recently he had an auction house where Alan bought some of the furniture for the house, including the antique dining table and chairs. The table is a large monster, apparently made from old ships' timbers, namely heavy planks resting on studded cruciform pedestals, the developing bloom in the polish indicates that the French polishing has been rushed and is quite fresh. The high-backed Windsor chairs suit the dining room, but I am not convinced of their antiquity, that is part of another story.

David was the person that Wendy had phoned, as Alan was dying in his room. For some reason the doctor or emergency services were not the first to be contacted. David told me that he was at the house within five minutes, and worked in vain to revive my brother for the fifteen minutes that the ambulance took to arrive. Last night he had been anxious for me to inspect the bedroom and stair carpet for stains that had resulted from Alan's demise.

I was told that Alan was due to go out with two friends for the weekly drink, but one was unwell and was going to give the session a miss. Later, Wendy said that Alan was unwell that evening so he stayed home and went to bed early.

*****

Now I became useful for the first time. On the arrival of Alan's daughter Susan, I was given the odious task of taking her to the bedroom she was to use; the site of her father's demise on the previous evening, his bedroom. The room with the carpet stain that the anxious David had asked me to inspect in the early hours, but by now there was no visible evidence remaining of its earlier existence. Why Wendy did not do this herself puzzled me at the time, but I did not question.

Saturday morning:

Susan was first to join me in the study and she told me how her night in Alan's room had distressed her. She had spent time sitting on the floor weeping when she was first left in the room alone, naturally distressed at having been given this particular room in the house when others were not in use. Hardly surprising, as her father had died in that same room less than twenty four hours earlier, the night before. In her distress she considered coming to find me, but unfortunately she did not.

When Wendy eventually surfaced, she asked me to register Alan's death when the certificate becomes available. A delay was likely, as a post mortem was anticipated.

The rest of the day passed with a succession of phone calls and a steady stream of visitors, as you would expect.

Wendy told us what she wanted on the day of the funeral. At the crematorium there was to be no vicar to conduct the service, there were to be no hymns or prayers. As there had to be some sort of ritual at the crematorium, Wendy and David were very eager to have me give the eulogy; they required me to demonstrate my collaboration. I firmly declined. I was so uneasy about everything that was happening that I wanted no part of what they were doing. I could not stand before Alan's friends and give my seal of approval to their proceedings.

No flowers for Alan except those picked from the garden by her. To top it all, there was to be no one back to the house for a wake. No one to celebrate his life: No good bye. Ideally there would have been naught to mark his departure. It would have been as if he never existed.

Had Alan's life and death been such an inconvenience to them?

Sunday:

Susan had slept in Alan's room again; his bedroom overlooks the secret garden and orchard, on the valley side of the house that is furthest from the road with its limited street lighting. There is little light outside to filter through the blackout lined curtains that hang at the window; the room at night is all but pitch black.

This morning she came to me in a state of confusion saying. "During the night I was aware of the presence of my father in the bedroom, I know it was him." She went on to say, "At one point, in the absolute darkness of the night, I could see the impression of his body on the bedclothes beside me. It was an indentation of him sitting on the right hand side of the bed. And I was aware of the form that was causing the dip on the bedding, it was transparent, but I was aware of it being there. It seemed to have an energy of its own, and it was generating a light, or lights; unlike anything I have seen before. I cannot explain it. I do not have the words. I do not understand it. There was not enough light to be able to see anything. How could I see it?"

"I could still see it when I got out of bed" In a state of confusion she told me, "I was trying to get to the light switch by the door. When I got there, I failed to flick the switch, I turned, and a feeling of confusion filled me, only to find myself looking at me, still lying on the bed. Suddenly I found myself back in bed, it was with a jolt; but the presence remained." Having had psychic experiences before she was not alarmed by Alan's visit, but the impression on the bedclothes baffled her, as did the form that sat beside her to create it.

"I do not know, but let's think about it, the image could take energy to create, so perhaps it was that energy that caused the phenomena to be visible." That was the best reply I could proffer to pacify her. Whether it was right or wrong, I had no idea, but it gave a sort of logical explanation for the image, and seemed to reassure her.

That evening after dinner the three of us retired to the study. This is the smallest and cosiest sitting room. At the back of the house, it is shielded on three sides from the elements by the valley, and closest to the stream and waterfall. Alan used to practice his psychic development and healing in this, the most psychically charged room in the cottage.

The aura around my head felt unusually large and active. I find it feels uncomfortable on occasions when people stand too close behind me. Tonight it felt highly activated, and I needed someone to smooth and soothe. Both girls understood, and I knew Susan would have been the person to help me, but Wendy insisted on coming to my aid.

Everyone has an aura and some people have the ability to see it, sometimes as a haze, but more frequently in colour. I have rarely seen it and then only as a smokey haze. The sensitive nerves on the palms of my hands can feel it. The aura is like an even halo, an inch or so around the skull. On occasions it can become distorted, irregular, and if you are sensitive, it can be gently caressed back into a symmetric shape. That is what I needed this evening. As Wendy stood behind me with open palms, I could not see what she was doing, but whatever it was, she was doing me no good. As her hands neared, I felt something I can liken to long needles, a foot from my skull and extending into my brain; each one, and there were many, were charged with continuous electric shocks and I fought hard to remain stationary. Susan observed my pained flinches with every advance of Wendy's hands. It was quite a relief for me when Wendy stopped; Susan took over and the discomfort ceased, but the aura was still active and I was unable to relax.

I took myself into the main sitting room which is neutral, but that was not enough to settle me. As I sat in the armchair I mentally asked, "What is happening?" "What is needed?" and similar questions, but I had no answers. Not understanding these feelings I tried to safeguard myself by thinking, "if this is a negative force at work, it has to go, there is no place for it here." But there was still no respite. The room had gone deadly cold, often the precursor of some manifestation, but I had no idea what was to ensue.

In desperation I donned my coat and left the house to walk the grounds and seek relief in the night air. Being early March it was cold outside and I walked down the drive to the gate not knowing what to do.

I had heard that some people get comfort and strength from hugging trees, and to the right of the entrance there is a large tree big enough for that. This had not worked for me before, but I had nothing to lose by trying. Hugging was a bit to forward for me, as we had not even been formally introduced, so I simply rested my hands on the smooth bark on that windy evening. I kept asking questions, but I gained nothing.

The cold was getting to me, so I started to walk back along the drive to the house, all the time asking, what is happening? What….?

I paced the rear courtyard until I finally re-entered the house through the kitchen, feeling bewildered and chilled. Susan met me in the hall and was facing me as I removed my coat. I started to pull off the jacket and felt my shoulders were 1½ inches lower than normal and the sleeves felt tight against my arms. Disbelief must have filled my face as I looked down to a stomach extended further forward than normal. I had taken on the stature of my brother. Shocked by this I exclaimed, "It is Alan, he has taken over my body." Susan did not seem unduly surprised; she simply helped me remove the coat. We hung it in the cloakroom and returned, a little stunned, to the tranquillity of the large sitting room.

Sitting quietly we spoke of what was happening, but all was not done. The temperature in the room was showing no sign of increasing. It was deadly cold.

Susan has, several times, told me that her father had foreseen his death, but he would not tell her the circumstances, as he felt if he did, it would provide no proof. No proof of what?

We both started asking with our minds what was happening, it was not long before I felt the jolt of Alan's return. He had re-entered my body again. I feel his anger. I am feeling his frustration of being taken from his own body. He is desperate to see the home he loved again. He has me leave the chair and go on a tour of the house; into the hall, the dining room, and into the servant's quarters' sitting room; this was the title we used to identify the room, there was nothing feudal about my brother. But, I am not comfortable and I call Alan a silly Bugger for dragging me around. With his beliefs and knowledge of the afterlife and with his new existence, he should know that he could go wherever he liked much easier without the use of my body. His soul needed to merely wish to achieve what he wanted, and it would happen. I do not think that my objection was well received, nevertheless I objected. He left and I returned alone, to the sitting room, to try to relax.

Susan left me to join Wendy and I missed what happened next.

As they were chatting over a cigarette in the main kitchen: Wendy was saying how she wanted contact with Alan. Bruce, the dog, who was with them, suddenly sprung to his feet, became alert and fixed his eyes on a spot in the space before him and started to whine, pining and making noises as if talking to someone like dogs do. But there was nothing there that the girls could see.

This passed and things were to quiet down for a while, return to normal, whatever that is.

Monday:

I had heard David tell Wendy on Friday that the lawyer could see them on Monday or Tuesday, but there was only an acknowledgement from Wendy. Having been isolated from all the arrangements so far, it was a surprise to be told that I was to go with her and Susan this morning.

Following Wendy's directions, Susan had left earlier on her own to deposit her car with the garage; she was keen to have her car seen by a mechanic before her return to Kent to retrieve her family for the funeral on Friday. There had been a problem on the journey to Devon and not wanting a recurrence she phoned the garage to arrange the repair that morning.

I was to accompany Wendy in her car, and collect Susan on route to the lawyers in town. We pulled into the forecourt and there was no sign of my niece or her motor; she had not been able to find the place, and had been driving in all directions trying to locate it and meet up with us, knowing that there was a fixed appointment.

She pulled into the garage in a flustered state just as we were about to leave, with both women believing the other was at fault. Quickly dumping the car with the mechanic, she clambered into the coupe to be driven to our meeting. Having parked in the practice's car park Wendy left us to go to the bank, a useful interlude for the women to calm down after the heated journey. Within minutes Wendy returned and we three walked to the offices. The reception was quite well furnished and we were comfortable as we waited to see the lawyer.

I did not expect to see Kaye come down the stairs to usher Wendy into the lawyers' office. Kaye, I had known for years. While I waited with Susan in the reception, I told her of the game of Trivial Pursuit when I had partnered Kaye against Wendy and Alan at the cottage. This was to be the shortest game I have ever played, Kaye is a bright academic young lady, and as luck would have it the few questions she could not answer, and there were few, I did. We all laughed as we wiped the board that day, but since then we have seldom played together and never repeated the success of that first game. No game was to be that short.

In due course Kaye returned to the reception and led us up through the building to join Wendy and the lawyer in her office.

Philippa introduced herself as the lawyer who would be working with Wendy to compile the probate papers for my brother's estate. She was not a tall woman, and her head almost remained at the same height above the floor when she returned to her seat. Chairs were found for Susan and I and the small talk revealed that Philippa commuted from the edge of the moors to work, and she had a keen interest in keeping horses. Although she is not tall, gravity had more than sufficient to pull on, and I recall thinking at the time that if I were part of her livestock collection, I would rather be lead than ridden by her - Strange how an image can be triggered.

Getting on with the purpose of the meeting, Philippa advised us that Susan and I were jointly, with Wendy, executors and trustees of Alan's estate and will.

Both Susan and I had a copy of my brother's will placed before us and instructed by Philippa to read them; a complicated document, in two parts, the like of which I had not seen before. Quickly I read the pages of the will before me on the desk, and as I finished, I looked up and it took a deliberate effort to check myself from saying, "Where is the rest of it?" Something stopped me from airing my impression then, but still I believe the papers offered that day were not in order. I had seen and dealt with about six different wills, so I was familiar with their general format, but this was quite different. It was not the construction that made me feel uneasy; the text was incomplete, a third part was not there.

The lawyer did not explain the contents of the will, as I would have expected, but that did not worry me unduly; it would be months before the probate papers would be finalised and ready for our signature.

Miss Philippa told us that once she and Wendy had completed everything, the probate papers would be sent to lawyers local to each of us, where they would be sworn. Susan looked puzzled by the proceedings, as it was all new to her. I suggested that we went together to the same lawyer. We live within a few miles of each other, so it would be quite convenient, and being accompanied may take away any anxiety Susan may have about the formalities. At my suggestion Miss Philippa's eyes flashed at Wendy's, but nothing was said.

The copies of the will were then placed in envelopes for us before Kaye was summoned to return Susan and I to the ground floor reception. In an attempt to reassure her as we waited for Wendy to complete her business with Miss Philippa, I explained to Susan what to expect her duties to include as an executor. While we talked, Susan told me that Kaye had not been able to look us in the eyes when she was escorting us. I had noticed this, and had deliberately started a conversation with her on our descent to the reception. I had made her look at me because I did not understand why she was not acting openly to an old friend.

Wendy, having completed her meeting, led us from the offices only to leave us to go again to the bank. When she returned we piled into her car and headed to her home, it was lunchtime. After such a strange morning, I needed a drink, but whether I had one, I cannot remember.

Whether it was Monday or Tuesday that the undertaker called is not important; that he did was essential.

Steve, a pleasant young man, suitably suited was lead into the study by Wendy. Susan and I were asked to join them. Once the introductions were complete we settled into the task in hand.

Steve's first action was to confirm that the funeral service at the crematorium would take place on the following Friday. The crematorium was fully booked until then and there had to be a post mortem examination.

An agitated reaction came from Wendy to this.

"Why does it take so long before he can be cremated?" she asked. "It is far too long to have to wait. If we lived in warmer climbs the service would be within 24 hours, some religions insist on it. Can you do it earlier?" And so the tirade continued, which Steve handled with professional calm assurance. He stressed the delay was quite normal, and when she calmed sufficiently, he continued his unpleasant task by telling her that Alan's body may need to be 'held on ice for up to two weeks after the service' He explained that this formality would not cause any delay to the service. Bewildered, she eventually accepted this saying, "I can live with that."

But Wendy was to insist that the coffin be removed from the chapel at the end of the service before the mourners leave. The screen or gates that normally close, leaving the casket in situ at the Torbay crematorium, was completely unacceptable. She vehemently insisted that Alan's body left the chapel first and accepted no compromise.

She continued to tell Steve of her wish to have no clergy, prayers or hymns, no flowers, and a friend from the local spiritualist church would conduct the service. Steve actively filled his notebook with Wendy's instructions and was quick to clarify anything that he was not sure about.

He opened his folder for Wendy to select the casket and was again the victim of another outburst, this time he could gain no guidance and was forced to withdraw the catalogue and decide for himself what to use. I had the impression that if he had suggested a cardboard box he would probably have been asked if a paper bag could be used.

They continued with a discussion about an announcement in the local paper, cars, and the order of events on the day. The mourners would follow the coffin into the chapel and so on.

At the end of the service, as we were leaving, Wendy wanted a particular song played; Steve noted the track number and left with the CD.

Steve's notebook had been put to use today. He had done a good job and it had been tough for him.

I was ready for a stiff drink, not coffee, and Steve had certainly earned one.

Whether he got one or not: Who knows?

While we are on the subject of Maunders, the undertakers; this is a good opportunity to add this little piece of information: Maunders were well known to Wendy and Alan because they had lived in the house adjacent to Maunders' premises when first moving to Devon; they had been neighbours for years. And it was Maunders who removed Alan's body on the night of his death and had it in their care until the Tuesday, when it was taken to the mortuary.

For those who do not know; there are strict, rigid procedures that have to be followed, which Maunders would have to know and adhere to. I will not bore you with them now.

They did not follow them in the case of Alan Hindley.

Who could have persuaded them to take such a risk, a risk that could seriously damage their business? What pressure was used, or was it simply a hand shake?

Wednesday afternoon:

Saw the arrival of the lady who was to take the service at the crematorium.

Shirley, the medium from the local spiritualist church joined Wendy, David and I to stand in the kitchen for a cuppa and chat, she was quick to make herself at home, she removed her shoes and earthed herself. She leant against the chest freezer while the rest of us used the oak kitchen units for support. It is a large room flanked on three walls with units and the freezer was on the forth, next to the entrance, so there was plenty of room to spread out.

When Alan refurbished the house he amalgamated several rooms to create the kitchen as it is today. To avoid major building upheaval, he put a wooden support pillar towards one end, only four or five inches square, but it is there and has to be negotiated. As we talked, I found that I could no longer see Shirley as the pillar came between us, the pillar had not moved, Shirley had; naturally I moved a few inches so that she was within my field of vision. Before long the pillar was between us again, so my move was repeated. On the third occasion I wondered whether there was something offensive in my appearance that made her use the column to obstruct her view. I can understand her actions if that is what she is doing, as I admit I seldom use a mirror on myself while wearing glasses.

At the allotted time of three thirty we left the kitchen to discuss the service in the comfort of the study.

I had been asked repeatedly to give the eulogy and on each occasion declined. David, who had taken over all the organising, could do this formality too. I sat quietly as the three talked for nearly two hours, sometimes about what was to happen on Friday, but mainly about anything else. Then out of the blue I heard someone say to me, "What do you think?"

Startled by the question, I replied; "This service is not really for me as I have already said my good byes to my brother, but I would like to have the twenty-third psalm read."

The look of alarm on their faces was unbelievable, and they quickly conferred amongst themselves in bewilderment at my request. What was this twenty-third psalm? They had already settled on reading the Lord's Prayer so I was puzzled by their reaction, almost alarmed, to this simple request.

I withdrew it, "It does not matter, do not worry. When Mum died I asked for it, but the version used was not the one I knew and that will probably happen again. Forget that I asked." I said, and they did.

They returned to their discussions and when they had finished David took me into the dining room to ask me about my brother's life. He needed material for his speech. I thought hard before giving him any answers, because he had to have the absolute truth in whatever he was told, I could give him nothing less. I told him about the shed roof being lifted by explosives, and how Alan earned pocket money playing find the lady with classmates and other chestnuts until he had gathered enough for his task. We drifted into more general topics. We finally spoke of soul mates and David reflected for a moment before he admitted, "I have finally discovered my soul mate."

I assumed that he meant his most recent wife, Jacqui, but out of devilment I looked him straight in the eye and asked, "Does Jacqui know?"

His jaw dropped and eyes came out on stalk and I collapsed in laughter, he recovered and joined me.

He had no idea how much I needed to laugh. I was desperate.

This was the signal to rejoin the ladies to briefly round off this afternoon. Shirley soon left and David clocked off.

Enough was enough and I want to talk about other things, so I phoned a friend who I had not seen for quite a while: He joined Wendy and me at a restaurant that evening, for a pleasant meal.

Tomorrow, Susan was due to return with her partner and the boys after leaving on Tuesday to make the journey back to Kent to collect them. The other houseguests were arriving.

Thursday:

It was to be the eve of the funeral: The reason for my being here.

Tomorrow Alan will be cremated and there are now a few jobs for me to do.

At last the death certificate can be collected from the registrar at Oldway Mansions, the local office, and I have been volunteered to undertake (no pun intended). I am quite grateful for a legitimate excuse to get away from the house and have time alone. This is the one real thing I have been permitted to do for my brother.

Earlier in the week I asked Wendy "How many copies of the certificate do you want? They charge about £3.00 for originals, and provide photocopies free."

"How many do you think I will need?" she asked.

"Normally about 6 originals should do, the DHSS keep one, but if you ask everyone to return them you should have enough." I replied. Having dealt with the mechanics of 6 deaths I have had some experience.

"Get one original and ten free photocopies. One original for the DHSS and everyone else will have to make do with copies." She replied dismissingly. In view of the treatment I had already experienced I was not going to comment further. There was no point.

Next day saw the number of original death certificates required increased to twelve on David's advice, but today was Thursday and nothing is normal here, so before I left I asked Wendy again. The number had changed, now it was to be nine originals plus a number of photocopies; Miss Philippa's specification. I was given instructions of what I had to do and set off to the Registry Office.

As I drove, I recalled that when I was first asked to do this job I had been warned that there was likely to be a delay in obtaining the death certificate if a post mortem was done. Nothing unusual I thought, but I was a little surprised when David ushered me out of the kitchen and into the garden on Monday to quietly tell me:

"There has been two drug related deaths in the Torbay area and the police are involved. The police naturally take priority in such cases and Alan's death certificate will be delayed as a result."

It did not bother me when I was to collect the certificate as my diary was not exactly full, not with just one date fixed within the next week, Alan's funeral, but I did think it odd that two deaths could cause such upheaval in such a large town. But what do I know of the workings of the West Country, as I come from London and the Southeast.

Then again, I recall David did draw me aside on another occasion to tell me that a second doctor was needed to countersign the papers, and none could be found to confirm the death. The third reason given to me for the delay was that there had been a lot of deaths in the bay, but there was no outbreak of influenza or anything else to thin the population.

Nobody knew whether the certificate would be available before I was due to return home next week. It was not until this morning when the confirmation arrived by phone that the death certificate was ready to be released; only then did I receive my final directions from Wendy.

Yes, I had been fed three different reasons for the delay. I thought it strange.

It is about a mile down the valley to Oldway Mansions, a neo-classical building that was once the home of the

Singer family, but now includes the offices of the registrar within its walls.

I made my entrance and followed the signs. I mounted the grand marble staircase to the first floor. Within minutes I was ushered into the registrar's office and a kindly lady entered the information I was giving into the inevitable computer. The question that had not been anticipated hit me with a jolt:

"What was his profession or occupation?" The registrar asked.

Occupation? Alan had not worked in the conventional way for years, he had renovated houses since he had been in Devon, but that was not his profession. Nor could I enter butcher from the days when he had the meat business. Photographer was probably the most accurate answer, but he had not done that for more than thirty years. People here would not relate to that. Looking confused I asked; "Do you have to put anything?"

"No I can put a line through that section if you like." She replied to my relief.

"That would be fine." I quickly replied. It amused me that this would buck the system slightly, which is what Alan had done all his life. This simple straight line could not have been more appropriate. He would have chuckled at this and I felt a warm glow and smiled sadly as I thought; 'This is all I have been allowed to do for you, Alan, but it's good, enjoy, Cheers bruv.'

I watched as she drew a ruler from her drawer and used it to guide her pen across the Certificate.

"Thank you for your help and understanding." I said to the registrar as I was handed the certificates, and I truly meant it.

I felt happier now than I had since this doleful business had begun a week ago. I drove back to the house knowing that I had been able to do something that would have amused my brother. It was to prove to be the only thing.

David had been working full time at the cottage since my arrival. He arrived to update Wendy with the progress he had made with Alan's affair, and now is busying himself in the grounds clearing an area on the other side of the stream. Wendy has made her recording of his working hours very obvious; daily asking me to confirm David's arrival and departure times before entering them in the diary she keeps by the telephone on the table in the entrance hall. Knowing that he is claiming from the DHSS I am surprised that she is committing this to paper.

I have had my coffee and toast to start the day and got some fresh air in the garden. Bruce has left his shelter and tempts me to play with him by offering me the rubber dog toy that he loves to retrieve. When he loses interest he dashes into the copse looking for animals to chase or into the orchard in pursuit of birds. He has the run of the grounds and keeps busy patrolling all his territory. Even through the night his surveillance continues, he triggers the garden lights as he passes the sensors.

Mid morning I join David with a mug of tea. We settle ourselves on the stone bridge that spans the stream just above the waterfall. The wall is wide enough to sit on and from here we can take in the views up the valley, and the course of the stream as it falls into the pool below before winding gently alongside the house as it flows through the grounds and beyond, towards the sea. Sipping at the tea we pass the time of day chatting, we talk about the last week and he suggested that I put pen to paper and write about my feelings, as therapy, I think. Had he conceived this account would follow, he would not have been so forthcoming, I am sure. Despite David's friendly facade it becomes obvious that he is abnormally anxious to know my intentions, and he even asks whether I intend to stay in contact with Wendy. My answers are uncertain as a result of what I have seen and experienced here over the week. On reflection, he was being inquisitive about matters that should have been of no consequence to him; he was hardly close or family. For all I know he may be now.

I feel there is something very wrong at the cottage. Wendy has changed in her attitude towards me and other friends, but I do not know what has induced it.

Alan has entrusted me to fulfil a duty: An obligation I would not wish. Should I complete my duty as executor and trustee as my brother had wished in his will, or do I not? I have been entrusted to perform this responsibility, but it would be simple enough to draft the letter to sign away the undertaking. I could sever contact with these people.

I know in my heart that Alan did nothing in his life without good cause; therefore it was somehow important to him that I am to play my part. Can I walk away? If I do, how will my action lay on my conscience? Do I honour my duty?

I am sure Wendy does not want me involved, but why? Her will mirrored Alan's when they were drafted. Although I doubt whether the wills she has made since do.

Is it her intention not to honour the wishes of my brother's will? The will, which Alan went to lengths to explain to me as we walked in the grounds; or has something happened here that I might question or uncover?

The image of Alan's face on the night of his death haunts her. Why?

Constantly she voices her need to visit the chapel of rest to see Alan, but she will have to wait for the authorities to release his body.

I am uneasy with my situation and that I am going to give serious thought to the future.

I leave David on the bridge to return our empty mugs to the kitchen.

Nothing is certain, except my uncertainty.

Back at the house, Susan was due to return with her brood. She was bringing sleeping bags for the boys and Wendy wants them to sleep on the floor in Alan's room with their parents.

That might have suited Wendy, but I could not stand by and see Alan's grandsons sleep on the floor on the eve of their grandfather's funeral; not when there are mattresses readily available in the house. I must admit that I was very surprised they were not given one of the other two bedrooms, being family, but both of those were for Wendy's friends.

I told Wendy of my intentions to give Susan and Peter the guest suite that I had been using. If you include the dressing area, the bedroom was almost three times larger than Alan's room to provide plenty of space for the extra mattresses. They would be much more comfortable.

It would take minutes to swap the bedding and transfer my belongings. Wendy would have to do nothing. Peter could help transfer the boys' mattresses later.

As I transferred the sheets and bedding I noticed that the ticking of Alan's bed was stained.

That night the young family had little rest. The guest suite that I had used since my arrival had gradually warmed, but on that first night, Susan and Peter with their oldest son, Luke, could not sleep for the deadly cold that enveloped the room; only little Jake slept on, oblivious to his surroundings. Maybe, if the brothers had been offered the two bedrooms that Alan named 'the boy's rooms,' they would have been more comfortable; they would have had beds. Alan would have then had his family in the appropriate rooms of his home.

Before Susan had returned to her home we had convinced Wendy that some catering should be done for people at the house after the funeral, even if it was only nibbles. I had been out with Wendy on a mini shopping expedition when she bought a few bags of crisps and nuts, one case of white wine and five cases of red wine, her normal falling down water. I topped this up with brandy and sherry. Susan and I had no indication of the numbers who were likely to come back to the house.

That reminds me; Wendy, who has a drinking problem, had drastically reduced her intake while Susan was here. I wonder if she will cut back again on her return?

Alan had been driven to distraction by Wendy's drinking and I had received many phone calls from my brother. The truth is, she did not have a problem drinking, she found it was easy and did it well; too well. Alan would tell me of the friends that they had lost and the embarrassment she caused when she had too much. The invitations he had to refuse; it had even cost him dearly in business, when she would open her mouth too far when under the influence: Although he drank himself, he could not cope with her alcoholism.

The house will be full tonight; as Cilla and Ian Baker, Wendy's friends, are arriving from Kent, and another friend, Barbara Ryell from the Midlands. It will be a take away meal of sorts, once they are all here.

I was weaned on crises and have learned that at times like these, food is essential and have tried to get something nourishing and tasty for Wendy to eat throughout the week. Her appetite was never great, but it had virtually disappeared. Most of her nourishment is coming from the bottle.

The sun is sinking below the yardarm and the glasses are being filled. Cilla and Ian and Barbara have arrived and are installed in the blue bedrooms in what used to be the servants quarters. Susan and Peter, with the boys, have done the same in the guest suite and it is time to eat. Fish and chips have been selected and I have been elected to drive to the fish shop at the back of the town with Susan as my aid to get them. While we are on our mission, the plates were to be warmed and the dining table laid. Well, that was the plan.

My part went well and we returned with the bags of piping hot food, I deposited them in the kitchen and took my coat to the cloakroom. Everyone sat at the table, place mats and cutlery were laid out and the fish and chips were brought through from the kitchen. Not on the plates that I had seen, as I left to go to the shop, nothing so civilised. Our fish and chips were in their polystyrene boxes, the plates had been returned to the cupboard and Wendy was proud to announce that the cutlery was the rough stuff they use in the garden for barbecues.

This was a good indication of what she thought of her guests. I had never seen anything quite like it.

There were to be more treats in store. For once the meal was over and the packages were being cleared away, I was to have Barbara bear down on me with flashing eyes. She had seen the food that was bought for the wake (I use the term loosely) and was saying firmly, "You have to do something."

If only she knew what we had been through to get what we had.

"I know, I know, but whatever I do is wrong. It has been the same all week. I can do nothing," was my frustrated response.

Nevertheless, it was not long before I was heading to the 24-hour superstores with Susan and Peter to buy the provisions for the unknown numbers of people who may come back to the house tomorrow. Alan was to be given a wake, but not by his widow.

This was blind catering on the hoof. We grabbed a trolley in Sainsbury's and trawled the isles for food. White bread, brown bread, cheese, crisps, biscuits, fruit and goodness knows what else. Paper plates, plastic glasses, it all went in the trolley. Someone back at the cottage had offered to make sandwiches in the morning, so ham was added to our list. At the deli counter the assistant cut slice after slice on the machine and we just kept telling her to continue cutting, and she kept turning towards us with a bewildered expression on her face to ask, "Is this enough?"

"Keep going, we will tell you when there is enough." Was our chorus in reply, and she would return to cut more. There was quite a pile cut before we released her from her task. And back to the isles to continue to fill the trolley, constantly throwing in serving suggestions and seeking ingredients until we had exhausted the useful stock at this supermarket. Through the checkout and back to the car to load the spoils, then a dash across town to another superstore for the other items we needed.

At the end of our second supermarket sweep we treated ourselves to a quick drink in a pub on the way back. We had done a good job.

Back at the house the food was unloaded into the second kitchen ready for the morning. We could relax until then.

After updating Barbara she pounced on me again, "You went to the pub, why did you not take me?"

Can't think of everything can you?

# CHAPTER 6

Friday morning, outside it is overcast and drab, a bleak mid March day.

David clocked on, or that is how it seems now. He had news for Wendy; he had been successful in organising spring flowers at the second florist in town (the garden blooms were past their sell by date). If I had known that flowers were being organised I would have ordered some for myself; this was, after all, my brother being cremated today. But there was no time left for that.

In the kitchen we are in a state of limbo, breakfast completed, we wait, anticipating the ritual we will all be part of later in the day. The food preparation was not pressing; there was time to take it easy. The blackened mini sausage rolls that Wendy had prepared yesterday were, much to her annoyance, now in the dog, and a fresh batch was in the oven. Wendy may have approved the charcoal topping but she was in the minority. Susan's eyes started to show signs of anxiety and I was ready to start the work, so I turned to her and said, "Do you want to start?" readily she agreed.

Within minutes we were getting organised in the second kitchen and as bodies arrive they were given their duties, even her boys, Luke and Jacob, set to. Cilla and Barbara became the sandwich factory. Peter, Luke and Ian were preparing salads, cutting quiches, loading plates and goodness knows what else. Susan keeping them supplied and helping wherever needed, and I was with Jacob sealing the prepared food in cling film, getting it to the table, procuring more serving dishes. At least I think that was happening, what was certain was the buzz of activity in that kitchen. Everyone mucked in and they prepared a handsome spread in an hour and a half. How they managed it so quickly was astounding. Extra brownie points for everyone; they were a terrific team.

Satisfaction for a job well done shone from the faces of Peter and Susan as they surveyed the abundant buffet that generously loaded the dining table and they were right to be proud, as they had organised the spread.

Calm returned, as then we had ample time at our disposal before the cortege was due to arrive, plenty of time to change our clothes and prepare ourselves for the main event.

Wendy was pleased to show me her flowers when they arrived, but I was sickened when I saw her shaky scrawl on the card where she had added to her name, those of Susan, Peter, Luke and Jacob plus, without any prior consultation, my name.

How dare she assume that I wanted my name added? It beggars belief. She should have asked.

The thoughtlessness of that woman was boundless, and to prevent myself from grabbing that card and ripping it to pieces before her eyes, I clasped my hands to my side. I clenched my teeth and walked away.

Since my brother had died, I had been treated appallingly by Wendy and I had witnessed her personality change. What had caused it I do not know, it may be the drink; something may have happened on the night of Alan's death. I have no idea, but whatever the cause, I did not like the result.

I took consolation from the thought that this charade would soon be over and I would be away from all of it. Just the duty of executor to fulfil for Alan remains.

Wendy had cut back on her alcohol consumption as Susan arrived on Friday last, she had taken far less than usual, but since Susan had left to collect her family the intake had increased. Her hands would shake throughout the day until she had her fix of modified grape juice.

Steve walked up the drive, leaving the hearse and car at the gate. This satisfied Wendy, but Susan and I insisted that both should come to the door; Alan should start his final journey from his home. As we waited in the hall to be summoned to the vehicle, Barbara turned to look deep into my eyes, and without hesitation put her arms around me; nothing was said. It was not anticipated; it happened and was very comforting. She joined the family in the car; others who had gathered at the house were following in their own transport.

Like all funerals, the slow drive following the hearse is interminable, and is worsened by the sight of the coffin so prominently displayed behind the glistening glass windows of the hearse in front. No matter how hard I try to look elsewhere, my eyes are drawn to the veneered casket ahead. My brother is alone there, among strangers.

Undoubtedly we each have our personal thoughts as we follow in procession through the seemingly endless winding streets of Torquay to Alan's final destination. I silently pray for strength.

After what seems like an age the cars turn into the grounds of the crematorium and climb the winding road that leads to the chapel, where we are to disembark to join other mourners awaiting our arrival. On this exposed ridge there was nothing to stop the chill wind reaching into your soul.

The coffin stood at the entrance to the chapel while Steve ushers us inside. This was not the order of the cortege that was planned when he visited the house at the beginning of the week; we were due to follow Alan into the chapel. Nor were we the first to enter, for as Wendy and I passed through the doorway, I was taken aback by the sight of the woman already seated on the pews adjacent to the exit door opposite. Two girls who I did not recognise flanked her. Who were they? Their eyes were anxious, but there was no acknowledgement as we walked past them towards our seats at the front, followed by Susan and Peter and the boys, and all the gathered friends.

Only when everyone was seated and settled was the coffin carried solemnly to the dais before us. Shirley took her place at the rostrum and started her simple service, to be relieved while David gave his eulogy, and I reflected that it was such a pity that he did not complete any of the stories that I had told him yesterday, his eyes centering on Wendy for much of his delivery. When Shirley returned to the stand, she finished with something I had seen on a previous trip to Devon when friends who practice spiritualism visited the cottage. She had the congregation close their eyes and imagine they were on a walk in the countryside, beside water and looking into a pond before retracing their steps; but there was something else, something odd about the route she was leading. I remember finding it strange. I took no part in this exercise, as I was calm enough.

The doors to the crematorium furnace opened and Alan left the chapel, as the doors closed behind him, I heard the uncontrolled sobbing from Wendy beside me. Whether it was remorse or relief that induced it I still wonder, there have been few signs of grieving from her before; a minute in quiet reflection before we filed out past the unknown woman and two red-eyed children alongside the exit.

Wendy held court in the niche opposite that, which now housed her flowers, the card proudly displaying her name alongside mine and Susan and her family fluttered in the cold wind. It stood defiant at my disdainful glance. We all shivered in the cold as slowly the queue progressed towards Wendy, and she was in no hurry. Eventually we did leave, but I did not see the departure of the unknown threesome.

As we leave the crematorium I am inwardly willing serenity and peace for us all.

Our silence during the journey back to the cottage was broken only by the idle babble of Wendy. We craved silence and I was not alone in wishing her further.

Cars and friends covered the forecourt of the cottage as we were driven up the drive. We all needed to seek shelter from the weather that showed no sign of improving. The wind was cutting and rain was in the air. People shuffled from foot to foot and rubbed their hands to keep warm while they nervously waited to get into the house, but Wendy, who had the only key, was oblivious to their discomfort. The cold was having its effect on the bladders of some, and they transferred their weight from foot to foot, not solely from the need to stay warm.

Eventually she got the message and finally used the only key to our comfort. We all fell through the front door, into the hall where some relieved themselves of their coats, some headed to toilets to relieve themselves in other ways, and all the loos were taking the first rush of guests. Teas and coffees were being prepared, glasses were being filled and the house was alive with the hubbub of chattering people. They were spreading everywhere, in the hall, kitchen, and sitting room. The dining room echoed with the rustle of cling film as it was swiftly removed from the prepared dishes of food. Thinking of 'swiftly removed,' Shirley, who had played her part at the service, had shed her coat, but not the shoes, perhaps she decided to keep them on for a quick getaway.

Some of Alan's true friends did not make it back to the house, but it was good to catch up with all those that did, for it must have been the Christmas break when I saw many of them last.

Andrew was here with his wife; they are a sweet couple. They had been to the house since Alan passed away and I recall how badly Andrew had reacted to the loss. On his first visit he was completely bowled over, and looked to me as if he had part of his skull removed. A strange description, but nevertheless the most accurate I can proffer. He had grown very close to my brother, who had become his mentor, training Andrew in the art of healing. I was relieved today to see him looking more complete.

During the afternoon I chatted with Max, a colourful character who loves people. He has a prestigious hotel in the bay and took time out when Wendy and Alan first moved in here to snag the rooms. Snagging is something done when refurbishing a building to pinpoint the thing that needs doing to complete the project.

I had made the curtains and been involved in the planning and design, therefore I had an interest in his views, and I have to admit that the way he did it was a joy to watch, little got passed his eagle eye.

Being in catering, he looked toward the table today and said to me; "Wendy has worked hard to prepare the food." I did not comment I was not going to shatter his illusion and tell him that she had done nothing; there had been enough upset this week.

Bill, a long standing friend of Alan's had motored from London directly from his work to be here today, so I offered him the use of my bedroom to rest and freshen up before he returned to London. Wendy was not so charitable; he had changed from formal garb into something more casual to relax a little. She, announcing to all in sundry, too much detail of the confidential nature of his work, then continued very loudly for all to hear in the crowded kitchen.

"I see you have not made any effort in your dress today Bill."

"Neither have you Wendy. You look like you are wearing the curtains." He immediately replied. Sadly, this was a very good description of the wide striped cream and black shirt and pleated skirt that she had donned for the day. He retired to another room and had little contact with her until he left to start his drive back to London for his work shift that night.

Cilla and Ian, Wendy's friends, had arrived yesterday, and stayed in the farthest bedroom in the servant's wing overnight, and she was telling me how the soap and toiletries that she put on the basin in their room kept returning to her suitcase unaided. Each time she reached for the soap that she had placed on the basin it was gone, the same happened to her towel. She was confused to find them once more back in the case. We laughed about it, but I did not tell her of the other strange events of the week. That would really have worried her.

She would not traverse the corridor on that landing alone; Ian was summoned to escort her. The feeling of a presence and the eerie cold spooked her. She was not alone this week in experiencing that phenomenon on the landing that led to the 'boy's rooms.'

There was to be no more paranormal activity today, just socialising with the people on this plane.

# CHAPTER 7

One by one we drifted into the kitchen to prepare our respective teas or coffees and toast on Saturday morning and then consume them in the study. Barbara and I were the first, and I was glad to have time alone with her. We had met only once briefly several years ago, but there had been a natural bond between us on this meeting, like the meeting of old friends. Something likened to that of soul mates that I had talked of with David. The subject of Alan's other lady came up and she told me how Alan would frequently ring her to talk of his dilemma; the relationship was still active, maybe not physical, but Alan would meet his lady on the evenings that he met up with his mates for a drink. I wished that she had told me earlier because I would love to have thanked her for giving Alan some pleasure in his life. Wendy gave him little in recent years. I was due to leave for home in an hour or so. I know that, years ago she lived just up the coast in Brixham. If my memory does not fail me, I was a guest at a dinner party at her bungalow before anything was known of Alan's relationship with her, but that was years ago. As I recall she had two daughters; perhaps these were the three females in the chapel. Given time I could trawl the town in the hope of recognising the place in an attempt to find her, but time I have not: the road to Kent beckons. So for now my gratitude to the mystery lady will remain unsaid.

Barbara was also to tell me of my brother's intention to give his girlfriend one of the houses that he planned to build at the top of the paddock. How I recall reflecting on what Wendy's reaction would be if she had her husband's other woman living on the brow of the hill overlooking the cottage, their home. Naturally I did not voice my thoughts. What could you possibly say?

Cilla and Ian are to stay with Wendy a day or two longer. I smiled as I reflect that Ian will be kept busy if he has to accompany Cilla along the landing to the bedroom. I would like to be a fly on the wall.

Barbara was the first to leave on her homeward journey. I followed with Susan, Peter and the boys in convoy as we plan to stop half way for a meal together. Just as we are about to head towards the gate, Jacob, the youngest, asks to join me in my car and with his parents blessing, he straps himself in the seat beside mine. His chirpy, cheeky manner makes for a good companion as we negotiate the road that heads eastwards. Halfway home and I leave the main road and watch the startled reaction of those in the car behind as I motor down a lane, unfamiliar to them, but I know of a pub with good grub, and it is calling us.

Walking through the door into the pub our senses are greeted with the hubbub from the busy bars, the busiest being the restaurant, which is heaving. Below the low heavily beamed ceilings, the tightly packed tables are filled to capacity, leaving only the scrubbed trestle table in the bay window that had been dressed with cutlery to advertise food to passers-by.

I have by now been far too long without eating properly; it has also been a long time since I have been amongst normal people who are going about their normal lives, socialising with friends, and enjoying being with their families. That is precisely what is happening in this country pub. This is exactly what is required and now that I am here, I intend to stop for a while.

I got permission to use the only unoccupied table for our party, and we swiftly squeeze ourselves around the table in the window. The publican's display yields to the heavily laden hot plates of homemade pub grub that we get from the carvery, and the assortment of liquor filled glasses.

Steak and kidney pie, potatoes and vegetables with sturdy gravy, and a pint of real ale may not be gourmet eating, but it does wonders for my metabolism; this is comfort eating with substance that my body has been craving for too long and now joyfully receives.

Throughout the meal I notice the glances from fellow diners. We are obviously strangers in this little backwater; just a few hundred yards from one of the main arterial routes to the West Country. Maybe we have broken with convention by taking over the display table, whatever the reason for their interest; it will not detract from my enjoyment of this interlude and I tuck into the pie, sup the bitter and enjoy the company; feeling the warmth building in my body.

Feeling fully fortified and refreshed, we make our way back to our respective cars in the car park to say our farewells and make the rest of the journey to our homes.

Alone, as the miles passed below the swiftly rotating wheels, there is plenty of time to consider the events that took my brother away and how he was dispatched.

I had seen all those people in Devon who had been part of both our lives, who knows whether I shall see any of them again.

I have lost my only brother. It was not altogether unexpected. But why should I feel so uneasy about his death? I have seen the death of loved ones so many times before, this is not a new experience for me, but in some way this time it is different. Perhaps it is the chain of events leading up to the night of his death, which I knew about; the request for the family tree or his aggravated manner when we last spoke. No, it is not just that; neither is it the treatment that I and other's had received from Wendy, nor her personality change.

During this last week in Devon I have heard several accounts of Alan's death; just as I have been given several reasons for the delay in the release of the death certificate. Wendy had said that Alan was home that night, as he felt unwell; his drinking companions said that it was because one of them was ill. But that aside, if Alan had the heart attack in his bedroom how could he call out for help? When a heart attack strikes, exhaling is unlikely and shouting would be, at least, difficult. His voice would need to be very strong, as it would have had to travel by a very convoluted route to be able to reach Wendy, who was in the main kitchen on the floor below his bedroom. Any sound would have diminished drastically on its journey and on its arrival; it would also need to compete with the television or radio which Wendy would normally use. I seriously doubt whether anything could have been heard.

In event of a heart attack the normal reaction would be to phone the emergency services. But when Alan was struck down, Wendy had acted as if she were appearing on "Who wants to be a millionaire?" She had 'phoned a friend,' namely David.

Where had Alan actually died? Was it in his chair in the study, on the floor of his bedroom, or in the chair there? I had been told each of these versions, but which is correct? If he died on the floor, how did he arrive on his bed? You are, by now, fully aware how my brother always tried to buck the system in his life, but who would have expected him to be able to take things to this extreme. Normally you die in only one place and stay put, you do not die in several. Wendy wanted Alan's body removed from the house, but who had actually taken it? Was it the undertaker or the ambulance men? Why was David so concerned to have no visible trace of stains on the stair or bedroom carpets in the early hours? What has actually happened in Devon?

As you can gather, not only my intuition tells me that all is not as it seems. Only inconsistency is consistent. In the deep recesses of my mind a nagging uncertainty of the manner of Alan's death haunts me. That is where it must stay for now, because I have to get on with my life. Within hours I shall be home. Post will need attention. Washing has to be done. Then work. This has been like every other major event in my life; a turning point. I am simply at the end of a chapter and about to turn over another page.

# CHAPTER 8

So I am back home after one traumatic week. Certainly while I was away, I knew full well, that my life would never be the same again, but what lie ahead could not be foreseen.

Cooking, cleaning and all those mundane chores await my attention. Unopened post and junk mail had been neatly arranged in piles on the kitchen worktop by a neighbour who had kindly kept an eye on things in the house while I have been away.

As the kettle is boiling I unpack the case and sort the dirty laundry ready for the washing machine, which is quickly put to work on the first load.

I am sipping a cup of tea while opening the array of envelopes and packages that have arrived in my absence. The discarded advertising letters, envelopes and packaging forms a formidable heap on the floor beside the table, I reckon the waste material amounts to about half of a tree. That rubbish is bagged up for disposal and what remains on the table is stacked according to type and priority. I listened to the myriad of messages on the telephone answering machine, deleting the crud as I go. Tasks completed, I know I am home, but apart from getting some food and a drink, a strong one, all that remains to be done today is relax and let the dross broadcast on the television numb my brain for the rest of the evening. Tomorrow I will re-establish myself fully.

I am not to know that the routine I planned to organise for myself was going to be elusive, and not form part of my life for quite a while.

*****

I was uneasy with the way Wendy had treated me after Alan's death. We had, after all, been there for each other in times of need for so many years. But throughout the week she had been, on occasions, stand-offish at best, and frequently extremely rude.

Notwithstanding, I was not the only person to have received bad treatment from her. Bill, who had travelled between work shifts in London to be at Alan's funeral, had been on the receiving end of Wendy's vicious tongue. Susan had to endure the nights sleeping in her father's bedroom following his demise, along with other unpleasantness. Wendy had mentioned giving Susan a keepsake that had belonged to her father; there were a couple of things Wendy apparently wanted Susan to have; but Susan never received anything. When she mentioned it to me I tried to console her with the idea that she had her memories and no one can take those away from her. Alan's car that Irene tried to acquire immediately after Alan's death, would have benefited Susan, but she could not bring herself to mention that to Wendy; Susan would have paid for the car; nevertheless it was all too soon. Looking back, there are so many similar unpleasant instances. Everything related to my brother was tainted.

Incidentally, Wendy's friend Barbara, while we were in Devon, had told Susan and I that we should have full access to everything as executors of Alan's will; we should be fully involved. Having observed our situation Barbara was quite aware that we were excluded from everything. She also knew Wendy's lawyer had not explained the will.

I had expected Wendy's lawyer, Philippa, to perform this courtesy, as Wendy had previously told Philippa that Susan had not had any prior experience of dealing with the affairs of anyone deceased. We were deliberately told nothing except that, in the fullness of time, we would each be summoned to separate lawyers to authenticate the papers that they would prepare. That was obviously intended to be the sum total of our involvement in the procedure.

Wendy had told me during the week following Alan's death that she was preceding with the purchase of the freehold of the plots, which formed part of the grounds, leased from the previous owners of Shorton Cottage. I was puzzled by her haste and I had assumed that this packet of land would, by reading Alan's will and wishes, be part of his estate, therefore Susan and I should have been involved in any transactions as executors and trustees. Wendy had been so curiously covert in her recent undertakings; all this contributed further to my motivation to get legal advice.

It was within weeks of Alan's death that Susan and I first had an appointment with my lawyers in order to gain reassurance, and to enquire about our responsibilities as executor and trustees of my brother's estate. This we felt was fully justified as a result of Wendy's callous behaviour since Alan's death, and her wilful self-reliance that was tantamount to deliberately obstructing our access to anything relating to my brother's estate and will. We needed clarification about our duties and liabilities.

I had previous dealings with this legal practice when they handled the conveyancing of the two properties since my divorce. Michael had taken on the problems with the Council Tax on the first house in Cuxton Road and then, with the second house, the house builder's permission for the conservatory was overlooked before completion of the purchase.

Neither incident could be classed as negligence. I have seen that Michael is very good when looking at the grand picture, but he has been known to falter on the detail. None of us are perfect. His practice is housed in offices that consist of two high street shop units, built about 1900, with several floors above. The receptionist announced our arrival to the lawyer who was to see us today, and the person, who was to help us, swiftly greeted us. This was to be the first meeting with this neatly turned out lady, who by her tidy business-like clothing, grooming and manner gave the impression that she would miss nothing in her work. All the '*i*'s' would be dotted and the '*t*'s crossed with precision, no detail would be missed. Reassuring qualities for what may lie ahead.

Jane treats us in a friendly efficient manner as she shows us to the large office on the first floor above the reception. From the two front facing, lofty sash windows we can see the 1960's office block opposite, it contains the local government departments and Crown Courts. The edifice obstructs the view of the river Medway; but not completely, as either side of the squat tower, the vista unfurls to reveal the curves of the river as it meanders up and down stream. Inside the office there is a hotchpotch of miss-matched furniture and filing cabinets, as you may expect to see in a lawyers practice.

Jane settles herself behind the large mahogany table while offering us the use of jacquard upholstered mahogany side chairs. She arranges the six A4 sheets of photocopied paper that makes up Alan's will and wishes; the contents digested, she raised her head to look at us, and I look into her eyes to see that the somewhat coy persona conceals an astute lively brain. She started her explanation of our duties and liabilities as executors and confirms to us that we would become responsible for anything that we put our signature to in its' execution.

Apparently our duties are to include our confirmation that everything submitted to the probate office is correct, and we are entitled to have a full disclosure of everything that is used to compile the probate papers to enable us to do this. So far there has been no divulgence; we know nothing. More importantly, we would be equally responsible should we put our signature to anything that proved to be fraudulent; we would be held equally as liable for the indiscretion as the person who instigated it would.

Turning her attention to the contents of the will and wishes before her, Jane broadly outlines the intentions they contain. Everything was as Alan had told, namely, that the house and everything would form a trust for Wendy, which would in the fullness of time be handed down to Susan and finally to the boys. It would be safeguarded for their use. Nobody, not even the taxman, could deprive them of the fruits of his life's efforts. Jane's answers to our inquiries are considered before they are delivered. Throughout our meeting she analyses the contents of the papers spread in front of her. Her body language and facial expression indicate her slight unease with what she is reading, but she says nothing about what she is contemplating. She told us that she would be conferring with Michael later to seek clarification of some of the detail.

As Susan and I left the lawyers' office we were invited to contact Jane or Michael again should we wish. Jane undertook to fully brief Michael about our meeting. I was pleased to have Jane involved with our case; her work would be meticulous.

What I had learned today strengthened my resolve that there could be no deviation from the norm on any paper that I put my mark. My wish for clarification today had been fully justified.

Following our meeting with Jane, Susan and I were still very uneasy about everything that had followed Alan's demise. Neither of us had peace of mind.

Wendy had such a change of demeanour. It was not just the way we had both been treated while in Devon, nor was it the tawdry funeral arrangements. There was also the covert way Wendy was handling Alan's will, plus we had been given different accounts of the events surrounding Alan's death. Normality, integrity and common decency were playing no part in the saga we were being drawn into. Little wonder I felt apprehension. Nothing felt right: Nothing made sense.

Within days of our appointment with Jane I had a phone conversation with Wendy, who told me that she is about to exchange contracts on the purchase of the two plots of land in the grounds that were previously leased. Her delivery was defiant and had an underlying unpleasantness that I could not define, but had experienced similar recently from her. How could she, within days of cremating her husband, buy or sell part of his estate? As executors and trustees, Susan and I would need to know of this. Furthermore the furnace at the crematorium was not yet cool; no dust had time to settle. This was not normal behaviour; it was all too soon.

I was alerted earlier, when I was in Devon, to the sincerity of Wendy's intentions when she had delivered the line "I am doing everything for the boys." She stood on the main staircase and proclaimed this in a surreal manner. What prompted her to do this puzzled me at the time. Maybe it was her conscience, but that I doubt. There were echoes from the story of Norma Desmond in Sunset Boulevard when she, in the final act, loses her contact with sanity and readies herself for the filming of her close-up on the grand staircase. Norma would then have been taken away for treatment.

I faxed Philippa, the Devon lawyer dealing with the estate to inquire of the details of Wendy's proposed land purchase, and was amazed to receive her reply by fax within an hour. She wrote that her company was not involved with the property deal; strangely it did not form part of Alan's estate, but those few questions that I had asked were important enough to produce her rapid reaction. Her swift written response included the undertaking to give a full disclosure of the details of Alan's estate; she has, to date, not honoured her undertaking.

Even after the appointment with Jane, at our lawyer's office, the will remains an enigma. I have read and re-read it many, many, times and still it looks incomplete and shoddy; the numbering of paragraphs is not quite correct and the text does not, in total, make sense when it is read. This is not logical, knowing how Alan would scrutinise legal papers in every detail.

While I was involved in my protracted divorce he would help me with the correspondence, and that revealed to me how detailed he would be when dealing with legal matters. He had after all, spent many years fighting various firms of lawyers who were negligent in dealing with the conveyancing of the purchase of Cecil Road and all that followed. Sloppy work done by the legal fraternity had cost him thousands of pounds and even more hours, even years, of anguish while he was alive and I am sure he would not wish anything similar to happen as a result of his will after his death. His will would have been constructed to do exactly what he wished without any complications.

Incidentally, while I was in Devon Wendy had repeatedly said, "The will is very clever." I could see no evidence of cleverness in the papers that I had been given as Alan's will.

I expected to see an immaculate document. His will should have been the slickest ever written.

The document presented to me is not.

*****

They say two minds being greater than one; Well Susan and I spent time discussing everything that had happened. We came to the conclusion that Wendy was about to make a serious error in judgement in her handling of Alan's estate, she was not going to follow Alan's wishes. Susan had read the relevant tax laws, and a fraud may also have been on Wendy's agenda. Were we to sign the probate papers Wendy was preparing and any sharp practice had been perpetrated, we would be held equally responsible in law.

It was time to contact Michael's office for his advice and assistance.

Because of my work commitments it was Susan who initially contacted the lawyers' office to get an appointment, but Michael had a full diary, as you would expect, so we would have to wait a while before seeing him. During the evening Susan phoned me to tell me the date of the appointment and we discussed the events again, and it was strange how we simultaneously came to the conclusion that Alan's death might have been induced.

Next morning I contacted Michael's office and the appointment was brought forward. Michael rescheduled his time to accommodate us, two o'clock the next day.

A copy of Alan's will and wishes, and my notes of the events in Devon were in my briefcase for the meeting. Arriving slightly early, the receptionist greeted us with cold efficiency. Michael was lunching in his office, but I stopped the receptionist from interrupting him, what we were about to tell him was likely to affect when he would be able to get another meal. I certainly had no idea of what was to happen next, this was very unfamiliar ground for me.

At the allotted time we were ushered into the office on the first floor by Michael and introduced to Jane again. She was joining us for the meeting.

For the next hour and a half or so we studied the will and unloaded the facts, as we knew them. It would be futile to repeat much of what you are already aware. I gave my account and Susan made her contribution to the debriefing. She mentioned additional observations that she had made during her visits to Devon following her father's death, which included the stained bedding that was on the high shelf in the cloakroom, adjacent to the ground floor toilet/laundry room. All the time, both Michael and Jane were making comprehensive notes, page after page of their A4 pads were being covered with the tiny script that I have seen other lawyers use. Periodically Michael would ask questions and steer his enquiries' and it was not until the end that he voiced his opinion.

He suspected a conspiracy of sort, what exactly that was he was not letting us know, except, he thought David Hart was involved and the conspiracy did not end with him, in truth, he was not sure of how far it did extend.

He was to see a friend who was a retired senior police official for advice. If this were to be a case for the police it would be channelled through the head of the Kent police to the head of the Devon constabulary, then down through the ranks to trusted officers. Michael and Jane had ideas of their own about this case and they were going to keep those to themselves; we were not to be told.

Shock at being taken so seriously, added to the thoughts racing through my mind as we exited the office and joined the rest of humanity in the High Street. I had expected to be shown the door much earlier, but no, we had been interrogated for almost two hours. Michael's attentiveness illustrated that he thought, as we did, that all was not well in the county of Devon.

The following weeks stretched into months and in that time Susan and I had additional trips to see the lawyer to discuss what was being unearthed about Alan's business. Those first visits followed the format of the first briefing session with Michael conducting the proceedings while busying himself, taking copious notes of all that was said. Jane sat in and echoed Michael in her task of recording on paper all those precious details and from time to time adding her thoughts and requests. Each interview lasted, as the first, almost two hours; and as you can imagine, lots of information was exchanged.

Michael was interested to know more of Alan's elusive friend, and as Susan and I were about to leave his office he reminded me that he suggested that I contact Wendy or David the next evening to get the woman's name and address. As we shook hands, his vice-like grasp of my hand was almost uncomfortable; he asked which person I would be phoning.

My reply was, "I will sleep on it." I was unsure.

I have learned that when I have a problem that makes me feel uneasy, a tried and tested method that yields the best results is literally to sleep on it: Exactly as I had said to Michael. That night in bed I mentally requested whom I should phone that could lead me to the identity of this woman.

As I awoke the name of Alan's friend Andrew was in the forefront of my mind. He, like the lady I sought, lived somewhere in Brixham, that much I knew, but I had neither his address nor surname. I did know that he had started to teach art in an adult education centre, but which one and in what town I knew not.

There was no alternative for me than to follow the lead I had been given overnight. During the day a list of Adult education establishments in the Torbay area and the towns within a thirty-mile radius was compiled. My heart sunk as I prepared myself to dial my way down the list before me; this was a crazy caper with such a very slim chance of success. I was looking for a needle in a haystack and I doubted whether anybody on the other end of the line would co-operate. Anyone I spoke to would think I was crazy.

Here goes. I braced myself and planned what I would say before dialling the first number on the paper before me.

I said, "I wonder if you can help me, I am looking for an Andrew who teaches art to adults and he wears a small ponytail. He was a friend of my brother Alan, who died a few weeks ago. I am afraid I do not have his full name. Can you help me please?"

The first call was, as I had feared not fruitful so I continued to the next number. I repeated my speech, thinking what an impossible mission this was. The lady listened until I had finished my routine and she said, "Is that you Peter? This is Mandy, Andrew's wife. How are you?" This to me was nothing short of amazing. Who would expect this to happen, it was beyond my comprehension that this had worked, and so easily. Mandy and I chatted a little and she told me that Andrew was at home looking after the children; she gave me the home number and address, and then suggested that I call him a little later.

That evening I was on a roll and before long I was talking to Andrew, he was fully aware of my brother's relationship. He not only knew the lady, she was a very close friend, but he was not going to tell me more without her approval. He would ask her permission before giving me her name and address, which is understandable. As the phone was returned to its resting place I recalled my mixed feelings. The pleasure of talking again to Andrew and his wife, Mandy, who frankly I feared had gone from my life with the exit of my brother; but I was bewildered that they had been traced so easily, and that they aid my quest.

Several years earlier I had been with my wife Brenda, Wendy and Alan to a dinner party held by Alan's lady. This was before Alan had started his extra relationship. There was another couple at the meal, and although I cannot remember who they were, I have a nagging feeling at the back of my mind that it was Andrew and Mandy.

Andrew phoned me with the news that he could not give me the details I sought, so the woman remains an enigma. I asked whether she had been at the funeral and he told me that she was not, but one of her daughters had been there, accompanied by a friend; but I am sure he was not being completely candid. The identity of the lady flanked by two girls seated in the crematorium chapel, as we arrived, remains unknown. Nevertheless we had a chance to talk a little and he told me of his shock at the death of my brother, that I had so readily witnessed when I saw Andrew in Devon, and how he was not aware how ill Alan was. Alan had trained Andrew as a healer. How I would have loved to voice my doubts about the circumstances of Alan's death, but this did not feel like an appropriate time.

On reflection, I had achieved much in locating the route whereby I could make contact with the other woman, if it was essential later. Secondly, I had located and made contact with Alan's prodigy. The third outcome came out of the blue from Andrew, the healer, who indicated incredulity, as he had no perception that Alan was so seriously ill; ill enough to die.

Unbelievably all this had been achieved without contacting Wendy or David, who I knew had the information I sought, and I had, by not contacted them, avoided ruffling their feathers.

If only I had those transcripts of our meetings with my lawyer, this section of the book would be so much easier to complete and I would be able to give you so much more detail. As it is I will greatly condense those lengthy meetings to provide their essence, that will save being weighed down by the minutiae.

Between meetings, it transpires that Michael and Jane had been busying themselves, making inquiries and obtaining copies of the relevant documents; while Susan and I did similar. We pieced together the facts as they became available and tried to understand Wendy, and the motivations that resulted in her actions.

It was the day before one of these meetings with Michael. Susan and I had spent time together discussing what we felt we would need to discuss and had returned to her home to make some notes for the next day. There was a lot to put to paper and it seemed impossibly complicated as we started.

Susan sat before the computer, ready to transfer our thoughts onto the keyboard. She can touch type, so it would have been faster for her to operate the machine, but it was not long before she turned to me and said, "I cannot do this."

We swapped places and I settled myself before the screen and started typing. My two-fingered technique (not those two fingers,) is not the best, but eventually our words were forming on the screen before us. I became engrossed by the task and recall thinking how our notes were so different from what we had proposed earlier in the day. The format was simplicity itself, nothing like the complicated clauses and sub clauses that we had envisaged. As I worked, the screen filled with our notes and I became totally immersed in the task. My eyes became riveted to the computer screen; they no longer looked down to the keyboard, as they would have normally, to seek the location of the keys.

It was then that I realised, I had been touch-typing. Remarkable, as I do not have that skill. "I am touch typing!" I exclaimed to Susan, "but I cannot do that."

But that was not all. Stranger still, I became aware how the precision of the text faltered when I thought about what I was doing. Immediately I became conscious of my actions while typing, I made mistakes. Teachers of touch-typing could explain that as a natural reaction, but they could not account for the way the words were being compiled before my eyes. That day, text was not as either of us had intended. It was far more economic and concise.

Touch-typing still eludes me, but stranger still, I have occasionally not recognised what I have written myself, while working on this book.

It became obvious that it was Wendy's intention to ignore the wishes of my deceased brother and exclude Susan and her boys from ultimately benefiting from the fruits of Alan's lifetime's efforts.

Allow me to take this time to explain Alan's intentions in his will and wishes that were deposited on Susan and myself by Wendy's lawyer in Devon.

When I first was handed a copy of these documents in that tacky office in Paignton; I scanned them. Although the wishes were as Alan had explained to me years earlier, while we walked in the grounds of Shorton Cottage, something was amiss. I stopped myself from asking Philippa, Wendy's lawyer, for the rest of the document once I had read it. To this day I doubt the authenticity. Instinctively I felt that they were incorrect, incomplete, something was missing and that initial concept remains steadfast with me even after the months that have followed. On close inspection, there is at least one error; namely the numbering of the clauses and why is Wendy's niece mentioned on one page? She is not mentioned elsewhere as an executor or beneficiary. Knowing how exact Alan was with any legal papers that he signed, I doubt whether he would have endorsed these.

The will and wishes, placed before Susan and myself by Philippa, indicated that we were to be the executors with Wendy, and we three would ultimately become the trustees of the trust to be set up with the proceeds of Alan's estate. This trust was envisaged to safeguard Shorton Cottage and holdings, so that in time it would pass from Wendy to Susan and ultimately to her two boys, Luke and Jacob. Alan's intention to instigate this course of action was to safeguard and protect the assets from tax liabilities or possibly any shortfall in tax payments that may have been made during his life. He would, after all, bedevil the establishment whenever he could. Why should he stop beyond the grave?

Alan was also very aware that Wendy had very little business sense and she had, on more than one occasion, cost him dearly by opening her mouth to the wrong people and at the wrong time. Perhaps her alcoholism was responsible for her loose tongue.

The proposed trust was to be administered by us three to provide accommodation and an income for Wendy during her life. Then, on her death, it would be Susan who would become the virtual caretaker for the boys until they were of an age to be able to benefit from their grandfather's estate.

It was early August when Wendy arranged for her lawyers to send proof copies of the probate papers, and tax declaration form to Michael. The contents revealed precisely what I had expected. Wendy had no intention of complying with my brother's Will. She presented a sham. The estate was merely listed as a few thousand pounds; all houses and land were excluded. In addition both her and her lawyer in Devon had failed to provide the requested comprehensive disclosure I requested in April.

A letter accompanying the probate documents sought the approval of Susan and I, and had we sanctioned them, the originals together with the original Will would have been sent for us to sign and 'swear'. These papers had already been approved by Wendy and upon our agreement she would sign and 'swear'.

Unbeknown to me at the time, Susan had received and rejected the same. In addition Wendy's friend Barbara phoned Susan to tell her, that it was in her best interest to sign the papers. Barbara went on to reveal that she had been shown everything while in Devon and she was reassured that Alan's Will was being followed as he had intended. Barbara advised Susan to visit Wendy before the end of the summer school holidays, or Wendy would change her intentions. Additionally Barbara reported that David Hart had 'his feet well under the table at Shorton Cottage' and his influence over Wendy increasing; hardly surprising having observing him and Wendy while waiting for Alan's funeral.

Being an executor is not a pleasant duty; it is something I have had to do too often. I feel bound to do all I can to fulfil the obligation that has been bestowed on me by my brother. It is a final act of decency, a means to respect the wishes of the dead, but it seems in this instance, if Wendy is to have her way, there will be no honouring of her dead husband or his final wishes. No allegiance from her, the person, with whom he chose to spend his time on earth.

I withheld my endorsement.

# CHAPTER 9

As Christmas approached I had a letter from Susan, who wanted me to contact her. She was eager to get me to join her at the lawyers to find out how far he had progressed and if he had as she suspected, not put his full attention into dealing with the case.

Ideally she would have liked me to agree to transfer to another legal practice, but I was not prepared to sanction that at this stage; it would involve additional costs which she, no doubt, would require me to settle from my funds.

I joined Susan at Michael's office where she set to heavily interrogate him about his progress. Watching the exchanges it was clear that Susan was far from happy with what she was being told. It became obvious also, that Susan had independently been in Michael's office since our last joint meeting. She also revealed the result of her investigations with the Devon Constabulary, about the normal procedures taken by the police and ambulance services in the Devon area, and voiced her understanding that these had not been followed in the case of her father's death. Michael was to seek clarification.

The most important aspect came about as a result of the revelation concealed in the documents brought to the office by Susan. Minutes before leaving home, she had received, by post, a copy of the deed relating to the sale of one of the building plots; it had been sent in error by the Land Registry in answer to her request for the documents relating to Shorton Cottage. Michael was puzzled when he read this to discover Tosser's of Exeter compiled the papers, these were the lawyers used by Wendy and Alan for property transactions. I would like to have witnessed his reaction had he realised that the signatures were witnessed by people using the address of Eastleys, the lawyers who have been instructed by Wendy to oversee the administration of Alan's will. Susan has, since our meeting, sent Michael a copy of those recent deeds and drew his attention to the two legal companies involved.

There have been many anomalies and numerous coincidences since this torrid saga began and this one is quite curious. Consider if you will; the fact is that there are numerous legal practices in the West of England and it just so happens, that all parties involved in this transaction, sale and purchase, are using the two companies previously used by my brother and his widow.

She also gave an account to Michael of her contact with the Devon Constabulary. They had confirmed that no record of her father's death had been logged with them as it should have been, had normal procedures been followed.

The meeting ended with an undertaking, at Susan's instigation, that Michael provide her with copies of the correspondence that he was holding; I understand from a copy of the letter written by Susan, subsequently, that he has not fulfilled that commitment. He has however acknowledged the coincidence of using the same two lawyers on the deeds.

*****

The gloom of winter is passing. The daffodils are in full golden glory in the gardens to herald the start of the warmer weather. Fresh green buds are bursting on the trees and shrubs. Nature is waking from its slumber. Spring has been formally confirmed with the altering of the clocks to British summer time and we are feeling the benefit of the longer days and sunsets an hour later.

The anniversary of my brother's death has passed and his will and wishes are no closer to fulfilment. What is to happen to the fruits of his life toils? They are not, as yet, being distributed as he intended? Whether they will be, only time will tell. From what I have gathered so far, it seems that his widow can, with the blessing of the legal system, ignore her husband's will and wishes. If this is so, it can only be yet another example of the immoral way the law works in England; certainly decency and justice plays little part in it. There has been no communication from Wendy or her lawyer for months. Nothing since I rejected her proposal to disregard Alan's last will and testament by refusing to sign the probate papers that Wendy had had prepared.

Four weeks had passed since I delivered a letter to Michael's office asking for his clarification about the present situation, but no reply has been received as yet. His silence is deafening.

But all has not been still. Susan has been frustrated by the situation and has written to the head of the Devon police telling of her uncertainty about the circumstances surrounding her father's death. She also, in her letter, outlined the conversation she had with the Devon police earlier, when she sought clarification of the normal modus operandi when death happens. Her prime concern is the police involvement at the time of a death; the procedure that was not, according to their records, followed on the day of Alan's demise.

Thus far, only an acknowledgement has been forthcoming from Chief Inspector S.D. Lander, the Staff Officer of the Chief Constable of Devon. They have passed the matter on to Chief Superintendent McGrath at the Paignton establishment that is an office just 50 yards from the end of Shorton Road, the road that leads to my brother's house.

Now that the investigation has returned to the place of its origin, or at least within walking distance, it may be time to start the final act to put Alan's house in order.

We have lived through a chain of events that started where they are now, in Paignton.

All that needs to happen is the final joining of the links. Is this too much to ask?

The words of the poet S. J Heaney could not be more appropriate to honour Alan's trust.

"Within new limits now, arrange the world
And square the circle: four walls and a ring."

# CHAPTER 10

# A Log of correspondence with The Devon & Cornwall Constabulary

Thank goodness we had the insight to keep logs of events and correspondence as they were to become invaluable in the years to come.

My first correspondence with the Devon Police was in November 2002 when I sent a letter, as I thought, to the Chief Constable, but the address I had obtained from the Internet was not correct and my letter was forwarded to a Sergeant Griffiths of Chudleigh Police, Newton Abbot.

It was a couple of weeks later when I received a telephone call from Sergeant Griffiths. Searches were made by him and no information was logged to say that the police had been called to, or visited the house or Torbay Hospital at the time of Alan's death. The procedures for a sudden death were explained to me; they had not been followed. Furthermore, the ambulance and Doctor's procedure were not standard. The sergeant advised me to contact the Coroner at Torbay Hospital, and the Chief Constable in Exeter.

I was to contact the Coroner first; both written and verbal exchanges took place in the weeks that followed, and it was early in 2003 that a letter was sent to the Chief Constable, Maria Wallis. I voiced concerns regarding the matter that Sergeant Griffiths of Newton Abbot had checked his records and was unable to find any information logged to say that the police had been called to, or visited the home of Alan, or Torbay Hospital at the time of his death. Sergeant Griffiths' opinion was that I should take the matter further by writing to the Coroner and Chief Constable Wallis and supplied the address. I received a card from Maria Wallis which simply stated: Your correspondence has been forwarded to Chief Superintendent McGrath at Paignton.

Within a couple of weeks I had sent a letter to Chief Superintendent McGrath explaining that I had feared my father had not died of natural causes, and I wanted to share information I had with him. His reply came within days and I was informed that the matter had been forwarded to Inspector Blackhouse at Paignton Police Station, and I would hear further in due course.

Six weeks passed and I had heard nothing, so without further ado, I wrote to Sergeant Backhouse with eight points that needed further clarification. These matters related to The Coroner's Report, the Initial Report to the Coroner, and the Request for Post-Mortem; all had anomalies.

It was to be a further seven weeks before I was to receive a letter from a Detective Chief Inspector K Tilke, detailing findings from his investigation in reply to points raised in my letter of 27 May 2003.

My reply followed, voicing my concerns that such a serious matter had been taken so lightly, furthermore, I had not been interviewed regarding allegations made. A copy of my letter was also sent to the Chief Constable.

September of the same year I followed up my letter to Tilke with another. This time the content focussed on anomalies surrounding Alan's will and wishes. I included the fact that this will, without the wishes, had been sworn at Bristol Crown Court, without my knowledge or agreement.

I needed to wait only a week or so before I received his reply, whereby he writes to acknowledge papers received dated 7 September in connection to Alan's will. He states the original file has been forwarded to an officer for independent review prior to considering further enquiries they will conduct. He adds that as soon as he has a result he will let me know their intended course of action.

A letter sent in October to DCI Tilke regarding his previous letter dated 16 September, which had stated I would be informed of the intended course of action, also expressed that Peter Hindley, brother of the deceased, would like a meeting with DCI Tilke and would be prepared to go to his offices. The Chief Constable was also kept in the loop.

Silence followed…

Four months had elapsed and we were now in 2004, moreover the silence was deafening. By involving my then MP, Jonathan Shaw, a letter was sent to a Chief Inspector S D Lander, Devon and Jonathan received a rapid reply.

On 10$^{th}$ March 2004, two years after the death of Alan, Peter and I kept an appointment at Paignton Police Station with DI David Taylor. We left relevant correspondence and a detailed account. The interview lasted almost three hours, he took notes, but not everything was discussed. DI Taylor undertook to study everything submitted and would let us know his findings.

As requested by DI Taylor, both Peter and I sent a letter of authorisation to him for access to any documents we were entitled to as executors of Alan's will.

It was late April when I sent a letter to Jonathan Shaw MP in reply to his correspondence dated 26 April. I explained that Peter had received a telephone call from DI Taylor, and an appointment was arranged for the two of us on 10th March at Paignton Police Station.

Jonathan had felt it necessary to contact Superintendent McGrath, and in his reply to me he not only stated this, but also, he would forward me his reply.

A reply was forthcoming from Superintendent McGrath and the letter acknowledged receipt of Jonathan

Shaw's letter dated 30 April 2004. McGrath apologises for the fact that he has not received a response as stated in the letter dated 19 February 2004 from the Chief Constable's office. He states he will make enquiries into the matter and ensure he receives a reply in the near future.

It is this push that eventually instigates a letter received via Jonathan from DI Taylor at the end of May, a day earlier than a telephone call received by Peter from David Taylor. The phone call was to inform Peter that two police officers would visit him and I on the 1$^{st}$ or 2$^{nd}$ June 2004, and he gave their names; this was not honoured. He stated during the phone call that the two detectives were assigned to work on the case for two days a week until it was reviewed.

It was 3 June 2004, more than two years after Alan's demise that DC K Chapman interviewed me, and DC Youngman interviewed Peter, at my address, separately and independently. The statements were taken and they were edited to the extreme by the officers. We were told that they were assigned to the case full time and that we would be kept fully informed. They did not do this in reality.

During the week ending 12 June 2004, both Peter and I had a brief message left on our respective answering machines from the DC's to express that they were proceeding with enquiries (nothing more).

The next contact was received by Peter, a phone call from DI Taylor; he stated that the papers were being passed to Superintendent Every, who would decide what was to happen. He confirmed that the establishment had been investigated i.e., coroner, doctors and ambulance, and he also referred to 'legals'. Notably he made no mention of witnesses. Nothing specific was forthcoming, other than DI Taylor told Peter to expect to hear from DS Every within approximately 3 weeks.

Another month elapsed and twice I telephoned DC K Chapman, one of the young officers who was sent to interview us and take 'statements', to hopefully gather some update of their progress. She was not available.

A reply to my phone calls did come; it was a couple of days later. I explained that the tax date had been altered regarding Bush Construction, a company set up shortly after my father's death. I asked about interviews that DC Chapman had carried out. I was told that they were extensive and many had been interviewed. DC Chapman was unable to give me any more information at present because the file was with the Superintendent awaiting his decision. I was told that when they came back I would then be able to receive information about the inquiry. The delay was due to many murders and deaths which were taking priority.

Once again the silence is deafening and in October Peter sends a letter to DI Taylor, which reiterates a conversation he had with DI Taylor, when he told Peter on 10 March 2004 that he would be kept fully informed of the progress of the investigations. DC Youngman, the other young officer to visit, had given a similar undertaking on 3 June 2004, when he took an edited statement at Chatham, Kent. Furthermore, he refers to a telephone conversation on 19 July 2004 when he was informed by DI Taylor that he could expect to hear from his organisation within 3 weeks. To date he has heard nothing.

One month later Peter corresponds with DI Taylor again, this time enclosing a letter received from one of the people that we understood had been spoken to sometime earlier, namely, Joan Tabram (Alan's mistress).

Peter had been previously told by DI Taylor to have no direct contact with anyone related to the events in Devon, and this was someone heavily involved with the deceased.

It is this letter received by DI Taylor that appears to induce him into action to reply, and 12 October, DI Taylor apologises for the delay in providing him with a comprehensive response to the allegations put forward by both Peter and myself. He adds that this delay is entirely due to operational demands over the last 12 months. He goes on to say that once all the facts have been properly reviewed by Detective Superintendent Newberry, he will be in a position to provide him with a comprehensive update.

It is three days after receiving Taylor's response that Peter receives another letter from Joan, where she states that she had been interviewed by the police recently. This, by the tone of her letter, was the first contact she had with them; this interview occurred after the matter had been virtually closed by DI Taylor on the 19 July 2004.

DC Chapman attempted to contact me on the 20 October and my return call failed to find her available, as she was busy in an interview, but would call me back the following day at 4pm. It was, in fact, three days later when I received her call. I was told the enquiry was still going on and the Superintendent had got the file. I was told that it was his decision and she only completes the reports. Moreover, I was told that we would hear a decision in the next couple of weeks.

Two weeks later, and nothing… I attempted to call Kay Chapman but she was unable to take my call. We did not have long to wait though, as four days passed and both Peter and I received a letter from Detective Superintendent Stuart Newberry where he ends his letter with: as far as the Devon and Cornwall Police are concerned the matter is now closed. Nowhere in this letter were any questions or concerns addressed or answered.

The undertaking to be kept full informed totally ignored; DI Taylor's undertaking, during our meeting with him, to meet again when the police work was finished, again totally ignored.

This reminds me, DI Taylor, during that interview in his office in Paignton, all those months ago, instructed us to have no contact with anybody related to events in Devon: Looking back, this instruction would be very useful to anybody wanting to engineer the outcome of this investigation: Certainly, we know for sure that two police officers felt strongly that something was very amiss, and one of those Officers wanted to continue with the case; he had the case taken away.

Incidentally, it is not unknown for the police to be less than honest; I have personally seen it; I have experienced it, and there are many instances where evidence has been altered by them to suit their cause, many case histories, which have involved Freemasonry and police officers of all ranks. It is common knowledge that many within the police are in the brotherhood: It is a fact that they can and do, on occasions, use or abuse the fraternity. All this is extensively documented elsewhere; it is in the public domain. It also must be said that there are many honourable men and women working within the ranks of the Police. Incidentally my dead brother was, for a while, a Freemason; certain of his friends were Freemasons; I have reason to believe David Hart is a Freemason.

It is not an organisation I would join, although, I have been, on several occasions throughout my life, invited to join their ranks; I have had pressure put upon me to become a Freemason, and experienced their displeasure when I would not comply, but I am not a team player, never have been, and by then had enough experience of life and survival to know they could not, and in the event, did not, beat me or cause me any harm; although it could be said that they tried.

My solicitor, Michael French, when he began to learn of the case, felt that a conspiracy existed and of an indiscernible size; he recognised something we did not. But remember the legal trade is absolutely saturated with Freemasons, and it's possible he has had to succumb to their pressure. It can be considerable.

Who knows, perhaps the brotherhood has been at work throughout; events are undoubtedly of the correct style, as many will recognise.

# CHAPTER 11

# A Log of correspondence with Eastleys Lawyers

You will recall from earlier reading that contact was made with Wendy's lawyer, who dealt with Alan's estate. What follows will help to establish the contact that we had with them over a period of three years. Our intentions are to give you the facts as we received them in order for you to make your own conclusions.

It was on 2 April 2002, two weeks after the demise of Alan that a fax, and letter was sent to Eastleys requesting that we be kept fully informed on all matters as they occur. Secondly, that we require a copy of the papers and deeds relating to Shorton Cottage and its grounds, plus any other goods and chattels relating to Alan's estate, and finally, enquiries were made by us about land that we believed was being purchased by Wendy.

Within minutes Peter's fax sparked up and their reply arrived, it simply said: "Yes, you will be kept fully informed."

It was to be four months later in August of 2002 when Eastleys wrote to Michael, our lawyer in Chatham, enclosing completed probate papers. These documents, the standard probate paraphernalia, were forwarded to Peter and I for our perusal.

It was in September that Michael was to write to the lawyers requesting relevant information and documentation; this was due to queries being raised, by both of us, that the information given in the form IHT 200 was incomplete.

Silence....

Very unexpectedly, and completely out of the blue in

January 2005, some three years later, an introductory letter was received from Eastleys by both Peter and I. In this correspondence a meeting was offered should we feel it beneficial. Furthermore, and I quote: '…if I can be of any further help, or should you have any particular query then please do not hesitate to get in touch.' It could not have come at a more opportune moment.

The moment was seized and my reply was forthcoming, which expressed my concerns; it read as follows:

*Further to your letter of 13/01/05, which was surprisingly sent to Peter Hindley's address, I would appreciate if you would amend my details on your file to the address supplied to your office, at the time of my father's demise.*

*As Executer and Trustee of my father's will and estate, I understand from the High Court in Bristol that his Last Will and Testament was finalized when probate was granted in October 2002.*

*I now require justification for such a breech being that I had no prior knowledge nor, did I give my consent for this to happen.*

*I received, from your office, written confirmation that I would have full disclosure and access to documentation regarding my father's estate. Your office has not replied to numerous requests, but has seen that this matter is concluded without involving Executors and Trustees; this has led to my Father's will and wishes being ignored.*

*I am dumbfounded at the shoddy work carried out by lawyers practicing under the Eastleys banner, which relates to all aspects of my father's will.'*

Their reply was rapid and their response was regrettable as they explained an error had been made in contacting me, but none of my concerns were addressed. My following letter reiterated my previous, with the addition of: *'If you feel an initial meeting would be beneficial, I would be only too pleased to oblige, as it is imperative that my late father's estate is handled as intended.'*

Receiving no reply I wrote again and it was a good

month before a reply was forthcoming; it merely stated that they are waiting for instructions from Wendy. They waited. I waited. April arrived, and so did the postman.

I was instructed by Eastleys that £12,800 (before expenses) is being held on deposit with the firm. This amount is offered to me on the understanding that it is to be equally split between the two boys. I am given 14 days to say to the contrary, and then requisite documentation will be drafted.

Obviously, my prime duty is to honour my father's intent and wishes, and not, to jeopardize the fruits of his life's toils and they are informed of this; as they were in my previous correspondence. It was at this time that they forwarded to me a letter dated 16 October 2002, supposedly written and sent; but was never received by any party including our lawyer prior to now! How could this be? It needed to be investigated and was. The following is taken from the reply which was dispatched:

*"Firstly, I have to reiterate that at no time have I or Peter Hindley advised your office that we decline our responsibilities as trustees and executors. Should your files, as you indicate, contain documentation which relinquishes our rights as trustees and executors then, I can assure you they are fraudulent.*

*I have copies of correspondence sent to your office which quite clearly states that we wish to be kept fully informed and, a complete disclosure given to us in order to be able to carry out our duties. Should these documents be missing from your files I would be only too pleased to send you copies.*

*Finally, you indicate in paragraph one, '…it is now too late…' please inform your client that there is no time limit regarding this case due to the apparent mishandling of my late father's will and estate.*

We are well into May when £12,800 (before expenses) is offered yet again with a clause requiring me to sign an indemnity. In no uncertain terms my recourse was delivered, *"Surely, if I am to sign either indemnity you propose that would negate the purpose of my father's will and wishes; that is, ultimately his grand children, Luke and Jake should benefit from the achievements of my honorable father, namely Shorton Cottage et al.*

*Referring to your letter sent to Mr. Hindley, dated 16$^{th}$ May 05, paragraph five relates to the 'letter of wishes', which you will be aware, was not included with the will when lodged with the High Court in Bristol.*

*I insist you do nothing until we have a meeting of all the trustees and executors. I would put to you that two of the three named executors and trustees are in accord and seek your co-operation."*

According to their response in June the total sum for probate purposes were sworn at just over £14,500. The money was offered again in return for that indemnity in favour of Wendy.

My next correspondence proved to be my last, as there has been no further contact with Wendy's lawyer to date. It was 10 June 2005 when I wrote, "You have not grasped the fact that Mrs. Wendy Hindley has made false statements in her probate submission and tax declaration. Under these circumstances I instruct you to do nothing until we have a meeting."

# CHAPTER 12

# LOOKING AT THE EVIDENCE

I don't know about you, but I need time to look at, and assess the evidence and information we have collated thus far. I'm sure there are many questions that will come up that will require answers in order to enable us to fathom out the true extent of any crimes that may have been committed.

**CORONER'S REPORT**
According to the post-mortem report the cause of death was 'ascertained' as:

1a. Haemopericardium 1b. Myocardial Infarction.

For those who are not sure what these terms mean they are as follows: Haemopericardium is a rupture to the lining wall around the heart, which causes a build up of blood around the heart, and if not operated on immediately, will inevitably lead to death. Myocardial Infarction is a heart attack.

Both the above causes have been thoroughly discussed with those of the medical profession, and as I understand it from a retired senior surgeon, known in this particular field.

Haemopericardium is usually caused from a severe blow to the chest, often sustained in car accidents or from a fall from a great height, and if not treated immediately, then the likely outcome would be Myocardial Infarction. It is clear that Alan had not been in a car accident or fallen in his final week, so what had caused this?

A logical question must be asked: Had there been a fight during the days before Alan's death whereby he received a very heavy blow?

Other curious points to look at are: The statement that the spleen had a moderately soft purple cut surface. Is this bruising? If this is the case then the question is raised, had there been a fight during the days prior to, or on the day of Alan's death?

Alan's height, which is stated at being 5'8", yet he was known to be 5'10 ½": Had he shrunk by 2 ½" on the way to the Morgue?

**WILL & WISHES**

Wendy has lodged the probate papers in Bristol, not Exeter or Plymouth, which would have been the normal course of action; moreover, the papers did not include the written wishes of Alan. Wendy has acted as sole executor, even though we were not advised, and it transpires that there is no trust to be trustee of, although the will and wishes clearly states that there should be one, and who should administer it? Alan's wishes have been ignored (both written and verbal).

It begs the questions: Why has Alan's wife not followed his Will and Wishes? And why was Alan's will not perfect when he was so particular, especially with detail?

The Will lists as a beneficiary, Samantha, a relative of Wendy, but there is no indication of how she should benefit. Now this is a puzzling fact because Alan had no time for Samantha, Wendy's niece. Why would he include her in his Will, but not the wishes?

I wanted a second opinion of the will from an independent lawyer, and visited an elderly Gentleman, whose long standing and well known legal practice was located in Maidstone. The upshot of my meeting was the instruction to find the rest of the will.

Has his Will been tampered with?

Have sections and-or paragraphs been removed?

Have sections and-or paragraphs been added?
Have 'they' wrongly numbered paragraphs?
Has a name been substituted or added?

## FORENSIC REPORT

Suspecting that the Will presented to both of us and the court was not The Last Will and Testament that Alan had signed, we approached a well known, reputable, forensic expert, who was an ex-employee of the Metropolitan Police at New Scotland Yard with considerable expertise.

The forensic expert examined the Will, which had been submitted to Bristol Probate Office. The tests were carried out in his laboratory; this followed 5 months of pursuance until we eventually were able to get the necessary documents released to him from Bristol Probate Office (Crown Court).

His findings were: 'I reached the conclusion that the questioned signature is probably not genuine, and is likely to be a good freehand copy of a genuine signature.' Would this now be evidence enough for the Devon police to 're-open' the mess that was unraveling before our eyes?

## PROBATE

In early August 2002, five months after Alan's death, a letter was sent from Eastleys lawyers to our lawyer, Michael; it read:

*'As arranged, we enclose copies of the probate papers namely the Oath and F.200. Please confirm your Clients are prepared to sign and 'swear' these, and we will let you have the originals plus the Will.*

*Mrs. Hindley has approved these, so as soon as we hear from you we will arrange for her to sign and 'swear'.*

It is clear from the above letter that we were expected to put our seal and swear to the courts of this country that we had performed our duties of executorships, and that the information given was a true account of Alan's estate.

Probate papers were submitted without our knowledge in September 2002. How was this possible?

We had been denied access to all Alan's affairs by Wendy, Eastleys and Tozers lawyers. Tozers were asked for relevant documentation to be released to us by our lawyer; they were not forthcoming. Alan had used this firm of lawyers when dealing with property transactions.

Probate papers state that the gross estate passing under the grant amounts to £16,027, sixteen thousand and twenty seven pounds; this includes life insurance policies amounting to £12,388.00. Had Alan died a pauper?

### MONIES

Bank and Building Society accounts show virtually nothing, yet we have knowledge of omitted bank accounts. Alan had no known regular income and he would not have anything from the DSS, money from the state, nor would he qualify for a pension on retirement, therefore how could the household bills be paid? Wendy had occasionally, during the marriage, worked, and may qualify in her own right for DSS.

Alan had been developing and building properties for some time before his death, and although we have copies of deeds in excess of 20, we are also aware of other properties that existed. Not only did he build and convert properties in Devon but also Kent. Anyone knowing Alan would know that he was a very frugal man who would travel to save a bob or two!

## MORTGAGES

When Alan was planning the building of the 6 houses in the grounds of Shorton Cottage, it was his intention to use his money to finance the mortgages of the purchasers; he knew he had the funds to do it.

But he was not to live long enough to follow his plans through. Wendy would have known of his intentions and had made it blatantly obvious when she announced to all in sundry, before his funeral, of her intention, "to carry on Alan's work."

She certainly built the last five houses, but did she arrange private mortgages for the buyers?

It is unlikely for number 20 Lammas Lane, as that transaction looks correct, but the others are questionable. They may have declared small mortgages, but is there a second hiding in the shadows?

It is quite likely when you consider that all the houses are on record as being well above the price of others on the same road, and not by just tens of thousands of pounds. Also most of the five are owned by people in the building or construction trades; trades known to do work 'under the table', therefore the money is not always declared to the tax men. As a result, they are unlikely to be able to produce statements to verify their actual incomes to a bank or building society: The purchasers may well have the income to repay a very large mortgage, but they could not produce proof of it.

If they were to borrow hundreds of thousands of pounds they would have to look elsewhere.

## BUSH CONSTRUCTION

We discovered that Bush Construction existed when I employed a Private Detective, from Argus Investigation Services, to visit the grounds of Shorton Cottage in order to assess the amount of new development that had occurred within the grounds.

It all began when, eager to know of developments in Devon, namely Shorton Cottage, I searched the Internet, and two detective agencies in Torquay were displayed to me. It was the second one I approached, who proved to be the right one for the job.

After I gave the gentleman on the phone a brief outline of the position I found myself in, and explained that I needed somebody to visit Lammas Lane, adjacent to Shorton Cottage, reporting back to me on the progress of development concerning the new builds; I was told that it would be possible and told the cost. All was agreed and, this is where it gets interesting, the detective went straight to the properties and made inquiries with those he could find available. I hadn't even written the cheque, two payments, half as a down payment and the remainder when the job was completed.

It gets better still because not only did this detective do the job I had requested, but he also furnished us with other details that, until that time, we did not know. One point of interest was the fact that he had been told by an inhabitant of one of the new builds, built in the grounds of Shorton Cottage, that the property had been built and sold by the 'couple' residing in the big house, as they pointed down to the cottage.

While this was all going on Peter was oblivious to my actions, and was left feeling dumbfounded when he received a telephone call from David Hart, the gardener, acting like a madman, as far as Peter knew, accusing him of all matter of things he know nothing about. So incensed was Peter when the conversation ended that he penned a letter to David which was dispatched immediately, and he waited for my explanation when next speaking to me.

You can imagine the conversation I had with Peter when I returned home from work the day of the detective's visit, and I was eager to tell him what I had done the night before, only to be told of the day's events. I couldn't believe the detective had worked so fast, surpassing himself he had gathered so much more information. Needless to say I only needed to write one cheque, and within hours I was so much more informed, as indeed was Peter. We did chuckle.

I received a copy of the letter that Peter had sent to David prior to my phone call, which has been included in this book.

*Dear Mr. Hart*

*I was traumatised by your phone call from Shorton Cottage on Wednesday evening, 18 February 2004, when you enquired whether I had instigated the visit to Shorton Cottage, of a person to value the property, and you're questioning about the matter of the doubtful title of Shorton Cottage. For the record this was not my doing.*

*I am extremely distressed and offended that you felt it necessary to ask.*

*I observed that you were involved with the administration of my brother's affairs at the time of his death almost two years ago, and are therefore in a better position than me to know anything relating to my brother's estate.*

*As you are aware I am one of three named executors and trustees of his estate I have been prevented from executing the serious and solemn duties associated with either task.*

*Since being presented with a photocopy of documents said to be Alan's Will and Wishes, I have requested from Wendy Hindley, the lawyers Eastleys of Paignton and Tozers of Exeter, various documents and sight of the original will. I am fully entitled to these for the task I was charged to perform, but they have not, to date, been forthcoming.*

*Furthermore, I was in no position to put my signature to the draft probate papers a year or so ago. Obviously with the absence of the requested information, I was unable to verify their substance. Incidentally, it should be noted, the draft did not conform to my deceased brother's wishes, written or verbal.*

*You mentioned in your conversation that I was a trustee, but to the best of my knowledge there is no trust to be a trustee of, if you know better I would welcome your input.*

*It is with much regret that I have to say that I have been prevented from the duty and honour of executing my brother's wishes. I am sure that Alan's will has not been administered as he would have wished, and the fruits of his lifetimes work and achievements have therefore been futile and sullied. I look forward to the day when his house will be put in order and he is duly honoured.*

*Yours sincerely*

Bush Construction was set up by Wendy three months after Alan's demise; Date of Incorporation 14/06/2002. Why?

Was this done for all, or some, of the six properties built in the grounds of Shorton Cottage, namely 12-22 Lammas Lane?

Was it for the two new builds behind 21 Milton Street, Brixham, which was in Bush Construction's name?

The two building plots in Shorton Cottage grounds, originally leased from the Willoughbys, but immediately after the death of my Alan, Wendy purchased the freehold at maybe an inflated price. Subsequently, Wendy sold a number of plots to Bush Construction, namely herself; although these are a little difficult to identify as house numbers were replaced by plot numbers, and the submitted plans were not lucid. Could this have been a deliberate smoke screen?

An accountant was shown some of the figures within the returns submitted by Wendy, but he suggested that they had been compiled to indicate nothing. Could it be part of a master plan? It almost mirrors the lack of registration with the land registry of some of the new houses built and inhabited on Lammas Lane.

Some years later I was to approach our detective friend again, this time in the search for Ellie Waugh, Joan's friend, who had supposedly seen Alan's will. Although again, he was eager and willing to work for a price, and I paid him the first half upfront, he fell deathly silent.

I only spoke with him on two occasions, one to arrange the job, and one to get a progress report, whereby he advised me that he thought he was making good progress and was due to visit an estate agent, whom he was sure, would have the information for me. I was never to hear from him again nor did any further money change hands.

Some years later we managed to track Ellie down.

# CHAPTER 13

# MYSTERIOUS MISTRESS

As you will recall, Alan's mistress, Joan Tabram, was contacted with the help of Mandy and Andrew Cooper, close friends of the deceased. Joan had relayed, through Andrew that she was not ready to speak with either of us – Alan's death was still too raw; it was to be a whole year later, when Susan received the first contact with Joan via a telephone call. There was a relationship to be built and this is where it began.

In addition to various meetings with Joan, there have been many letters, messages, and correspondence that has been forwarded through a third party, Teresa Emberson; a close confidant of Joan's, who has been on hand to provide Joan with an ear to listen and a friendly shoulder to cry on, as well as receptionist to our phone calls, and Postmaster for our letters.

Many letters received from Joan included notes and love letters exchanged between Alan and herself during the four years prior to his death. Amongst the numerous letters, notelettes, and cards received was one letter, whereby Joan pens her account of the facts as she knows them. There were twenty in total.

Joan reveals in her own hand a very interesting picture which begins with the words: Alan was a very wealthy man who lived in a mortgage free property, namely Shorton Cottage and the attached land being used for the new builds already belonged to him. The two additional plots, which Alan bought from the Willoughbys was for about £85,000 the pair. As far as Joan was concerned he had issued two cheques, one dated March 2002 and the other April 2002, and she had witnessed this take place. After all, Alan was in a financial position whereby he could afford the building of all six houses, which he had the planning permission for, without borrowing! His preferred intentions were to 'build one', 'sell one', but he hadn't really expected it to work out that way. The plan was to arrange personal mortgages for any buyer who was looking to borrow.

One of these new builds was finished and on the market before the demise of Alan, and had been for a considerable time. The cost for the build came in at about £75,000 – Oh yes, they were not your average size and Alan had expected a £200,000 profit on each house. As a point of interest, the first house, number 18, was sold after his death and slightly surpassed his estimation.

Over the years their relationship had continued to flourish, and according to Joan's words 'Alan also had sufficient funds to buy a small flat (for us to get away from it all). This in fact did not materialize. So we rented. There is no property belonging to me as David seems to think!! Had this gone ahead, Alan proposed to use the money from the reverse level house he had built on Central Avenue, in the rear garden of his cottage in Cecil Road.'

According to Joan, and I have no reason to doubt her, there were many arguments between Alan and Wendy, and apparently during one of these rows, brought on by Wendy leaving 'messages' on her answer phone, Wendy had told him "she'd take him for every penny he had."

Alan said, "She's in for a shock. It's all going to Susan and the boys." Although he said, he wouldn't see her without a roof over her head.

'Regarding Alan's wishes - Alan wished to divorce Wendy and had made this clear to her, but she didn't want that - of course. As you know, Alan led his own life. They only lived under the same roof....

Furthermore, Joan continues, 'I have letters from Alan

confirming his wish to divorce Wendy. I will make these letters available to Susan.' She did do just that and we have copies of them all.

A further point made is: 'I truly believe that David and Wendy are 'uneasy' as things have gone quiet. They fear that Susan and yourself will in time uncover the truth - they really want you 'off their backs' hence the <u>attempt</u> to pay you off with £12,000 split between the boys - a mere pittance! I believe another will exists. . At the time of this will - 2<sup>nd</sup> Sept 1998, Alan had no future plans with me, and we had only met early summer that year.' It would seem from the last remarks that Joan would have expected to have been named in his will as a benefactor.

She concludes her list with the words, 'Finally - one more fact, probably the most important one. Alan had not been ill for several weeks before he passed. His health and happiness had improved by the day - he had never felt better - he told me that.'

**Taken from another letter:** '…When I met David he seemed very keen to tell me that Alan's will was very simple, 'a mirrored will', as they say. He said it was on <u>one sheet</u> of paper and everything was left to Wendy.'

'Whenever Alan left the jeep it was a long 'ritual'. He'd remove <u>several</u> 'passbooks' from his inside pocket and locked them in the glove compartment - then double check - then lock the jeep - then double check… Alan would reply "There's a small fortune there young lady…"

'Alan said "shall I build a double-garage in front of Shorton Cottage - on the right hand side?"… "Well I want to buy a Rolls Royce - I had one once - I'd like another one… besides I want to lose a bit of money! Dodge the bloody Tax Man… Last time I wanted to 'lose' money - I bought two three bed-roomed semis over in Barton…"'

Received with the above letter was an enclosure of a letter sent to Joan from Eastleys lawyers dated 25 October 2004 regarding Alan's affairs.

We will return to Joan's involvement later.

# CHAPTER 14

# MY VISIT TO DEVON: 2 March 2006

It was as a result of yet another demand for more information and clarification from our lawyer, Michael French, that I made arrangements to visit Paignton, Devon on the 2nd and 3rd of March 2006.

At our previous meeting, on the 28$^{th}$ of February 2006, he asked for photographic evidence of the existence of the 6 detached houses that had been built on the grounds of Shorton Cottage, with their entrances in Lammas Lane. He made the suggestion to hire the detective again, but that would have been futile as he had previously undertaken a task, then taken the money and silently failed, but I had a good camera and could make the time for the journey, so off to Devon I went.

This was an ideal opportunity for me to meet with Joan Tabram, Alan's mistress, so Susan instigated contact with Joan via the normal intermediary, Terri (Teresa) Emberson of Preston, Devon. When Joan telephoned me to arrange the rendezvous she asked, "How will I recognise you? Will you be wearing a red rose?" Well, the situation was a bit 'cloak and dagger.' Joan went on to say that we would recognise each other; I had my doubts, for I thought at the time, we had only met once at her house some 5 years or so earlier. It was after the call had finished that I realised I would need to eat after the journey to Devon, so I left an invitation, via the intermediary, to eat somewhere, but that received no response.

I arrived in the Torbay area with ample time to settle myself in a quiet hotel on the outskirts of town, and take those precious photographs of 12 to 22 Lammas Lane before the light failed; they were all pleasant detached houses of four or more bedrooms. Sadly, number 12 encroached on the little ancient wood, which I remember from the plans, was not due to happen, but I was horrified when I crossed the valley to Shorton Road, and saw the huge retaining wall that had been built in the grounds of Shorton Cottage to prevent these new houses from tumbling down the hillside, and on to Shorton Cottage. I know that the original planning permission required that these houses were to be built on the natural terrain, and follow the existing contours of the site, but Alan had added soil to make the sites and gardens level.

Well, I soon had the required photographs so the next item on the agenda was the meeting with Joan. I had hoped that it would be well away from the scene of the crime, but Joan had selected 'The Ship' on Manor Way, Preston. The pub was within spitting distance of Shorton Cottage, and a few hundred yards from the house David Hart shared with his wife Jacqui in 6 Old Torquay Road.

Joan entered the pub by the rear door and looked completely different from what I recalled from our previous meeting, she was well dressed and had obviously been to the hairdressers and looked like a middle class lady of leisure, she certainly gave the image of having money, which surprised me as I understood her husband had not worked for years and she was not working either; but that was not the only surprise in store for me.

At my request we found a quiet table on the second floor, and as we settled in our seats she virtually verbally attacked me with, "What do you know?" She was very anxious to find out, but I did not feel it was normal curiosity, it was too urgent, too pressing, and I told her precious little: Please remember I have earned my living interviewing people, gathering facts and recording them: this is second nature to me and I would need those skills.

What Joan told me during that evening follows:

David Hart had phoned Joan about six months after Alan's death and told her that he knew where she lived, and he knew where the house was that Alan had bought her: Compton was the name of the village, it was the orange cottage that juts out into the road, and he had seen her Vauxhall car parked nearby. He told her that she had this car and her response was "I have loads of cars." Joan went on to tell me that David would have known where she lived in Brixham with her family, because Wendy would have told him. One thing was surely true; David had really unnerved Joan by this little exchange.

About the same time these two spoke on another subject; this time it was Joan who questioned David about the death of her deceased lover, Alan. Joan wanted to know what Alan was wearing at the time of his death and where he died. She was told that Alan was in his pyjamas and died in his bedroom, just in front of the shower room door. I do not know why or what importance it may be, but Joan told me that their friend and drinking companion, Vic Nicholls, had phoned Shorton Cottage at about midnight on the night of Alan's demise.

In the conversation that evening Joan said that she was 5'9" and Alan was 5'10;" this was near enough confirmation for me that my brother was 5'10 ½" and not the 5'8" that is stated on the coroner's report. On reflection, Joan, being Alan's lover at the time, would be very aware of his size.

Talking of Alan's body; there is a conflict here as Wendy had stressed that Alan was unwell the week of his death, yet Joan told me the exact opposite. In fact she told me that they were together for three hours (between 2.00pm and 5.00pm) the day before he died, and from the look in her eyes I would say it was a very rewarding sexual liaison. To use her words "He was absolutely fine, health wise."

Joan went on to say that she had phoned Alan from a telephone box at 2.30pm on the Thursday of his death, "and he was fine." Alan had taken the call on his mobile phone while he was in 'his jeep'.

It is puzzling that the two women closest to my brother give a completely contradictory assessment of his health. Normally people are more aware of a person's condition at such a time of crisis, and the memories are recorded accurately within the brain. But what is normal about the death of Alan Hindley?

Changing the topic, we talk of Alan's wealth: Joan wrote various letters which contained information on this subject, but this evening she was talking about everything.

According to Joan, Alan was a millionaire, and whether that is true or not, I do not know; if it is true it would come as no surprise to me. Certainly he had enough money to do as he wished without going to work and he was not receiving any money from the State, or a pension: He was not a drug dealer either, so money existed; it had to, to pay normal living costs: Another indication that money would have been in existence was the new car, a red Hyundai coupe, that Alan bought from the showroom for Wendy; this was paid for out of Building Society interest and it would take more than the interest on £1,449.00 to produce enough money to buy that new car. It was, after all, only £1,431.00 lodged in a Portman Building Society account, and £9.00 in a Barclays Bank current account, plus £95.00 in the Instant savings account that Wendy Hindley declared to the Probate Office. This £1.449.00 was supposedly all Alan had at the time of his death; not enough to pay the food and alcohol bill for one year, not to mention gas, electricity, and council tax on Shorton Cottage; and where would the money come from to pay for the petrol for the little Hyundai coupe, the 'Jeep', or the large Jaguar. Is this a case of major evaporation of funds? They did not live the jet set life or gamble, they did dine out, but that was modest, in pubs like the Blagdon Arms, not Michelin rated restaurants, and Alan spent Thursday evening in 'The Ship' with Joan, Vic Nicholls and Brian; then there was money needed for Wendy's alcohol; but no major frivolities. So where did the capital go?

Joan's jaw dropped when I mentioned the loan Alan instigated just before his death; she was genuinely aghast. She understood there were more than enough funds in the kitty to build all six houses, and buy the two plots in Shorton Cottage grounds retained by the Willoughby's.

It was also Alan's intention to give Joan one of these six houses, and money. At this point, I recall being told the same story by Barbara Ryell at Shorton Cottage, the day after Alan's funeral.

Talking of Shorton Cottage, Joan spoke of the drive that leads to the house with a strange enthusiasm, and she talked about 'the lovely oak front door' and the house generally; the enthusiasm was a little too much for me, she was hooked on the house and it felt as if she would have liked to become the lady of the manor.

We talked of other things relating to the House, but it was the dining table that was delivered on 18th December 1998, (she gave me this date), which was interesting for me. Joan could not grasp why Alan had spent so much; £3,000.00 buying the table at David Hart's auction rooms. As I have just said, the table was interesting for me: It had a history, especially the top, which was made from ships timbers. It was a large rectangle that rested on rustic trestles which gave the table more height than normal. Now I must clarify my interest, for it was not the table that puzzled me, it was the chairs that came with it, large Windsor carvers which Alan and Wendy believed to be antiques. This I am sure is not the case, the patina was wrong, it looked like modern sprayed matt polyurethane polish, even the staining showed no sign of aging; what is more, there was precious little sign of any stressing visible on the wood. These chairs looked like they had been purchased from a contract furniture manufacturer, and were typical of thousands that can be seen in pubs throughout England. But David Hart had convinced Alan and Wendy that they were genuine.

We talked on diverse subjects including Alan's spiritual healing and psychic abilities; Bruce, Alan's hyperactive Dalmatian dog, even the fact that Joan had been at the crematorium for the service. How well I remember the days before Alan's funeral, how Wendy had threatened to create a scene if Joan was present at the crematorium; but Joan was there with her daughter and a friend: Naturally Wendy would have seen and recognised Joan sitting at the back of the chapel when she entered, she would walk virtually in front of Joan, they were just a few feet apart with an unobstructed view of each other, yet Wendy showed no reaction, and did nothing. I have often wondered why?

Joan reminded me that Alan had owned two houses in Barton, an area of Torbay. I had visited these houses once many years earlier. Alan had bought them as an investment, with the intention to renovate them before selling them, but the housing market went flat and he rented them out. He had told me of the problem he had with the tenants and eventually sold the houses when the market improved.

At one point during the evening I went to the bar, and when I returned Joan handed me a scrap of paper on which she had written various names; most I knew but one or two were unknown to me.

As we left the pub that evening Joan waved at her drinking friends, Vic and Brian, who were sitting by the window, it was, after all, their normal evening to socialise here. I escorted Joan to her car which was parked on Old Torquay Road, virtually in front of David Hart's house; at the time I thought it strange after she had told me that David had made her feel so uncomfortable and threatened; I know now why she was so at ease here, but that part of this story is for another time.

On route to her car, we passed the Spiritualist church and I was shown the commemorative plaque that she had installed in remembrance of my brother: Strange that she had this done and not his wife, Wendy.

Then it was the drive back to the hotel to make more detailed notes of what had passed knowing that tomorrow I now had two extra tasks before I left Devon.

The first item on the agenda was to go to Compton and see whether I could locate the house that David alleged Alan had bought for Joan, but that proved to be a fruitless journey. I still had to make a small diversion to my second destination, I had the time.

Previously I have mentioned that I am not a trained medium, nor have I ever sat in a circle to develop these arts: Yes, I have been surrounded by people who worked and practiced in these fields and had seen quite a few who used all types of paranormal techniques. Using the term paranormal is difficult because, for me it is not paranormal; it is normal, everything is normal; I have been exposed to all sorts of phenomenon: I have come to accept that anything is possible. Having said that, I have obtained, by accident normally, several, what some might call, 'paranormal' skills, and one was going to be employed today. One might call it a form of dowsing, I would not know, as I am no expert in these matters.

I drove away from Compton and towards Barton, the place where Alan had, at one time, owned the two houses. Before starting off I had looked on a map for the location, but nothing was familiar; all I could do was drive to the area. I turned left to leave the dual carriageway (not by the exit I had planned when looking at the map) and concentrated on the two houses I needed to locate. I remember crossing a roundabout and descending down a road, it turned sharply to the right and at this point I turned left and climbed the hill, then turned left at the top and stopped the car, it felt right. When I walked the length of the road I knew this was not the place I was seeking. Returning to the car I drove another hundred yards and there was a small dog leg with a turning on the left, but I continued straight ahead, not far, just a few yards, then stopped the car and walked. This time the feeling was different and I noted the name of the road and the numbers of the two houses; I also took a couple of snaps with the camera.

My mood changed and I knew there was nothing more I could do here, so I set off to find the dual carriage way; not by the same route, and without referring to a map, directly back home to Kent.

This two day excursion did not end as you would expect because, Susan was eager to learn what had happened in Devon, and gain the information about the Barton houses; at this time I was not sure that they had been located, but it was not long before the telephone rang and Susan confirmed her findings gained on the Land Registry web site. The two houses my brother had owned were found, but with an unexpected bonus. One house was in Wendy Hindley's name; not the customary name of Alan Hindley: This was done to avoid tax, at that time Alan had too many properties in his name, and he did not like giving the State any more than he had too.

# CHAPTER 15

# CONFLICTING CAUSE OF DEATH

Someone has given me some unsolicited facts that I had not expected.

As I said earlier, I had two methods that would have facilitated the death of Alan which I had not discounted in my research, but now I will talk of just one.

Moving on sometime, Susan gave the cause of death to a surgeon who was adamant that the cause of death given was as a result of a strong impact; he gave a car accident as the normal occurrence for this, and continued by saying that death can be avoided if surgery is administered swiftly. Alan had not had a car accident.

What comes to mind at this instant is that David Hart told me that he was proficient in first aid, and that when Wendy phoned him (not a doctor or ambulance) at the time of Alan's death, David came to the house and tried to resuscitate him for 15 minutes. That would sound reassuring if it were not for the fact that he told me that if a person could not be revived within 12 minutes, all was lost. Not only did he allegedly work for 15 minutes on Alan; if he was not already in the house he would have had to add the time of the journey there, a distance, as the crow flies, of more than half a mile; even by the most direct route you would be looking at three quarters of a mile.

Thus the story does not hold water, any more than another story David told me, namely, that Alan had told him, just prior to his demise, what funeral arrangements my brother wanted after his death: That would have been so very, very out of character for Alan to have said that to David, I knew immediately that he was lying.

Now, just days ago, I received, quite unsolicited, confirmation that Alan's reported cause of death was normally as a result of a blow in the region of the heart, 'he must have received a blow in that region as that does not usually happen otherwise'. The writer had expected that this was the case, and sought confirmation from a qualified health worker before coming forth with the information. There is more, but that is for another day. Meanwhile, we can reflect on David Hart's story and what it is telling us. Was his account accurate? Was he being unrealistic by trying to revive Alan for "15 minutes" knowing his journey to the house would have taken five or ten minutes? Was he simply lying? Does his story place him at Alan's house at the time of his death?

# CHAPTER 16

# THERE APPEARS TO BE NO JUSTICE IN THE UK

What follows was received from a contact and is a brief account of the reality of the workings of the UK police and legal system; it paints an absolutely accurate picture of the system of law in very few words. I have deliberately not added the word justice to the previous sentence as it is an anathema to the legal trade. There is nothing new to me in what follows, but I fear a great majority of the British Public have no clue to the reality, and they should be aware, it is their right to know.

*"There appears to have been a deliberate programme of obstruction and miss-management of this case from the very beginning. This policy, coupled with poor investigative skills and tardy responses by the police, has proven to be a very poor foundation for all that has followed. As the investigation has stop-started over the years, due to your pushing and prompting, there have been wrong approaches by those who subsequently have taken up the 'baton' of the investigation. From an investigative point of view, great regard will be paid to the evidence of those who were immediately present at the time of death, or were closest to him at that time. Despite the obvious inconsistencies in the evidence of Wendy and the first-aider - David - the police will give them greater weight. Any inconsistencies will be put down to poor memory, shock or personal preferences to put out of the mind unpleasantness. The senior investigating officer will adopt an attitude of - "they were present and may be confused, but I will believe them rather than you, who were many miles away at the time." Right from the beginning the investigation has proceeded with wrong assumptions.*

*Leaving aside any involvement by the brotherhood, there are other 'associative organisations' that would have either directly or indirectly affected the path of the investigation. For example - police officers tend* to trust other police officers before they trust non-police, unless they have very good reason to do otherwise. Consequently, any further investigations by different police officers will precede on the assumption that what has already been done in the investigation has been done correctly. Only if you can produce cast-iron evidence of an earlier misdirection will they accept such a suggestion. I have personally seen this at first-hand from both sides of the 'mistake'. The honourable officers later appointed to the investigation have simply assumed that the previous case officers were also honourable individuals. Given the often too public antipathy towards the police, then you can see how this would work.

Then there are the legal associations. Even out with the brotherhood the legal profession [which is even fuller of brothers than any other profession, except possibly the Church of England] has a code of support towards each other. Anyone trying to sue a lawyer or barrister for malpractice knows how hard it is to find a legal advocate that will take the case on. Again and again the assumptions are that everybody else might be lying, but we don't lie to each other. On a practical level this sort of attitude does help in getting many cases resolved 'out of court' when the lawyers act as 'honest brokers' between the parties. Most of the legal people involved in the process of probate and etc. are probably more comfortable dealing with the 'professional objective police officers' than they are with 'emotional and unprofessional relatives'. I am not saying that you are either, but that the 'professionals' often view relatives as such and the tendency is to regard all as such.

I am sorry to say that with the passage of time, the numerous wrong assumptions, the obstruction, the delaying, the muddying of the water and any fraternal conniving this investigation is likely to either close with a decision unfavourable to yourself, or to drag on interminably without any satisfactory conclusion.

Not being a lawyer and having lost touch with the few police officers who were friends - I left the police in '96 - I am unable to see a way through this horrible situation. You have learned a little of how

*Hercules felt as he attacked the Hydra - of how for each head that was cut off seven others grew in its place. Where the heart of the beast lies I cannot see. It could be that Wendy does have more to do with this than meets the eye - possibly she has friends/family that were able to pull strings from the very beginning, but without it being seen or noticed. Just a guess."*

No, this is not fiction, it is reality stripped bare and exposed as it should be. I, from personal experience can find no fault in the above quote, in fact, there is so much more I could add, and will at a later date. Meanwhile, be aware, this is how it really is!

The police, lawyers, barristers, judges etc. are all in bed together with the sole purpose of perpetuating themselves. And they do it so well. Who pays for this? You do!

If you need confirmation you need look no further than this book and our Internet site; we asked for a legal representative to help us months ago, and to date, not one practicing lawyer has had the testicles to offer their services, although help has been offered from more honourable trades. Anyone working within the legal system with one iota of intelligence is fully aware that they prostitute themselves on a daily basis.

While we are on the subject of police and their duties, let us take a little time out and look at what actually happens daily in the United Kingdom and what the police actually do. What follows may be unbelievable, but as ever, it is all absolutely true.

Thinking initially about the drug issue and crime: Would you be horrified if I told you that from what I have observed, the police generally know the majority of drug users and dealers, big and small; but they do nothing? Possibly because they do know where to find these people, and if they were in fact arrested, they would be replaced immediately by someone new, someone the police would need to locate. Obviously it is easier to sit back and do nothing, and that happens daily. Could it also be that some officers are paid for their inaction; would there be anything new in that?

Have you thought about the police patrolling the streets in Panda cars? Well, in fact, unless I am very much mistaken and things have changed, it does not normally happen. The police are called to an incident and then return to their warm offices to await the next call out. When I unearthed this, I was shocked, but it was confirmed by so many working in the force.

If you want more there is the question of the gun culture in the youth of the Afro Caribbean. This will probably be a revelation. Everyone is aware of the drug culture of the Caribbean, but few, except those who live amongst it, know that gun ownership, in certain quarters, is the norm. Maybe these guns are licensed, but I very much doubt it from what I have been told. If they were they would be unlikely to be used for gang initiation, as they are. Yes, this is right, you read that correctly; initiates are driven through the streets in a car and obliged to shoot some innocent pedestrian before being accepted into the gang. It is true that it rarely makes news headlines, but it is not a rare event in certain areas.

The biggest problem I have is that I do have so much unpublished information about the police's day to day handling of crime, and I would find it difficult and very time consuming to work through it all: Perhaps on another web site or elsewhere?

You may think I am anti-police, but that is not the case. Many are very well intentioned individuals, but they can, and do, get very frustrated in their chosen careers. It could be the system, or the pressure less honourable officers may put on them. There is also, no doubt, the legal system and the way it frequently works in a way that has nothing to do with justice. All are valid reasons which contribute to bad policing. I would suggest that corruption within the force is no novelty either, and generally goes unchecked.

The most dangerous thing in my opinion is the way the police have engineered themselves away from the public they are there to serve. Just look at all the new shiny police offices being built on the outside of the town they serve; each one conveniently isolated from the centre, where people live and work, and are subject to criminal acts. Furthermore, if something happens and you need to visit a police station, you will normally find it is closed outside business hours. Do criminals work 9 to 5? Clearly the answer must be no, and they have even less reason to now.

This is nonsense when we need common sense and real policing; policing that works for, and in the community. Once the communication between the public and the police breaks down, their task will be impossible; regrettably it is so very close now.

You and I and every other tax payer in the UK are paying for what?

Nobody will accept responsibility for their wrong doings!

As you know, we have had serious problems when dealing with the police, and have always been told to refer it to the IPCC. You go to the IPCC and they are as incompetent as the police and will even lie to an MP if they see fit.

Although we have asked the Prime Minister, other Ministers, MP's, other government officials including the Commissioner of the Metropolitan Police, none of them to date will tell us, or has told us who the IPCC and Devon & Cornwall Constabulary are responsible to.

It would seem they can do what they like as they are not answerable to nobody, yet every tax payer in the UK contributes to their inflated wages. It would seem that we pay for them to do nothing, and they do it very well.

It has now been over seven years that we have been seeking honour and justice from the establishment in the United Kingdom, proving it to be useless. As you have seen, they can't even answer a letter sent to them or take any responsibility whatsoever.

# CHAPTER 17

Wendy has recently told Susan she has done nothing wrong. I must ask what Wendy has done right? Has she honoured my brother's Will and Wishes? Has she honoured her late husband? She says her many letters have been ignored. Not true. What letters? There have been no letters unanswered by myself or Susan. The only letter unanswered is one when our solicitor wrote requesting details regarding the probate; a correct and proper request when acting as executors, but on no occasion did we get a reply or the requested information.

Wendy Hindley talks of the truth, but she would not know it if it hit her in the face. If we are not telling the truth in this or any part of this, she or others would have taken us to court, but they all know what is written here is pure unadulterated fact, no lies, no falsehoods, simply the truth.

So what can be done to bring these liars and incompetents to book?

Answers on a postcard…

All this maybe a sign of a very degenerate society, which permits, some might say encourage, such immorality. Maybe it signals the end. This society will not be the first to crumble.

Why would you ask?

Wendy recently asked me a series of questions about Alan's death: What day? What month? What year? What time?

Why would anybody seek confirmation of the time of death? She was there. Why ask that question? Is it normal?

Because of the many discrepancies in the information she gave me earlier, I could not put my hand on my heart and answer. If it was anything other than the time stated, there would be no reason for her to ask. Why is the time of death important to Wendy? I could not, in honesty, give the day or year of my grandmothers' death, or any other person who was very close or dear to me. A great number of people would be the same.

Therefore, should we ask: What was the actual time of death of Alan, and why is it so important to Wendy Hindley? We know already that the place of Alan's death has changed more frequently than my underwear in one day! Are we to assume that the time of death is not as originally given? Maybe it is different by 15 minutes, maybe even more. It can no longer be assumed the stated time is correct.

What motive drove Wendy to seek my confirmation of time of death? What if I had challenged the original stated time? Would she have been aware that the truth is known? Maybe I do, she cannot be certain that I do not. If she is not worried, she should be.

Let us go back to the actions of Wendy, David, the undertakers, doctors, police etc. on the given night of Alan's death. None of the above followed normal procedures – fact!

The question that remains unanswered by all those involved, is why?

Another question that requires a truthful answer is where was the actual place of death? Too many versions have been given. It is not normal to die in more than one place.

Now we know the time (as we have suspected) of death is at best suspect – another lie? But for what reason?

Who can tell when a liar tells the truth? Even Solomon, with all his wisdom, would be hard pushed to know if Wendy spoke honestly. Meanwhile we continue to expose all.

# CHAPTER 18

I did have a little contact with Wendy after the death of Alan, there was a few telephone conversations; none were pleasant.

The first phone call came not long after arriving back home. Wendy was extremely keen for me to return the spare set of front door keys, which, inadvertently, I had returned to Chatham with; these were the set of keys I was always given when arriving for a visit. Not a problem, I could post them back the next day and I told Wendy such. As it turned out this was not all I had come away with. Wendy was very, very anxious for the return of the second item, one pink slipper.

In the cloakroom of Shorton cottage is the washing machine and a clotheshorse, and when gathering up our coats on our departure, I had also inadvertently included in my bundle, one newly washed, but still stained slipper; I immediately posted the two items back with a note. How I wish now that I had retained at least the slipper, never mind doing something about the blooded blanket, poking out from under a pile on the shelf that I saw above the coat rack in that cloakroom.

It was then some months after Alan's funeral when I received a phone call from Wendy, She took a sadistic glee in telling me that his ashes had been scattered, how they had been scattered, where they had been scattered, and who scattered them. Wendy told me that she had thought of inviting us, but decided against it. Not one single, solitary member of Alan's family was invited.

Apparently, it was a lovely summer's day; many people had been invited, Alan's ashes had been dispensed into different containers and each couple was given a 'pot' and told to throw him anywhere they pleased in the grounds. A splendid day!

Now if that is not bad enough, and extremely disrespectful in my mind, according to those that were present, shall we say, they were disturbed by this performance; it didn't leave a nice taste in the mouth, and some had found it a very difficult experience. Imagine this: There was Wendy carrying a large bowl containing the ashes along with an assortment of containers on a tray.

Those poor people present were being asked to take a cup, mug, beaker, glass, china or plastic container away, to dispose of, a portion of their friend, Alan's ashes. They all, many unknowingly, had aided and abetted the disposal of Alan's remains; perhaps Wendy could feel some sense of security in knowing that no trace of her dead husband could ever be located, no one person could locate all. It seems Wendy had much to be happy about.

The extraordinary ritual was not quite over because when everybody had returned to the rear of the house having done what was asked of them, Wendy emerged from the kitchen singing, and then telling them that there were 'seconds.'

Grotesque!

*****

I have been puzzled why Wendy had given a time limit of seven years for the executorships during a telephone conversation; I have asked lawyers and many others, but nobody has been able to comprehend this time limit; I have had the same response from all; blank puzzled faces.

But Wendy was adamant, seven years: Not any other number.

Reflecting back on something else, I was given the time limit that solicitors are supposed to keep and store their files and that is twelve years, although it is common practice to halve this to six years. Could it be that Wendy had been told this by Eastleys lawyers? They may have even said that the case could be opened at any time until the file was destroyed.

Presumably they would do their weeding just once a year; therefore if the execution of Alan's Will were to be challenged, it would have to be within seven years maximum (six years plus an extra part)

If no challenge was made before those seven years she would think herself safe. I can think of no other possibility.

Time will tell whether she is safe, for she is exposed and vulnerable; she may need to be constantly looking over her shoulder.

# CHAPTER 19

# MINISTERS & MINISTRIES

Jonathan Shaw, MP for Chatham and Aylesford has been turned to on many occasions when, with our entire muster, we were often unable to get a response from most government departments and Ministries. When collating and reading the untold documents and letters relating to our MP, an interesting picture evolves and certainly, some would say, show the United Kingdom's Establishment in a very poor light. It has obviously not been possible to include all documents in the following account of events, but it certainly does leave a bad taste in one's mouth.

**Letter to Gordon Brown and Others**

The following letter was sent to Gordon Brown, Prime minister; Harriet Harman, Deputy Leader and Party Chair of the Labour Party; Jonathan Shaw, my MP; Baroness Ashton of Upholland; Lord Charles Falconer and Sir Paul Stephenson, Commissioner of Police of the Metropolis, New Scotland Yard.

*9$^{th}$ May 2009*
*Mr. Gordon Brown*
*10 Downing Street*
*London*

*Dear Mr. Brown*

*My late father, Alan Edward Hindley, a wealthy man, unexpectedly died on March 14$^{th}$ 2002; his death is shrouded in deceit and conspiracy which enables the perpetrators to get away with murder, fraud and forgery.*

*I cannot apologise for the bluntness of my previous statement when* the evidence collected from many sources, including: a Forensic Expert, Mr. Michael Ansell BA, MA, MFSSoc., witnesses, the police and courts, to mention a few, all confirming my initial fears and subsequent beliefs.

All relevant and necessary routes open to me have been followed in order to seek justice, and over the past 7 years my every turn has been met by concerned ears and sympathetic tongues, which are deafened and silenced shortly afterwards.

With the copious files full of facts, figures and findings and a log of events since my father's death, my uncle, Peter Hindley, began the task of compiling a dossier which could be published on the Internet. Feeling that our story was in the public's interest, on May 16$^{th}$ 2008, we published our first blogs containing an account of our experiences as executors and trustees; what has been published to date is readable at www.myspace.com/saphireanimal; and www.howsafeisawillintheuk.com. All parties, involved and mentioned, were made fully aware before and during the publication, and I feel sure have read our entries. There has been no attempt to stop or challenge anything that has been made public; this also includes from those in the establishment. I am not surprised that all is silent when every word we have published is absolutely, true and correct.

Thousands have read our experiences and have shown much support and encouragement in our fight for moral justice. The experiences of others who have suffered similar or equally corrupt injustices have come forward to share their stories with us.

As you are head of this country, it seemed right and fitting to approach you in order to seek your expertise and support in seeking justice, not only for my late father but for the thousands who find themselves in similar circumstances.

Thank you for your time and I hope that you can find a way of helping me in this diabolical situation. I would dearly love to honour my late father and have his house put in order.

Yours sincerely,

It is now the 26th May, and all but one has failed to reply, they have not even had the common courtesy to acknowledge receipt of my letter.

It was this morning when I received my one reply, and that was from the Metropolitan Police, a Madhu Dodia from the Commissioner's Private Office; they did have the decency to acknowledge receipt, and they did concur that I have previously made this allegation to the police, then they stated the obvious,

*"However, for us to make further enquiries we would require further information on the circumstances surrounding your father's death."*

From the tone of the letter it is obvious that they have not bothered to read or digest what is written on the Internet or review and compare the information contained in the Devon and Cornwall Constabulary files.

Yesterday I sent an email to the Attorney General containing the same letter.

### More who do nothing!

I have received a couple of replies to my recent letters. Firstly, I have had a letter from Gordon Brown PM's office, which states, 'Mr. Brown has asked me to pass your letter to the Ministry of Justice so that they may reply to you on his behalf.' We wait…

It has been a month since I wrote to my MP, Jonathan Shaw and to date I await a reply.

Today, I have received the following letter from the Attorney General's Correspondence Unit in response to my correspondence.

*Thank you for your letter to the Attorney General, your letter has been passed to me for reply.*

The Attorney General does not perform in an investigatory function and is I'm afraid, unable to investigate your claims. If you have evidence relevant to your claims, then you should forward this to the police for investigation to see if a crime has been committed.

Yours sincerely'

Here is my reply to the Attorney General, which is self explanatory:

9*th* June 2009
**Recorded Delivery**

For the Personal attn: only of:
The Attorney General
20 Victoria Street
London
SW1H 0NF

Dear Attorney General

I am in receipt of the letter dated 5*th* June 2009, from your James Ross of your Correspondence Unit and note the comments. It is obvious from the reply the content of my letter was not fully digested and understood; had they visited the site, www.myspace.com/saphireanimal they would have known the reply given would be inadequate.

My letter to you dated 30*th* May 2009 was written as a result of advice, received from a person from within a high profile government office. Therefore, I am surprised that I was misinformed and had written to the wrong person. I am aghast that my letter to you has been treated so casually.

Your representative requires me to contact the police; this we have done, and found their service sadly lacking in the extreme. As a result we have absolutely no confidence what so ever in the Police or the

IPCC.

There must be someone in the United Kingdom, whom has jurisdiction over them both, a higher authority. I presumed, with your title, it would be you. If not, I'm sure you must be in a position to name and locate such a body or person to me.

I look forward to receiving your reply within 10 days.

Yours faithfully

I have received a reply from the Attorney General's Office dated 11 June 2009. Yet another department whereby our case is outside their responsibility, nevertheless they have suggested that we contact various people, i.e., My MP, the police and IPCC.

These are the departments that have now been sent a copy of my original letter to the Attorney General, who were mentioned in their latest letter: The Director of Public Prosecutions (DPP), The Director of the Serious Fraud Office and HM Crown Prosecution Service Inspectorate. Time will tell if any of these departments have any useful responsibilities!

Below is my reply to the Attorney General's Office:

*'Thank you for your letter dated 11 June, I note the content and have taken up your advice and contacted those parties mentioned that we haven't had contact with previously.*

*Had you read the website you would be fully aware that we have previously had dealings with: law firms, the police and the IPCC, and found them, at best, incompetent; the Internet site makes this absolutely clear. Therefore, as we do not have any confidence, what so ever in those concerns, we will not be contacting them.*

*Overall the orthodox system for dealing with the executorships and what followed has proved useless, and obviously urgently requires radical reform (much the same as the MP's expenses fiasco).*

We would be obliged if you read the information you have to hand, on the site and elsewhere. If you can fathom a course of action to put matters right for us, and all the other citizens in the UK, who we now know have had similar problems, we would see this as a first step in the right direction for justice, which is so sadly lacking. With respect we would suggest you pass the information of our case to all the heads of department so mentioned in your previous letter.

*Yours sincerely'*

### Response to letters

Although most have not replied to my recent letters, including the Minister for Justice, the Home Office, Commissioner of the Met Police, the Attorney General's office and many others, I thought you would be interested to know that I received a reply to my letters to Mr. Jonathan Shaw, my MP.

I had to ring his office and request that they acknowledged receipt of my previous letters while I was on the phone to them. A member of his office was able to confirm receipt, but initially unable to give me a response time, other than to say her backlog was 4-5 weeks; I had been waiting 6 weeks.

I insisted that I received a reply within a week or I would be ringing back. Within minutes of the call being terminated I received a phone call back from Mr. Shaw's office to say that a reply to my letters would be with me two days later. In fact, I received his reply the very next day. It read as follows:

*15 June 2009*

*'Further to your letters about your continued concerns regarding your late father's estate I confirm that I have now reviewed your paperwork.*

*The last letter I received from you is dated 19 January 2007 where you were still pursuing Devon & Cornwall Constabulary about this, but I do not have any further record from you detailing the outcome.*

*As I confirmed in my letter of 20 October 2006, if you can draw up a clear statement outlining the new evidence you have, I will refer the case to the Home Secretary.*

*I hope this is helpful.'*

Here follows the content of my reply:

*16/06/09*
*Dear Mr. Shaw*
*Thank you for your letter received today instigated by my telephone call to your office yesterday. I note and have fully digested the contents.*

*Thank you for reviewing the paperwork you hold. Obviously from your reply you have not read the website as requested in my previous letters, including my letter dated 1st August 2008, which has been overlooked by you.*

*You know something of what I have experienced with the shoddy investigation etc, by the Devon & Cornwall Constabulary and the IPCC. You will recall how incensed you were when you discovered that the IPCC had lied to you, as an MP, and told you that there had been a meeting, when in fact there had not. Regrettably, both of these organisations have been exposed as grossly incompetent in dealing with our problem.*

*Therefore, we have, as we told you we would, gone public with some of the facts on the website; people have the right to know how things work or not with the legal system.*

*You ask for new information in your letter, but I would respectfully request that whether it is new information, or that which is already at hand, makes no difference because we can prove, with documentary evidence, that the case was not handled as it should have* been, and in a professional way by virtually all parties; it has been a sham.

To make it quite clear to you, it is obvious that the faux investigation was a farce. Therefore it would be in everybody's interest for the job to be done properly, as it should have been done in the first place, and as soon as possible. If this requires the intervention of the Home Secretary, whom you mention in your letter, then so be it. Meanwhile we will continue.

Yours sincerely,'

And now we wait…

# CHAPTER 20

## 'THE UNTOUCHABLES'

I have been thinking about The Right Honourable Michael Wills, Minister of State's, letter dated 9 September 2009, to The Right Honourable Jonathan Shaw, and notice how much emphasis he gives to the responsibilities of the Police and their associates at the Independent Police Complaints Commission.

Whether he thinks we should contact these people again or not is unclear, but if he were to consider our abridged account on the web site, which he claims to have read, this account gives some of the experiences with these incompetent bodies, he would be aware that it would, once again, probably be futile.

Let us take time to recap just a few little items:

1. It took a year, and the intervention of The Right Honourable Jonathan Shaw to obtain an interview with the Police in Devon, Namely, Detective Inspector Taylor. In that interview relating to fraud and possible murder etc. he took a personal phone call on his mobile phone from his daughter. He stated that he/the police were worried about being sued (note, the facts we have disclosed here and elsewhere could have induced the same reaction, but to date not one person has made any such approach to us; we are not surprised as we are disclosing reality, the truth, facts). When told that according to Wendy Hindley and the gardener, David Hart, Alan died in various places, we were told that was not significant. Taylor said that we would be kept informed; we were not. Taylor said we would have a meeting at the end of the investigation; again, we did not. Once he phoned me to tell me that the case was being reviewed by another officer, inferring that as far as he was

concerned the case was closed; during that phone call Taylor said the police had spoken to various members of the establishment and medical people, but deliberately omitted to mention any friends or family of the deceased, I immediately knew that essential work had not been done. Not being reassured that a thorough investigation had taken place I immediately asked Taylor whether he was satisfied with his work; this really rattled him and confirmed my suspicions that he was not: These suspicions were confirmed when I learned that some weeks after that phone conversation, the police took the first statement from Joan Tabram, my brother's mistress, and an important player in the saga.

2.The IPCC, or to give them their full title, The Independent Police Complaints Commission. At Susan's first meeting with two ranked IPCC officers at the Police Headquarters Exeter, Devon. both officers agreed that she was correct in complaining about the way the police had handled the case; this outlook changed subsequently (not the first time we had experienced a change of heart, it had happened within the Devon and Cornwall Constabulary more than once, and we have noted and recorded those officers and instances; it is also worth mentioning that those police officers who wanted to work on the case were never permitted to). Via the IPCC we learned of a Police letter to us that never existed: That the Police denied the existence of one letter that they had sent to us, but we were able to provide them with a photocopy (this brings to mind some of those reported instances of police altering evidence). The IPCC also managed to give Susan a brother; quite a surprise to her and the family. When Susan's mother was asked about her son, she could recall giving birth to no such person and being forgetful is definitely not one of her character traits.

3.Returning briefly to the Devon and Cornwall Police and the different stories given by the widow, Wendy, and the gardener: Initially Alan's place of death was said to be in his chair in the study, within hours, that was to change to his bedroom where he was reported to be heard crying out in pain, by Wendy, who was in the main kitchen. Two things do not work here, firstly as I understand it, if you are having any form of heart attack, you inhale, it is impossible to make a sound. Secondly, because of the geography of the house, and one wall in particular is in excess of a foot thick, the sound would not carry, and even if it did, it would have to compete with the radio or television which Wendy would turn on automatically upon entering the kitchen. We also understand that much, much later, Widow Wendy's statement gives the place of death, which had moved to the main staircase. But, back to the original locations for Alan's demise; the study: were Alan died in his chair, that was followed by death in his bedroom, the first place here was in the chair, then on the floor in front of the shower room door, then yet again he died on the floor in widow Wendy's arms, after which he managed to get onto his bed unaided; the last act puzzled widow Wendy. I am not alone in being puzzled as to how he died in so many places. But all this is normal and acceptable to the Devon and Cornwall Police Constabulary (or Cooperative) and furthermore gets no reaction from the IPCC. Why?

And now no reaction from the Minister of State; but he of course says he cannot comment. Why? And of course he says he is not responsible. So I ask," Who is responsible for the Police and IPCC then?" Can somebody, anybody, tell me who is responsible?

All this and more leads me to ask, "Has anyone got the balls enough to take responsibility in their position of authority and trust?"

It seems not so far:

If we look at the few replies received to date, from those in trust and authority, we see a pattern emerging.

We now know it is not the Minister of State, the Right Honourable Michael Wills who accepts responsibility, and he is, in his letter, speaking on behalf of the Minister of Justice (Jack Straw), plus the Home Office (Alan Johnson), and the Attorney General (Baroness Patricia Scotland). So in one letter alone, four parties do not take any responsibility.

We can continue:

Roger K Daw, Principal Policy Advisor of the Crown Prosecution Service, in his letter dated 14 August 2009, has already said this case is outside their responsibility and finishes his letter with the useful comment *"...there is nothing further that I can usefully add to the response that has been provided."* So yet another not responsible!

Stacey Oliver, Intelligence Unit of the Serious Fraud Office says in her letter, dated 5 October 2009, *"....we have concluded that this matter is not a matter which is appropriate for investigation by the SFO..."* and then goes on to suggest contact with the following: the local police (she is wrong there) and Department for Business, Innovations and Skills, also Consumer Direct plus, the Office of Fair Trading and other irrelevant organisations; we can only conclude that she is greatly removed from the real world, or living in an alternative dimension. The end result is the same: not our responsibility *"...In certain situations the information you have provided may be retained on our database for future reference..."* civil servants wording for 'it may be filed'. This is another case of 'Nothing to do with me; not our responsibility'. So, yet another not responsible!

Assistance with this case was asked of the most senior police officer in the United Kingdom, namely the

Commissioner of the Metropolitan Police, but the reply from his office said that he is not responsible for the actions of the Devon and Cornwall Constabulary, so naturally a letter was sent to his office on 6$^{th}$ June 2009 asking him, as senior officer, to act; to date there has been no acknowledgement or reply. So, yet another not responsible!

You may think that if you contact the Prime Minister, he will help or take responsibility, if so you are naive, because sadly, that is not the case; his staff of civil servants reply on his behalf telling you that the matter has been passed on to an appropriate Ministry. By now we all know where that leads, yes, straight into the 'in tray' of an employee of the State, who takes no action or responsibility. So, yet another, not responsible!

Returning to the Minister of State's letter where he indicates that the Police Constabularies are answerable to nobody except themselves, and the same applies to the IPCC, therefore, would that mean, as is frequently said in the media and beyond, that the United Kingdom is now a police state?

# CHAPTER 21

# TURNING TO YOUR MP

I wrote the following letter to Jonathan Shaw, my MP, requesting his support in gaining responses from ministers and others who continue to ignore our plight.

***HAND DELIVERED***
*11/07/2009*
*Mr. J. Shaw MP*
*411 High Street*
*Chatham*
*Kent ME4 4NU*

*Your Ref: SS/JS*

*Dear Mr. Shaw*

*I have enclosed copies of recent correspondence to various parties, who have to date, not had the common decency to reply. Therefore, I would ask you to forward them in the stamped addressed envelopes enclosed with your covering letter requiring a response from these officials.*
*I have also enclosed a self addressed envelope for your confirmation, or, should you not feel able to co-operate with my request, then you can tell me the reasons why, as I understand that these parties are obliged to respond to my MP.*
*Thank you in anticipation.*
*Yours sincerely*
*Susan Goodsell*
*Ps I look forward to receiving your reply to my letter dated 17/06/2009*
*Enc...*

Today 8th August I have received a reply to this letter it reads as follows:

*'I refer to your recent letters and confirm that I have followed-up your correspondence to the various parties concerned.*
*I enclose a copy of these for your information. Please note I have written to Rt. Hon Jack Straw MP, who is now the Lord Chancellor and Secretary of State for Justice, as the Ministry for Justice has superceded the Department for Constitutional Affairs.*
*I will of course send you copies of their responses once received.*
*I hope this proves helpful.*
*Yours sincerely*
*Jonathan Shaw MP'*

I note from the correspondence that follows (copy of letter sent by my MP to members of the establishment) that my enclosed letter to all parties does not appear to have been forwarded on as instructed.

*'My constituent, Ms. Goodsell, has written to you directly about the death of her father in 2002 and the concerns she has regarding executorships following a police investigation and IPCC review into her complaints.*
*Please can you respond to Ms. Goodsell's concerns, and also determine whether there are any further avenues open to her to be able to resolve this matter.*
*I hope to hear from you soon.*
*Yours sincerely*
*Jonathan Shaw MP*
This letter was sent to the following people:
Sir Paul Stephenson – Commissioner Metropolitan Police

The Rt. Hon Alan Johnson MP, Secretary of state for the Home Office

Mr. Kier Starmer QC, The Director of Public Prosecution

The Rt. Hon Baroness Scotland QC, The Attorney General

The Rt. Hon Jack Straw MP, Lord Chancellor and Secretary of State for Justice

Please note that not included in this list is The Rt. Hon Harriet Harman MP, Deputy Leader of the Labour Party, which was requested. Why not?

My reply to Mr. Shaw's letter follows:

*09/08/2009*
**HAND DELIVERED**

*Mr. J. Shaw MP*
*411 High Street*
*Chatham*
*Kent ME4 4NU*

*Your Ref: SS/JS*

*Dear Mr. Shaw*

*Firstly, I would like to thank you for your letter in response to my correspondence dated 11/07/2009, and the subsequent letters you sent on my behalf to those who continue to ignore.*

*After reading your letter I am uncertain as to whether you have forwarded copies of my letter with your letter to the various parties, and would be grateful if you could confirm one way or the other. I am also puzzled as to why you omitted to write to Rt. Hon Harriet Harman.*

*Thank you for what you have done so far and I look forward to receiving the considered and constructive replies in the near future.*
*Yours sincerely*

# CHAPTER 22

# GOVERNMENT RESPONSE

We have sent letters to various establishment departments and government officials and their responses have started to land on the door mat; my first impressions are:

The Serious Fraud Office, letter from Stacy Oliver of the Intelligence Unit, is a farce. They have obviously not done their homework, and it seems are as competent as the police and IPCC, namely, totally incompetent. Telling you to contact your local police shows that they know nothing of the case; after all you live in Kent, and the problems lie in Devon, and you know from personal experience that your local Police will say it is outside their area (it makes me wonder whether it is worthwhile committing a crime within the remit of one constabulary and living in another - seems to me one option of avoiding police action; they don't need much of an excuse). The Fraud Office letter goes on to invite you to contact Consumer Direct; how that applies to this case puzzles me: the same can be said for Department for Business, Innovation and Skills. At this point I feel like asking for some of the substance the writer has been taking, because it seems to have taken her into another dimension and cannot be legal. As for the Citizens Advice Bureau, I have never found them useful when dealing with problems.

From the way the letter is constructed I would suggest it is nothing more than a compilation of standard civil service paragraphs, and an expensive waste of tax payers' money. Yet another letter from those versed in justifying how to do nothing. But worth exposing her; the letter is transparent to anyone reading it, anyone who has half a brain cell.

The same can be said for the Crown Prosecution Service letter from Roger K Daw, Principal Policy Advisor, who gives the impression that they do not soil their hands with anything; having said that, it is worth noting they give the impression that they only look at cases given to them by the Police, but are " independent" of the Police: Thinking of "Independent" we know from experience of the Independent Police Complaints Commission, which is supposedly independent of the Police, that the only thing "Independent" with them, is in their name.

The Minister of State's letter headed Ministry of Justice and written on behalf of: Jack Straw, Minister of Justice; Patricia Scotland, Attorney General and Alan Johnson, Home Secretary, ends with the writer, Michael Wills, Minister of State, giving permission to Jonathan Shaw MP, to pass the letter on to you!

They seem to have done their homework, but have made errors

1. That I wrote the blog alone. (At least they read and digested some)

2. They mention forgery, but make no reference how to bring the forger's to book or expose them. Is forgery a private or criminal matter? Surely it is criminal.

3. IPCC can be overruled by a judicial review: How do you get a Judicial Review?

4. As for Lawyers: Eastleys have been negligent in providing information and canvassing us as a client of another lawyer; as for our lawyer, Michael.......

And these comments are purely after an initial glance at the three letters.

# CHAPTER 23

**Reply to Minister of State's letter**

Further to receiving the letter from the Minister of State on behalf of the Minister of Justice, the Secretary of State, and the Attorney General, I have hand delivered the following to my MP, Jonathan Shaw, to forward to all parties requesting a meeting.

*Dear Mr. Shaw*

*I have now fully digested the contents of the letters you forwarded to me from the various government departments. I am now enclosing letters for you to forward to the appropriate people.*

*Thank you in anticipation.*

This is taken from the enclosed letter that I wish him to pass on to all the above parties.

*'Having fully digested the contents of your letter dated 9$^{th}$ September to Jonathan Shaw; I require a meeting with you at the earliest possible time in order to clarify matters.*

*I look forward to receiving your reply with an appointment within the next 14 days.'*

The following letter was received in response to my letters requesting a meeting with each of the Ministers who corresponded with me last.

*'I refer to your recent letter including those that you would like me to forward to various parties asking to meet with them to clarify matters, and I confirm that your requests are unlikely to be successful.*

If you wish to clarify matters you will need to put these in writing, and I will certainly send these on with a covering letter from me as appropriate. Can I please point out that the Rt. Hon Michael Wills MP said in his letter, dated 9 September, that he responded to me as the Duty Minister and any further correspondence needs to be addressed to Ms. Bridget Prentice MP, Parliamentary Under Secretary of State.

When I have your more detailed correspondence I will write accordingly and send you the responses in the normal way.

Yours sincerely
Jonathan Shaw MP'

6/12/2009
Mr. J. Shaw MP
411 High Street
Chatham
Kent ME4 4NU

Your Ref: SS/JS

Dear Mr. Shaw

Thank you for your letter dated 22$^{nd}$ November; I was dumbfounded by its contents in reply to my letter dated 25 October.

From your letter it would seem that you have done nothing with my letters, which I asked you to forward to the various parties, therefore I feel that you have failed miserably in your duties as my Member of Parliament.

You say in your letter that you need more information before you would consider any further action; this is unbelievable when you have been fully aware of my problem since our first correspondence on the matter in 2004, more than 5 years ago. You have had knowledge and access, via correspondence, a meeting and the Internet since. Therefore by requesting more information I can only assume you wish to hinder *progress; you have more than enough information already.*

*I require your confirmation within 10 days that you have complied with my request and sent my letters to all the named officials, without exception. In addition I have enclosed a further letter, as you indicate, to be forwarded to Ms. Bridget Prentice MP, Parliament Under Secretary of State.*

*I look forward to receiving confirmation and convenient appointments from all parties very shortly.*

*Yours sincerely*

# CHAPTER 24

# OBSTRUCTIVE BEHAVIOUR BY OUR LAWYER

The following letter was sent to our lawyer, Michael French requesting the files for our case to be released to us, as it has been more than seven years since he took the case on. There would appear to have been very little action on his part, and no real progress made by Michael French in all these years, he has been unable to achieve any tangible results, and it would seem from the following that he intends to continue to obstruct us in our endeavour to put Alan's estate in order.

**Recorded Delivery**
*Mr. M. French*
*Michael French & Booth Hearn*
*52 High Street*
*Chatham*
*Kent ME4 4DS*

*Reference: Alan Edward Hindley (deceased)*

*Dear Mr. French*
*We urgently require you to give me the file(s) you are holding related to the above matter; it will be convenient for me to collect all the papers relating to this case on Monday 7th December at 4pm.*
*Thank you in anticipation*

Monday 7th December: after finishing work I arrived at Michael French's office to collect the files in their entirety. Marilyn was the only one on duty in the front office, and I greeted her as I usually would, with a smile. At first Marilyn appeared to be unsure as to why I should be there, but after informing her I was there to collect the files she explained that Michael was not in the office and asked me to take a seat while she ran upstairs to speak with someone. The person she spoke to was a gentleman called David, I know no more about him other than that. To cut a long story short, the files were not going to be ready for collection that day, or the following. I produced a pre-typed letter which expressed my regret that he, Mr. Michael French had again been unable to comply with my requests, and stated that I would call again tomorrow the 8$^{th}$ December, by which time I expected them to be ready for me. I required a signature from Marilyn as she was taking receipt of my second letter. My copy of the letter was signed and she took a photocopy of it for Michael. I was told that I would have to wait for the files until Friday 11$^{th}$ December at the earliest. I eventually agreed and was instructed to ring on the Friday morning before collection.

This is the second letter that Marilyn signed:

**Hand Delivered**
*Mr. M. French*
*Michael French & Booth Hearn*
*52 High Street*
*Chatham*
*Kent ME4 4DS*

*Reference: Alan Edward Hindley (deceased)*

*Dear Mr. French*
*Further to our letter dated 3$^{rd}$ December requiring you to give me the file(s) relating to Alan Edward Hindley: Regrettably you have not*

*complied with my requirement, therefore I will return tomorrow, Tuesday 8$^{th}$ December, at 2pm to collect all the required documents.*
  *Thanking you in anticipation*
  *Yours sincerely*

I rang on Friday morning as requested to by Marilyn, I was told that Michael wished to see me and could I make an appointment to do so. "3.30 today would be convenient," this was the only choice I gave, and the appointment was made.

At 3.30 I arrived at Michael's office and Marilyn rang through to Michael to say his client had arrived. Michael appeared from the back room as usual, shook hands and led me through to where he had just come.

Needless to say, I did not leave with the files, but I did leave with a firm undertaking from Michael that by the 23$^{rd}$ December 2009, I would receive, in writing, Michael's proposals for moving our case to its conclusion. He said he was going to give me a detailed plan of his intended actions and outcomes, also the time frame these actions would take. He shook my hand in confirmation of his undertaking. By now, all these years later, it came as no surprise when the 23$^{rd}$ came, and passed, without any contact whatsoever from the unreliable Mr. French.

# CHAPTER 25

# MEETING WITH MP

I received a letter from Jonathan Shaw MP, who is also a Government Minister, requesting to have a meeting with me on 15$^{th}$ January 2010. Naturally I accepted by phone and letter, which follows:

*Mr. J. Shaw MP*
*411 High Street*
*Chatham*
*Kent ME4 4NU*

*Your Ref: SS/JS*

*Dear Mr. Shaw*
*Further to your letter dated 15 December 2009, I would like to confirm that the appointment to meet with you at 17.30 on the 15$^{th}$ January is convenient for me.*

*I certainly hope that after our appointment you will be able to then arrange the meetings I have requested with the previously named ministers.*

*I look forward to what I expect will be a very useful meeting with you on that date.*
*Yours sincerely*

At the meeting Jonathan told me he had no power whatsoever, and he was unable to facilitate a meeting with any of the required ministers, and he still retained my letters to them in his office. He made it quite clear to me that he had spoken with the ministers and, incredible as it may sound, they required more information - A useful delaying tactic, which we've seen before. All the Ministers were fully aware of what has been published on this website and believe it or not, he told me that they, the Ministers, could do nothing, they were powerless.

At this point should we ask if they are powerless, why are they in their position of power and privilege, which we all pay for in our taxes?

To my astonishment, during this meeting Jonathan produced a log of correspondence and his involvement in our case, we must presume that would include any dealings with the various other ministers, and he kindly offered to give this to me. I accepted. The document was within an inch of my hand when his colleague, who was taking notes, stopped Jonathan in his tracks and said that a copy should be taken for their records, and then sent to me.

I had observed Jonathan's colleague reading through another copy of this same document, which he then put into the pile of papers he was holding on his knees. When I immediately challenged his colleague, as he was blatantly lying, he had no need to make another copy as he was looking at a second, Jonathan said it had taken his wife many hours to compile the log and wanted to have his own copy; his complexion changed.

On reflection, a word document is saved on the computer it was produced on as normal office practice, and it is well known that Government and Civil Servants do everything in triplicate. Therefore, we must assume that Jonathan's assistant saw something on that log which would have been dangerous to expose.

The following letter has been sent to: Alan Johnson MP, Michael Wills MP, Jack Straw MP, Baroness Scotland QC, and Bridget Prentice MP and a copy has also been sent to Gordon Brown, Prime Minister and HRH Queen Elizabeth II

'Dear …

At the request of the Rt. Hon Jonathan Shaw MP, I had a meeting with him on 15$^{th}$ January during which he made me fully aware that he had discussed some of the issues which require your action, and that you are fully aware of what has been published to date on my continually expanding website.

He also advised me that you could do nothing: This is totally unbelievable. I would respectfully suggest that if you were at all motivated you could, and would act to correct and resolve matters: Certainly it is within your remit to instigate change to laws and act in other ways when you think necessary; and **now** those actions and changes are needed and imperative. The system you are responsible for is not working, not for the ordinary people, not for those ordinary people who you represent and work for. Please remember this is certainly not an isolated case, I have received documented information of many others since the web site was started.

I look forward to a mutually convenient appointment with you within the very near future to move things forward.

Yours sincerely

PS. For your information a copy of this letter, with others, has been added to the 'howsafeisawillintheuk.com' website.

Cc. HRH Queen Elizabeth II
Rt. Hon Gordon Brown PM'

**Quote:**
"There is none as daft as those that want to be."

# CHAPTER 26

# QUICK RESPONSE 23/01/10

I have just received my first response to the last letters sent to and requiring meetings with: Baroness Scotland, Attorney General; Bridget Prentice, Parliamentary Under Secretary of State; Michael Wills, Minister of State; Jack Straw, Lord Chancellor and Secretary of State for Justice; Alan Johnson, Secretary of State for the Home Office.

The Attorney General has once again passed my letter on to James Ross, of the Correspondence Unit, the content of his letter follows:

*'Thank you for your recent letter to the Attorney General's Office, your letter has been passed to me for reply.*

*If you wish for laws to be changed then you will need to contact your local MP and put your concerns to them, as they will need to take this forward in parliament on your behalf.*

*In my previous letter to you dated 11 June 2009, I informed you that the Attorney General's Office is unable to offer any legal advice or any assistance to individuals, also I provided you with the details of the other various government departments that are ideally suited to deal with the issues you raised.*

*That stance has not changed I'm afraid, and I can only refer you to my previous letter for the correct course of action for you to take.*

*Yours sincerely*
*James Ross*
*Correspondence Unit'*

Received in the letter James Ross (one of the Attorney General's minions) tells me that my Member of Parliament is the one I should approach to get the law relating to the executor's execution of the Last Will and Testament changed: Which is just one thing that is needed, as the law, as it stands today, is a sham, and makes the making of any Last Will and Testament a futile waste of time; executors can, and do, ignore the Will, and indeed the Wishes of the deceased daily (the Law permits it). If any members of the legal profession or Government tell you otherwise, they are simply lying.

Now why did my Member of Parliament, the Rt. Hon Jonathan Shaw, a Minister in this government, tell me that he can do nothing to get this obscene law changed when I attended his surgery at his request recently? He must have been aware of what he can do, and that this will fall within his remit to act.

We already know that my MP, Jonathan Shaw, also a Government Minister, has told me in person, that he holds no authority or influence, and Mr. Ross has seen it necessary to remind me of various government departments suited to deal with the issues I raised: These so called 'government departments' either ignore my letters, or deny any responsibility or authority whatsoever.

Now, I find myself in a quandary, which leads me to ask the question: Who actually holds the power and authority in this country, the United Kingdom?

The existing establishment dictates that it is not with Royalty, but lies with Government, yet, from the 'horses mouth', the members who form Government, your MP's and Ministers, not to mention the Prime Minister, Gordon Brown, have all made it very clear that responsibility, authority and power is not theirs to use, which begs the question: Are these Ministers and Members of Parliament in a position of privilege without having or taking any responsibility; if this is the case, they are holding their position under false pretences.

If these government officials are no more than puppets,

then who are the puppeteers? Who are the real 'Masters'?

Frightening thought - that makes you and me nothing more than fodder! But to who?,

As this is only the first reply I have received it will be interesting to see if, as now expected, the rest of the puppets within the government ministries follow with similar replies.

Is there anybody in the United Kingdom capable of doing anything honorable? It would seem, to date, that there is nobody!

# CHAPTER 27

# SOLICITOR IGNORES SRA (SOLICITORS REGULATION AUTHORITY)

As you are aware, we employed the services of a lawyer, Michael French, of Michael French & Booth Hearn. He refused to release our file when it was obvious that he had made no attempt to move our case forward during the 8 years he controlled it.

After 2 months of failure in our attempts we employed another lawyer to retrieve the file; he failed to, so in desperation we went to the Legal Complaints Service of the Solicitor's Regulatory Association (SRA), who obtained an agreement from Michael French to release our papers immediately.

Needless to say he did not honour his word! He has snubbed the authority of the SRA by his inaction.

Today we discovered that the Legal Complaints Service had prematurely closed their file regarding Mr. Michael French.

Letter sent to SRA by fax and post as follows:

*Legal Complaints Service*
*Victoria Court*
*8 Dormer Place*
*Leamington Spa*
*Warwickshire CV32 5AE*
*29th March 2010*

*Dear Ms. Sexton*

*Further to our phone conversation this afternoon, regarding the release of our papers from Michael French, I was aghast that you had prematurely closed the file. As you are aware, we wrote to you on 24$^{th}$ March 2010, voicing our doubts that Mr. French would release our file. Further to that I wrote to you today, confirming Michael French's non-compliance; this letter was faxed to you at 8 o'clock this morning.*

*As agreed today, during my telephone conversation with you, you will be reopening your file and contacting Mr. French tomorrow, Tuesday 30$^{th}$ March, in order to gauge why he had not honoured the agreement he had made with you to release our file on Thursday 19$^{th}$ March 2010.*

*As agreed I will be phoning you on Wednesday morning for your update.*

*Yours sincerely,*

## LAWYER CONTINUES TO SNUB THE LAW SOCIETY.

Although I have received a letter from Michael French some days ago, which he was instructed to do by the Law Society, whereby he agreed with them to release our file. To date, he continues not to comply by withholding the dossier.

Today I telephoned Michael French at Michael French & Booth Hearn's offices as I had been instructed to do by Ms. Sexton of the Law Society. Michael French's receptionist, Valerie, was about to connect me to Mr. French until she knew my name. Then I was told that Michael French was not available, 'he was with a client'. Why are we not surprised?

We have passed this information on to the Law Society for their records because they need to be kept fully informed.

## Update on File Release from Lawyer

We've been advised today that Michael French, our old lawyer, has released our dossier to our new lawyer. It arrived in three separate parcels: Whether it is complete or incomplete we know not. Nevertheless, the Law Society's lawyer's complaints section has already closed both files they've opened on this subject because, they say, the word of Mr. French is sufficient. Strange, as they also know from a 'Control' where they instigated certain sanctions against him for his mishandling of another person's estate, and non compliance to their instructions.

Unfortunately it was a painful experience dealing with the Law Society (SRA); it has caused unnecessary and considerable concern and aggravation, and exposed gross inefficiency.

What follows is the letter I have written to the Chief Executive, details given to me by Ms. Sexton.

*15 April 2010*

*www.howsafeisawillintheuk.com*

*Ms. Deborah Evans*
*Chief Executive*
*Legal Complaints Service*
*Victoria Court*
*8 Dormer Place*
*Leamington Spa*
*Warwickshire CV32 5AE*

*Your ref: CRO/116991-2010/CCC*

*Dear Ms. Evans*

What follows is an edited account of the appalling service I have experienced recently within your organisation. The manner in which our case was handled by your employee, Ms. Saima Sexton, was incredibly unprofessional and I feel I have been lied to repeatedly. Ms. Sexton was initially bubbling with enthusiasm and ideas for future action. Within a week, without receiving any concrete outcome she had closed the file.

It has come to our attention that the SRA has published a control, issued on Mr. Michael Edward French dated 3$^{rd}$ March 2010, published 6 April, where it makes it quite clear that this same lawyer has acted unprofessionally and dubiously on another client's estate. Nevertheless, today Ms. Sexton was completely prepared to accept the word of a liar.

She was fully aware that he did not forward our file within the deadline that he agreed with her. In fact, the final two or three files have only arrived with my new lawyer today, and there has been no opportunity as yet for him, or me, to validate the contents and confirm whether they are complete.

I would also like to draw to your attention the fact that, during the first phone call I had with Ms. Sexton, she told me she was fully prepared to organise, if necessary, officials to visit Mr. French's premises to retrieve the file. Whereas today she told me that she has no means at her disposal to carry out such an act; this is just one example of your appalling service.

After she had closed the file we advised her that Michael French's conciliation had failed because he had not released any papers whatsoever, as we had warned her in my letter dated 29$^{th}$ March 2010. She decided to open a new file, Ref: CRO/117945-2010/SS and instructed me to telephone Mr. French during the week commencing Monday 5$^{th}$ April to get him to comply with the agreement she had made with him. What the hell am I doing your job for? Surely, this is complicating the situation and unethical.

*I am obliged to ask what you intend to do to halt any similar repetition of such appalling mishandling in the future? To date, I have not completed and returned your Customer Feedback Form.*

*Yours sincerely,*

We await their action…

# CHAPTER 28

# 15 May 2010: THE GUILTY TRY TO COVER THEIR TRACKS!

For years now we have been monitoring the Land Registry's entries for, amongst others, Shorton Cottage and its building plots, and new build houses in Lammas Lane, and we can tell you now that within the last two weeks, three completely new entries have appeared:
They are:
    1. DN481974 for 18 Lammas Lane, Preston, Paignton, TQ3 1PS
    2. DN472885 for 14 Lammas Lane, Preston, Paignton, TQ3 1PS
    3. DN for 22 Lammas Lane, Preston, Paignton, TQ3 1PS

What puzzles me is why these should suddenly appear now: If you were to look at these recently published entries it would appear that these properties were registered years ago, and if that is the case, why is it only in the last two weeks that they appear on the Land Registry's site? They did not exist there before: One thing is absolutely certain, and what we can prove is, these three entries are very, very recent.

One has to ask why is it that all three properties are finally legally registered and published at this time. If we believed in coincidence, and we do not, it could be simply coincidence that these deeds are published now.

Could it be the late publication of these deeds is something other than a coincidence, and we can't think of a motive for such action now.

Please remember, those parties involved in the original execution of Alan Hindley's Will and the registry of related properties, namely Wendy Hindley et al, are aware that we are actively working towards having the late Alan Hindley's Will and Wishes executed as **he had wished,** and that we will also be having a meeting at the Ministry of Justice shortly to discuss this and other matters?

We have openly published these facts globally, here and elsewhere. Wendy Hindley and her aids will be fully aware of the situation they have placed themselves in. Could it be that they are now trying to limit the damage to themselves? One has to ask: Could it be that they are trying to make our task more difficult?

If this is so, they will fail.

# CHAPTER 29

# A MEETING AT THE MINISTRY OF JUSTICE

Further to my letters of 16$^{th}$ January 2010, to Jack Straw MP, Bridget Prentice MP, and Michael Wills MP about the laws relating to Wills and Probate, I have received a letter from the Ministry of Justice.

Bridget Prentice is the Minister for the Laws relating to Wills and Probate, and has expressed that she would like to help resolve our case as far as she can, and has requested that I telephone the Ministry of Justice to make arrangements to meet with her officials.

Needless to say, I will be excepting their offer to meet, and hope it will be the productive meeting that is needed to protect the many who will have their will and wishes ignored after their death.

## MEETING AT THE MINISTRY OF JUSTICE CANCELLED

For more than a year we have been trying to get appointments with various government ministers in order to get changes to inheritance laws that are so badly needed, to move our case forward, and to expose to the relevant Ministries, the diabolical shortfalls in the departments they are responsible for. Some, but not all you have read.

We have, during that time, sought help from Susan's current Member of Parliament and Parliamentary Minister, Jonathan Shaw: It could be said that he has been 'almost' cooperative: 'Almost,' but not quite; in aiding our requests to meet with Government Ministers.

This week we finally had the first signs of positive action from a CIVIL SERVANT at the Ministry of Justice;

and an appointment was made to meet with one or more CIVIL SERVANTS at the Ministry of Justice's offices in Petty France, London for today, 9th April 2010.

This appointment was made on Tuesday of this week with full knowledge that there was to be a general election, yet yesterday we received a telephone call from Kirsty Milliam (the person who made the original appointment) cancelling the arrangements. The reason was given as the impending election of members of parliament.

I have been obliged to accept a new appointment on Friday 21 May, which will prove extremely inconvenient for me (they are fully aware of this); obviously this is yet another unnecessary delay.

The Ministers and Civil Servants are proving to be so efficient in finding ways of avoiding work and their responsibilities.

Had the intended meeting been with the appropriate Minister I could understand the delay, but it is not: It is to be with CIVIL SERVANTS, namely Kirsty Milliam and Paul Hughes, whose position is not resultant on any general election. CIVIL SERVANTS are NOT ELECTED; they normally have a job for life.

Am I expected to believe that the Ministry of Justice ceases to do anything for the duration of a general election?

Taking this scenario one stage further, do all Government Ministries stop work now while awaiting the election and selection of the new Ministers? I think not.

If this is the case, the employed Civil Servants are, in effect, only occupying their respective offices; they are not working, it would be a sort of paid holiday break, hiding within their cupboards with their cups of tea that we, the tax payers, are paying for.

Do you find this acceptable?

# FINALLY, MEETING AT MINISTRY OF JUSTICE

## MY AGENDA

Meeting at Ministry of Justice, London on 21 May 2010

1. The Wishes of Alan Edward Hindley regarding his estate are to be put in order and adhered to. (The will submitted is a forgery, signatures also).

2. A fully transparent and comprehensive investigation into all matters relating to Alan Edward Hindley's demise and the mishandling of his estate (must include all parties involved at the time, and since).

3. Investigations must be overseen by Government at ministerial level.

4. The law must penalise ALL those parties who have aided and abetted Wendy Hindley.

5. Laws must be changed now so that a Last Will and Testament is followed to the letter.

6. A person's Human Rights to continue after death: If someone abuses the trust by misappropriating a person's belongings or wealth, it is an offence; as the law stands today this stops after the final breath.

7. Severe penalties put into place so that abusers of executorships are punished by the state (criminal offence as well as civil).

8. Forgery of Wills to have appropriate Laws and very severe penalties, which are enforced by the state.

9.  Changes to the inheritance laws to be retrospective.

10. Ministry of Justice to hold executors responsible.

11. Solicitors and other parties are now taking money under false pretences when they draft a will, and do not advise their clients that executor's can, and do act as they wish; therefore they do not adhere to the deceased wishes and will. A will can be said to be not of merchantable quality, because it is not fit for its purpose. The Law Society and lawyers to immediately stop advertising their services for drafting a will under the pretext that when they draft wills, they are resolute. (At present this is blatant misrepresentation because they know it is not so). Any will can be 'broken' within minutes should the executors wish it. Therefore it contravenes normal consumer laws.

12. Create a Central Bureau where the last will and testaments can be deposited should people wish.

*****

Now during that first meeting at the Ministry of Justice, I presented to Paul Hughes and Kirsty Milliam the outline agenda, which you have seen earlier.

All these topics, without exception, were thoroughly discussed and accepted as reality.

But the Civil Servants admitted the only way forward was to get the media involved, and letters of protest sent to government offices. The more letters they receive the quicker they could react.

Therefore, what they were actually saying is that if they receive no letters of protest they will do what they do best: namely NOTHING. (Remember 'NOTHING' is exactly the same technique the Freemasons use when they are under serious threat).

WHAT DOES THAT SAY FOR THE ETHICS AND HONOURABILITY OF THE BRITISH GOVERNMENT?

It says it all!

I found it incredible that Mr. Hughes said that everything that could go wrong for us, has gone wrong. He went on to say that normally a person has one thing that goes awry and they eventually give up the fight to get justice: Sounds like those in a position of power rely on it, and I am sure they do. It is a tried and tested technique which has worked for them for a very, very long time; that is, until we arrived, and we will not stop until our task is done, in its entirety.

The Government and the Police know what needs to be done and corrected; perhaps it is because this is the first occasion for them, (Paul Hughes said this was a horrendous and a unique case) and those in power are unsure how they can proceed. Perhaps they have forgotten how to do actual constructive work: So now the GOVERNMENT and the POLICE have the PROBLEM; they know what the problems are, and they have the wherewithal to rectify all, and they also know they are theoretically responsible. They will need to find the solutions, but that would involve doing something, and that sets another problem; they have forgotten how.

It was suggested that I contact the Press: This sounds good if you are naïve; it is a fact that the press and media of the United Kingdom can be silenced by the Government and the Police, and it is an everyday occurrence. Our case is not one that either party, the government or the police would benefit by; its mass exposure would be very embarrassing; they would not like to see it published: It exposes too much corruption etc. in the establishment from top to bottom.

Paul Hughes asked me how long I had been working to get Alan's will executed as he had wished and I told him it had been 8 years; his response was a calm statement that it would probably take a further eight years. With that, I advised him that was not a problem and that there were people waiting in the wings to take over from me; which is absolutely true. I will work until the job is done, after all, this is not an isolated case, it may be an extreme case, but it does not stand alone.

In addition to the above, the following points were also discussed at the meeting:

AOB (Any Other Business)

- Police – Are not answerable to anybody, and nobody takes responsibility allowing corruption to take place at all levels – Police State!? Incompetent and/or corrupt officers must be brought to book. The same must be said for those members of the IPCC.

- IPCC – Are NOT independent (police officers investigating their own colleagues cannot possibly make them independent). This needs to be changed to fit its description.

- Bristol Probate Office - needs scrutiny; it has proved itself obstructive and unethical at the very least.
- Undertaker, Coroner and Doctor involved, also need close scrutiny.

We have been told by many that we are experiencing a conspiracy; it did not dawn on us until our old lawyer, Michael French of Michael French and Booth Hearn, Chatham, Kent told us that he recognised a large one. How and why he recognised a conspiracy leads to another question or two; but let us not get diverted.

If this is a conspiracy that we have experienced, it has spread like wildfire in many quarters and, from our research, we find there is only one organisation diverse enough to encompass all parties. It may be that the club is on the whole, enrolling good men and true, but to use a phrase "it only takes one rotten apple in a barrel…"

It is well documented that the same organisation has many members in most, if not all, professions and it saturates the Legal System, and the highest halls of power.

That hall of power includes the Ministry of Justice. I can confirm that Mr. Paul Hughes appears to be a member of the Catholic, quasi Masonic Order, namely the Knights of Columbus, located in St James, London: He made that apparent during our meeting.

You might be wondering how I can make such a bold statement. The fact of it is, that during my meeting with Paul Hughes, he made a point of making sure that I was aware that I was not only meeting with the chief advisor to the Minister of Justice, Kenneth Clarke, but also a Freemason.

Whether this was done to intimidate or threaten me, I do not know, but either way, it did not have the desired effect. It only went so far as to confirm to me that yes, we really were dealing with masons that run from top to toe in the UK establishment, and they are at the very heart of government.

Let us hope he comes from another barrel, not a rotten one; a fresh and pure one.

Time will tell.

His actions will reveal all.

But I came away thinking he would do nothing more than locate the ministry responsible for the police.

I am still aghast that these two very senior Civil Servants could not name who is ultimately responsible for the British Police Force's actions: Every name they suggested had written to me denying any responsibility. Some that I have approached include: the Home Secretary, the Prime Minister, CPS, Attorney General, Minister of Justice and even the Commissioner of the Metropolitan Police (the most senior police officer in the country).

This is amazing, bearing in mind the importance of such a post in a democracy.

Maybe we are right in saying that the United Kingdom is a Police State.

England boasts worldwide that it has the best Police Force, and that it also has a Justice System second to none.

Regrettably this is not the reality, as we have proven to them, the Ministry of Justice and others. The Thousands of readers around the world who have visited our web sites are just as aware as we are that this is actually false propaganda issued by the State.

At the meeting these two Civil Servants found themselves in a very embarrassing position when they became aware that the Person responsible for the Police was, at best illusive, or HORROR OF ALL HORRORS, NON EXISTANT. They were obliged to urgently set themselves the task of trying to find this phantom of the police via the Houses of Parliament.

The other task, which was imperative for them, was to contact Her Majesty's Courts Service, Probate Office in Bristol, Avon, who had given them false information on our case, but that is another story, for another day.

Meanwhile, we await the name of the Government Minister who is responsible for the Police, as it is essential for a meeting with him or her now.

Or, if it is a phantom that is responsible, then we actually do live in a POLICE STATE.

Well, it has been two weeks since my meeting with Paul Hughes and Kirsty Milliam at the Ministry of Justice on 21$^{st}$ May 2010: Ample time to reflect on that session which lasted two hours; ample time to digest what was said, and what was actually meant.

As you know, the two Civil Servants set themselves the task of locating the Government Minister responsible for the United Kingdom Police, and once discovered, advising me of their name and title; but to date we have heard nothing.

- In earlier correspondence the Home Office denied responsibility for the Police: This would be the logical Ministry, as the two Civil Servants agreed.
- We have previously asked the Commissioner of the Metropolitan Police, the most senior police officer in England, (although in what way he is 'senior' is unclear) but his office states that each Constabulary is responsible for itself. They have not given a direct answer to my question.

So have these Civil Servants been chasing through the corridors of the Houses of Parliament on a fool's errand?

If their silence is any guide; the answer is YES.

Yes, we have in the United Kingdom a police service without any control over its actions: Consequently, I suggest, the UNITED KINGDOM must be a POLICE STATE.

There is, at the time of writing this and publishing it worldwide on the website, no governmental control over the police, no minister that the police are answerable to; the police are answerable to nobody, except themselves.

# CHAPTER 30

# THE ETHICS OF LAWYER'S

Let us start with our obtaining the legal dossier: For this we were in contact with the Law Society's Legal Complaints Service and after some forceful actions on our part, Michael French of Michael French and Booth Hearn, Chatham, Kent finally released our file to, what was to be our new lawyers: Gullands, 16 Mill Street, Maidstone, Kent, ME15 6XT. The file went to them with a lien, but more of that later.

The Gullands legal practice came heavily recommended, and with Susan's first direct contact with them they indicated they were prepared to take up the baton and work, and work quickly. But first they would require a payment of £1,000.00; to read the file; this is not a typing error; yes, **one thousand pounds to read the dossier**. They also required officially authenticated copies of domestic bills and passports, and that company's condition to be signed before starting work.

In order to speed up the process it was agreed with Mr. B. Leroy Bradley of Gullands that my copies could be certified by the Maire, an active State Official of the Country in which I live (but there will be more of this later).

What followed shortly after was a further demand from Mr. B. Leroy Bradley, for what appears to be further reading of the file, and very little tangible work, of £551.00: That was during June 2010 (no receipt has been received to date for that money, which was paid by return of post), but it must be said that he ultimately did not read the entire dossier, nor did he read those parts that they read thoroughly or comprehensively. In addition he did not tell us one very important fact, a very important basic fact which would be obvious to anybody within the legal profession dealing with probate; but today I can say no more about that because it is 'work in progress'.

Mr. B. Leroy Bradley of Gullands did provide a letter which Susan took with her to the meeting at the English Ministry of Justice, which has been mentioned before. It was after that meeting we assessed the situation, and decided not to proceed at the time with Gullands, as all their advice indicated that it would be very expensive and probably fruitless, so Susan wrote to Mr. B. Leroy Bradley on 31 May 2010, advising him that we had chosen not to proceed with anything at that time as follows:

*"Thank you for your letter dated 20th May 2010, which I found most useful......From the contents of your letter I gather you are hesitant to act at the moment ...."*

*"When I am in a stronger position to proceed I will contact you...."*

Obviously this letter gives clear unambiguous instructions to Mr. B. Leroy Bradley to do nothing.

On 24 June 2010, (one month later) Mr. B. Leroy Bradley wrote an unsolicited letter to Susan advising that time was rapidly running out and we would need to act soon if anything was to be achieved: If we needed to act with such urgency why did he wait a month before writing to Susan?

This letter read as if it were written in anger, so Susan asked for an appointment to find out what she had done to infuriate Mr. B. Leroy Bradley, and why he found it necessary in the letter to distance himself from any contact with the Ministry of Justice (we never asked or expected him to have any direct contact with them). During that meeting he undertook to provide me with a receipt for the money I had paid him; fortunately I did not hold my breath while awaiting the arrival of that receipt, because I would by now be dead, buried and cold in my grave; that promised receipt has never arrived. Personally I can think of no legal reason for not producing a receipt, but I can think of reasons outside the law.

The following letter was sent 30th June 2010 to Mr. B. Leroy Bradley after this meeting:

*Dear Mr. Bradley*

### Re: Mr. Alan Edward Hindley (deceased)

*Thank you for the informative meeting on 29 June 2010.*
*We have been seriously considering your advice and agree that it is not logical to proceed through the courts. Therefore, I would ask you to return our complete file, obviously, that also includes the file you received from Michael French and Booth Hearn.*
*I look forward to receiving my files in the very near future, or if you prefer I will willingly collect them.*

What followed was amazing; during early July 2010 I rapidly received several faxes and letters from Mr. B. Leroy Bradley stating that the photocopies of my passport and household bills, certified at the Mairie, were invalid and that I had to provide a further set, certified by a Notary. I refused to adhere to his unreasonable requests as it had been two months since he had accepted the documents, we were proceeding with nothing as far as he was concerned; and I was fully aware that the certification of a document by any Maire in this Country would be challenged by no official or authority within, or outside the State bureaucracy: Whether Mr. Bradley's harassing action was induced by our refusing to proceed with what, he told us, was a potentially pointless course of action through the

Courts, I have no idea: But the tone and frequency of his demands made me feel very harassed.

A third demand for more money, namely £700.00, was in Mr. Leroy Bradley's letter dated 9th July 2010; this was not an itemised bill or statement (we have never had those), the letter simply demanded more money.

What follows here is an extract of the letter Susan sent in reply to Ms. Golding of Gullands lawyers on 21st July 2010:

*"...I will be available to collect my file during week commencing 26 July 2010 when you will make it available for me."*

Again, just as in Susan's letter dated 30th June 2010, this letter gives crystal clear instructions, one could say they are 'idiot proof', but it still took numerous phone calls, faxes, and visits to both of the legal practices of Gullands lawyers, and of Michael French and Booth Hearn before we were able to gain possession of part of our dossier; note, Gullands lawyers covertly failed to release their part of our file. On Friday 30th July 2010, when Susan finally was able to collect our file from Gullands lawyers, they did not mention that they had withheld their section of our dossier, and to date, that has not changed despite numerous letters requesting its release.

Three months later, we await the release of our file from Gullands lawyers, 16 Mill Street, Maidstone, Kent, ME15 6XT.

Now let us say more about this latest demand for money, the money demanded after we gave instructions to stop work on 20th May 2010: We challenged this charge and received the following contradictory reply in the letter from Gullands lawyers dated 20th July 2010, from Ms. A. M. Golding.

*'Mr. Bradley has not billed you for work that he undertook since 20th May 2010.' In his letter dated 9th July, he draws to your*

*attention that further work has been done over and above that which was detailed in his original estimate. Having sent you his written advice on the 20$^{th}$ May 2010, together with his invoice, which was heavily discounted by over £2000 in the interests of proportionality, and with a view to the original estimate, Mr. Bradley received 3 pieces of correspondence from you and Mr. Hindley. You wrote on the 31$^{st}$ May 2010 stating that you intended to leave matters in abeyance. Mr. Bradley replied on the 24$^{th}$ June to emphasise points raised in his earlier detailed letter with reference to limitation issues. This prompted you to request a meeting with Mr. Bradley, which took place on the 29$^{th}$ June, where it was agreed that you would not incur the costs of pursuing this matter any further. The additional £700 of costs that Mr. Bradley refers to in his letter relates to work undertaken since he raised his last bill on the 20$^{th}$ May 2010, please be reassured that it does not relate to any work undertaken without your consent.*

The contradiction in that single paragraph could not be clearer.

So what should you believe when Gullands lawyers, write to you or give you advice?

I could not give a definite answer to that question, could you?

Certainly their dealings have caused me to lose all confidence in their practice.

There is a lot more to expose, but not today.

## WARNING

A word of caution here to anyone who is considering employing a lawyer in the United Kingdom: If they ask for money in advance to read your file etc. think twice about using that firm, and when you have thought twice, think again, and again, and think very, very hard before you proceed; or simply go elsewhere.

The reason I give this advice is because I changed lawyers during my divorce, and to one highly recommended practice, who charged me six or eight hundred pounds to read the file. Then, when the first hearing was due to be heard in Court they said it was outside their geographical area.

- Did they do anything useful?
- Did they achieve anything for me?
- Did they refund that money?

The answer to all of those questions is the same: NO.
For your own sake, please take heed of my warning.
Is this a case of déjà vu with Gullands lawyers?
Most certainly, yes.

# CHAPTER 31

## **COMPLAINT TO LEGAL OMBUDSMAN**

As a result of the unacceptable service we received from Gullands Lawyers, I contacted the Law Society's Legal Complaints Service in 21 September 2010, and on 8 October 2010 they wrote to me advising that they stopped dealing with new complaints "from close of business on 5 October 2010;" (It may appear that they are a little slow in opening their post): and they advised me that the Legal Ombudsman would be dealing with new cases. So then there was a delay, partially because I had surgery to my shoulder and had great difficulty in getting facts onto paper, but I managed to complete a dossier and sent it on 22 October 2010. Then I received a letter dated 30 November 2010 telling me that the case had been closed as they had heard nothing from me.

So on 6 December I sent a further copy of the dossier by registered mail. This also went missing, although, I was to run a trace on it and discovered that it had been delivered and signed for: Much later in the month both packages were located in the offices of the Legal Ombudsman. And ultimately as the month reached its close, I received a letter asking for my confirmation of their interpretation of the case; When I examine this letter I had the impression that had I approved what they had written, there would be no case to answer, and was unsure whether that was the motive or whether comprehension of the written word was not their forte. So I compiled a reply in what I loosely call 'idiot proof' fashion. This produced silence for months, despite e-mailing requesting progress information, but that was answered by a standard reply giving the reason for delay as heavy work load and holidays (the accent seemed to be holidays).

It was finally in March 2011, some eight months after I started, I received an e-mail giving their findings; Guess what! The Legal Ombudsman service considered that Gullands Lawyers service was as it should be; just as I thought they would; they are, after all, associates: The expression 'Birds of a feather, stick together' comes to mind.

But it is worth noting that the e-mail was one person's assessment, the same person who had misinterpreted the original dossier: This had not been formally dealt with by the Legal Ombudsman. I would have to request that service again within a limited window of time and if I were to proceed, the writer would submit his findings; presumably, that would then be rubber stamped by whomever, and all the rotten dealings of Gullands Lawyers would be judged as correct and proper.

In conclusion, I feel that this had been a complete waste of time dealing with an incestuous body: they had been as much use as a wet fart.

### **Missing papers**

Now here's something to think about: When I last visited the offices of Michael French, my original lawyer, he had reason to examine his file, which I had with me, the same file that was sent to Gullands lawyer. He stated then that papers were missing, papers that he had sent to Gullands.

This raises a question: Who has disposed of the papers?

Was it Gullands? Certainly Leroy Bradley had told me that Michael French had not worked on our case since 2002, which was not true.

Was it Michael French who had disposed of those papers? Rather a silly thing for him to do knowing how we recorded and kept everything relating to the death of Alan and the executorships; and what would he gain by this action?

Think about it for a moment and draw your own conclusion.

# CHAPTER 32

# MASONS AT WORK?

Returning to events around the time of Alan Hindley's demise, and those events that could be said to have continued, even up to today, I am conscious of the possibility of hidden forces that have been at work. It has been confirmed by many independent people that the normal formalities that follow a death were not adhered to: That is a fact; it is undeniable, yet nobody has justified why this should be, or taken action to discover why. Nobody has been brought to book or criticised. These irregularities have been ignored; by the police, their cellmates the "Independent" Police Complaints Commission, Government ministers and the like.

Can we assume for example, that the Police and IPCC, who are known to have active members of the Masonic Brethren in high ranking positions within those establishments of law and justice, have been, and are, obstructing the course of justice and protecting their own? It is well known that within Masonic orders, the Masons are obliged to help one another whenever possible should they find their brethren in difficulty. Is this what is happening in this case?

If this is true, then it could equally be said that those offending members are failing other orders of their non religious, yet worshiping society. As I understand it, their initiation and indoctrination rites require an understanding and acceptance of various rules and goals.

- For example the candidates for the Secret Master ($4^{th}$ Degree) is required to remain trustworthy.

- A Perfect Master (5th Degree) should revere and respect their forebears, and behave honourably.
- Provost and Judge (7th Degree) is about the importance of fairness and equality within any system of justice.
- Elect of the Nine (9th Degree) teaches the importance of serving others within society
- Elect of the Fifteen (10th Degree) indicates that justice will triumph eventually over unfair and unrighteous actions. (Time will tell).
- Elect of the Twelve (11th Degree) indicates that those who show honesty, and fairness, and honour will reap their rewards, and the corrupt will receive their just deserts. (Time will tell).
- Knights of the East or Sword (15th Degree) are reminded that it is essential to retain their integrity.
- Prince of Jerusalem (16th Degree) instructs the candidate to meet their responsibilities.
- Master of Vitam (20th Degree) tells of the importance of working with others to improve society. (Time will tell).
- Patriarch Noachite (21st Degree) teaches that one should not abuse a position within Freemasonry, and behave honourably and within the law; to respect justice which is administered fairly and correctly.
- Knight of the Brazen Serpent (25th Degree) recognises that suffering has to be endured, but good will triumph over evil. (Time will tell).

Obviously this is not a comprehensive diagnosis of the 33 Degrees within Freemasonry, but I think they particularly relate to the actions of the Police and IPCC who, I feel certain, that the practice of the arts of Freemasonry within the United Kingdom, at least, those that I have dealt with.

If you ask which of the above degrees has been honoured by those parties, and they know who they are, as I do in certain cases, I would have to say none have been followed so far.

Then the rituals seem to take another direction in Chief of the Tabernacle (23rd Degree) when the candidate is instructed to strive to aid his fellows, and to do good works **"in recognition of the Great Architect."** Surely this can only be interpreted as a religious teaching: Or perhaps I am wrong, what do you think?

Certain police officers within the Devon and Cornwall Constabulary, and members of the associated Independent Police Complaints Commission are Freemasons; would you think that their deity, the Great Architect, is pleased with their handling of our case?

If so, it begs another question: What sort of being is this Great Architect that they exalt in their lodge meetings?

What type of association or religion is it that these people actually belong to?

It cannot be denied that the Police and others have proved themselves to be, at best incompetent, and at worst... Well you know already, and words fail me now; I do not know where to start the description.

We have proof that they have failed in their duties and undertakings; they have not honoured their word; their work has been shoddy, it has been flawed. Corrupt is a word that also comes to mind. Without doubt, they have done nothing to induce confidence in their respective organisations; in fact, I would say, nothing to justify their existence.

This is not an isolated case; I could, and may spend weeks writing true accounts, which would need no embellishment to seem totally incredible, giving you countless instances of bad policing etc. Perhaps I should, as you should be aware of the truth.

You may feel that I am anti-force, but that is not so. I have spent much time with many officers who have wished to do their job properly; highly honourable men and women with good intentions. Yet these other rotten apples flourish, and gain power and influence within the organisation; for some reason they go unchecked.

There is nothing new in any of this. I met Chief Inspector Buggie (forgive me if I misspelt his name) a couple of times socially many years ago; as I understand it, he had retired early, and certainly at that time he had invested in Launderettes. Much later, via the media, I read that for some reason his finances were investigated; allegedly he could not have legally accrued the money that he had used to buy these businesses. Subsequently, he died before his case was due to be heard at the Old Bailey. Perhaps it could be said, "He was laundering money," but not in the way that that expression is used today.

Moving on to something quite different; this happened about the same time. I was witness to a crime and an investigating officer of the Metropolitan Police said to me, "Would you say that you saw a white mini clubman?" My reply was no because it would not have been true.

But these are minor incidences and of little consequence.

What the case relating to Alan Hindley clearly illustrates is unchecked incompetence at best, and probably something far more sinister within the Devon and Cornwall

Constabulary and the IPCC; and that 'the powers that be' sanction it by their inaction.

Which begs the anther question: Why?

Meanwhile nothing changes; sickening isn't it?

# CHAPTER 33

# NO F****ING ACTION

Please excuse me for breaking away from facts of the case, but I for one need a bit of a break, so may I thank all the thousands of readers for their encouragement and their assistance, not to mention the good wishes. Our thoughts are with all the friends who have told us of their stories (this is not an isolated case), you have touched our hearts.

We have had so many diverse and constructive comments: Thank you all. Many have given their opinion of what has happened with us; some have been courageous and mentioned murder. Recently I read somewhere that when dealing with murder much of the evidence is very frequently entirely circumstantial. Murderers are not known for broadcasting their wrong doings from the roof tops, nor do they do them willingly in front of keen-eyed witnesses, although, on reflection, they may share the experience with a fellow conspirator. Not a bad description when you think about it; it makes sense.

It was not my intention to mention murder when I started this thank you note, it just happened naturally, so while on the subject: I have been asked about Alan's death from the time when it happened; that is perfectly normal, but because of the varying versions of his place of death etc. I have answered that the fact that my brother died is of no great surprise, but the events surrounding his death could indicate that he was helped in some way, I know not how. People in difficult relationships do react differently; and certainly Alan and Wendy's marriage was not an ideal one. Having extra marital relationships can instigate drastic action: Divorce and crimes of passion are not rare events.

Now if you were to ask, the response would be different because of all you are aware of so far, and the other information we have been given that you, as yet, do not know, I would be inclined to answer in the positive, and even suggest the two methods that could have been used; methods that my research has not eliminated. I have been continuing my research as you would expect, and my latest findings only confirm that what Wendy Hindley started at the time of the death of her husband, has developed into a huge conspiracy to conceal the truth of her husband's death and assist her to bypass the Will and Wishes of the deceased.

I could easily suggest that she does not have the influence, or for that matter, the mental capacity to have done this without considerable help; help which most likely originated with the input of David Hart and his Masonic Brothers; but I would think readers would be fully aware of that, having read the story so far.

If I am completely honest, what follows does not come as a surprise, but the new information I have gleaned permits me to name certain parties, who I feel sure played their part.

On reflection, it is quite probable that our original lawyer, Michael French of Michael French and Booth Hearn, Chatham, Kent, by his actions, and lack of actions, could be interpreted that he was subject to outside influences. Wendy Hindley said, "He was no good." But how would she be so confident in her knowledge of him? As far as we are aware she has had no direct dealings with him?

Now we are aware of the very obvious procedures that he, as a lawyer would know, were not followed: Procedures he could have, and should have executed. And even today, as I write this, his lack of action continues; he has repeatedly been asked to release the case file, initially to Susan Goodsell and subsequently to a law firm: Note: it is standard practice, laid down by the ruling body of the United Kingdom legal system, to release such files without delay. Michael French's inactions can only lead to his downfall, so why should he choose such a path?

Could it be that when he first saw us and recognised, as he said, 'a conspiracy' which was large, that he had been used by these early conspirators to delay and try to halt our pursuit for honourable justice? Certainly his actions have followed a familiar pattern frequently recorded and employed by corrupt Masons, Probably he is, as we now suspect he is, a Mason; but we are not sure.

Moving on: It is the findings of the research which has motivated me to draw to your attention to a few who have been involved with this case.

We have frequently found that people who one would expect to be honourable in their employment have. on first sight of this case, said that it requires serious action; they have told us it is not normal or correct in so many ways. We have, for example, had Police Officers, and later Police Officers of the Independent Police Complaint Commission tell us just that. Strangely, almost all have changed their opinion (or had their opinion changed for them). From their performances I would suggest it is more accurate to say they have been influenced by their "Brothers" within "The Firm". Remember the priority of members of the "Brotherhood" is to aid their own, they each have to swear solemn oaths to that effect, but this same oath can, and is known, to be interpreted and used in a suspect manner; I put it to you, a corrupt manner.

But to give a balanced viewpoint, we have had contact with those that appear to be genuine and honourable Police Officers in the Devon and Cornwall Constabulary, and I would be likely to include Sergeant Griffiths of Chudleigh

Police Newton Abbot and Inspector M. Blackhouse, Paignton Police Station, amongst them.

But I would be inclined to think that DI David Taylor & DCI Tilke (more to follow) are of another caste, and probably members of the Brotherhood, Freemasons, and to use their own words, "on the square." Although I am not one prone to gamble, I would lay a pound to a penny that some, or all three of these Police Officers are Masons, and probably in the same lodge as Shorton Cottage's gardener, David Hart (why should I now think of Lady Chatterley's Lover?) and that those officers in turn will have had their "Brothers" in the IPPC, namely, Inspector Davison of the Devon and Cornwall Constabulary, and Marc Withers, Wales. We have observed these two following exactly the same pattern in their work.

They are, I would suggest, in the position to be free to put NFA (no further action; I use the polite version here) on investigation files that suit their cause; whatever that cause may be.

These later two groups certainly produced shoddy work; we have that well documented; but what if it is not only shoddy, what if it is also corrupt?

Should they be allowed to continue unchecked?

Who has the courage or influence to investigate them?

You will be horrified by our answer.

So far, by their actions, everybody in the Establishment of the United Kingdom we have contacted, does not have the intent, or power to act against this or similar gross incompetence or corruption; be it the Police themselves, the Independent Police Complaints Commission, the Home Secretary, Members of Parliament, Government departments or Ministers, Gordon Brown, the Prime Minister or even Her Majesty Queen Elizabeth II, to name but a few.

Do they therefore feel vulnerable in some way or are they tarred with the same brush?

Why is nobody able to take responsibility? All, without exception, are willing to take tax payers money.

As yet I do not have the answer to give you.

Thinking of other possible corrupt modus operandi:

I am reminded of the actions of the Bristol Probate Office.

If you recall, it took us some 5 months, and the intervention of government officials to get the deceased's Will released to a forensic expert. His findings confirmed our suspicions that the signature was, in fact most likely, to be a forgery. We have always felt certain the will was a document the deceased would never had signed, it is too heavily flawed. I had only known the deceased for some fifty year,s but that counted for nothing to those employed by the Devon and Cornwall Constabulary; unbelievable is it not?Yes, for five months Mrs. Peacock of the Bristol Probate Office delayed the release of the will; but she was, I presume, only doing as she was told by her boss, a judge, or a justice of the peace, maybe a civil servant. Could it be that he was being obstructive in an attempt to aid his "Brothers"?

Could it be said that in this case he was using Mrs. Peacock?

To use a familiar expression in an unfamiliar way: Was he hiding behind her and his own apron strings?

Or even worse, hiding behind one of his Brother's apron strings?

It could easily be said to be so. It is not an unheard of technique amongst the Brothers.

Why on earth did they not wish to grant two executors their right of access to the Will?

Why were they so intent on obstruction?

Why did they want to stop us seeing this document?

Did they realise it was a fake and wish to protect a third party or two?

Then you might ask: was it his presence in Bristol that caused Wendy Hindley to use his offices to lodge the Will and Probate Papers when there are two Probate Offices much closer to her home?

I would like to be proved wrong; you may well guess what I now think.

It must be said that I am not one who is a great believer in coincidences, yet throughout this sordid affair it could be said that there are plenty. Or are they synchronicities?

The more you unearth the more disgusting the image gets.

Nevertheless the overall image is becoming much, much clearer.

You can see it I am sure.

# CHAPTER 34

# FACTS

**Fact:** As you are aware from reading earlier, it took some 6 months and a lot of butt kicking to get Bristol Probate Office to release the Will to a forensic expert for examination:

**Fact:** Now you will also recall that following telephone calls to the Devon and Cornwall Constabulary when we were initially advised that all was not well in the house of Hindley around the time of Alan's demise; it took some 12 months of writing and butt kicking, even parliamentary intervention to obtain the one and only interview with the Devon and Cornwall Police on their territory. Would you say this is obviously idleness, incompetence or something far worse?

**Fact:** We have written, directly and via the junior parliamentary minister Jonathan Shaw to The Rt. Hon Alan Johnson MP, Secretary of State for the Home Office, Home Office, 2 Marsham Street, London, SW1P 4DF, asking for his direct help. It has been refused on shallow grounds.

**Fact:** We have followed the same procedures to request a meeting with the Rt. Hon Jack Straw, Lord Chancellor and Secretary of State for Justice, Ministry for Justice, 102 Petty France London SW1H 9AJ, but this has resulted, so far, in a classic response indicating the standard NFA.

**Fact:** We know they, and-or, their colleagues have read our web site and if they are in any way sensible, they and other government departments will keep themselves updated as there is so much more that they will learn: More to expose because people should know the truth.

**Fact:** We have been informed by the Home Office that they cannot get involved with Police matters. Yet it was within the remit of a previous Home Secretary, namely Merlyn Rees, who instigated an investigation into police corruption in London in 1978. Is it that this power has been taken away from the present incumbent of that same office? I think it is most unlikely. And if, as a result of the diminished responsibilities of the post, has the salary of this public servant been reduced proportionally? The answer surely is 'no' to these questions. So are we to presume that the author of the letter, an employee of the Home Office, is nothing more than a liar?

**Fact:** We have written (and had some replies) to the Metropolitan Police Commissioner; officially the most senior police officer in the United Kingdom. But his office advised us that he has no power or control over other constabularies. If this is so, (and the 'if' is a big one) I must ask why he has a different title and probably higher salary. If he is senior how does this manifest itself? Who, or what, is he senior to? Why has he a different title from other heads of Constabularies? Are we really expected to believe he is of no higher rank than any other head of any other constabulary and that he has no influence over them? The information we have been given by his office makes no sense. Perhaps he is simply more skilled at NFA?

Let us take just a step back for a moment. You may be wondering why we recently used "No F****** Action" as the title for the recent addition; the answer is actually quite logical, NFA is an abbreviation for three words used by the

Police when they choose to stop working on a case, they rubber stamp the relevant file with the words 'No Further Action' or 'NFA'.

We thought, because we are very familiar with the normal lack of movement from the Police and other state departments; "No F***ing Action" was in fact far more appropriate.

# CHAPTER 35

# READING BETWEEN THE LINES

We know the catalyst to this saga we find ourselves living through, but it is the other information we have gathered along our journey which has certainly been a learning curve; should I say a bloody great arc!

We have sought help from various Members of Parliament and Ministries as you know; we have become quite adept at accurately interpreting correspondence from them. Some replies are compiled from standard paragraphs which are most commonly used.

Over the years, I have known a number of MP's and 4 or 5 prospective candidates; of this latter group all but 1 was seeking election, not for the party they supported, but for another political party: If you take time to think about it, this is not a very reassuring concept and you have to question their motivation, it was the positions, not the policies, that were important.

I have also had dealings with elected MP's; of those there is only one I would consider to be honourable. In fact, he was for a time a Minister, but I fear he was too honourable to retain such an office for long.

Thinking of politicians I am reminded of the old joke:

Question: "How do you know when a politician is lying?"

Answer: "His lips are moving."

But seriously, what exactly do these standard paragraphs mean?

Recently a letter arrived from The Prime Minister's office, it said:

"The contents of your letter have been carefully noted." Or "I can assure you that a careful note has been made of your concerns…"

This is civil servant speak for 'NFA', in other words, it will be put in "the look and laugh file" (the equivalent of the waste paper basket). The only thing worth noting here is that all letters are logged according to their subject, so, for example, if it is a letter of protest, it may be used to assess the political implications.

Another letter from the same office said:

"Mr. Brown has asked me to pass your letter to the Ministry of Justice so that they may reply to you on his behalf." Or "…your previous letter was passed to the relevant Government Department"

This is civil servants shorthand for; the Prime Minister will be doing nothing, and he has forwarded your letter to another Minister or government department. It should be noted that this normally results in you receiving a reply after an extremely long, many months, wait.

**Helpful tips**

- Letters sent direct to Ministers or Ministries frequently remain unanswered.
- You are more likely to receive an answer to your request from a Minister or Ministry if you send your request, or question to the Prime Minister.
- Letters forwarded by your MP have a good chance of receiving a response, so use your Member of Parliament to forward your letters to the relevant Ministers or Ministries; although we have discovered that an MP cannot always be relied on to carry out this very simple task.
- If you use your MP to forward letters, or do anything else on your behalf, it would be advisable

to seek his confirmation, after 14 days, that he has cooperated.

If you experience long delays getting a response from your MP, contact his/her office and ask:

>1. How long he/she normally takes to respond to constituents (they don't like it).
>
>2. Demand a date when you will receive their response.
>
>3. If there is an unreasonable delay, stipulate an acceptable time (7 days should do it).

It is worth knowing that these officials have guidelines they are supposed to work within.

# CHAPTER 36

# LAW SOCIETY LOGO

I wanted to research something this morning so I visited the web site of The Law Society of England and Wales, plus the associated organisation Legal Complaints Service.

The banner for both organisations' home page have the same format: They give their respective titles followed by the motto: "SUPPORTING SOLICITORS".

In view of recent events that you have read here, and my past experience, I found this somewhat disconcerting.

Does their motto indicate that they actually exist to "SUPPORT" lawyers at the expense of the people, the lawyer's clients, rather than improve and regulate lawyer's standards? Does their logo reveal where their loyalty really lies?

From what I have seen so far I would have to say they are in fact, looking after their own, but I would love them to prove me wrong.

*****

The law society's web site logo "Supporting Solicitors" remains unchanged, but if you continue directly from there into the Solicitors Regulatory Authority's web pages you will now find a new logo; they are no longer using the same banners. All logos have been changed, and the site has been completely revamped and is no longer user friendly; it is confusingly full of civil servant jargon and gobbledegook.

The Law Society's action is yet another example of self preservation they have acted to save their own embarrassment from the exposure of the truth.

All join in the chorus: "Pull up the ladder jack, I'm all right."

# CHAPTER 37

# THE CREATION OF A GOVERNMENT MINISTER RESPONSIBLE FOR THE BRITISH POLICE

Some months after my meeting with Paul Hughes at the Ministry of Justice I was amused to hear on the television news that there had been created a new position; a Government Minister who would be responsible for the British Police.

So what does this mean? Simply that we were correct, nobody was overseeing the actions of the Police. We had exposed the fact that the Police were answerable to nobody except themselves.

Paul Hughes and his colleague were running through the government offices desperately trying to locate the person responsible for the police after my meeting with them. The Home Office would have been the logical answer, but they have no say in how the police are operating. The police may have been funded by the Treasury, but the Treasury had no control; in fact nobody outside the Police had control. We were correct in saying that Britain was, until the creation of this new Minister, a Police State.

The Government could not have that said of the United Kingdom so they acted: They acted to save themselves embarrassment. We were of course publishing our suspicions of a Police State, worldwide on the internet at the time.

Now what does that indicate? Does it tell us that the employees within the corridors of Whitehall can only act if they feel vulnerable; it would look that way.

But it tells us far more than that, for they have, following my meeting, done nothing to amend the inheritance laws; why should they?

They do not feel vulnerable, so why should the Ministries do anything?

Now there is more to this, as during the meeting I had at the Ministry of Justice it was obvious that Paul Hughes was very well versed in inheritance laws, he knew them like the back of his hand. Furthermore, he was fully aware of the European inheritance laws and knew that one in particular was appropriate for our case; unfortunately the British government has chosen not to include this in British law even though it would be a simple matter to do.

That has not changed. So this is a clear indication that the people within the walls of government and power are not motivated to help the people they serve and who pay their salaries, namely the British tax payers: It is worth remembering that the Government has no money of its own, it only has the money they have extracted in taxes.

This situation can be expressed quite simply; Pull up the ladder jack; I'm all right.

# CHAPTER 38

# THE GOVERNMENT OF THE UNITED KINGDOM HAS A PROBLEM

This case is now a problem that the Government of the United Kingdom needs to resolve if it wishes to regain its status as a credible, respectable democratic entity: And it is fully aware of the embarrassing situation it has, through its lack of action, placed itself.

We have, over the years, given them many opportunities to act, but they have sat on their hands and done nothing, they have taken no responsibility for the known flaws in the legislation and government departments.

If you were in their unhappy position, could you risk doing nothing, knowing that it too would become common knowledge and only create an even greater embarrassment.

Now my friends, we are not the ones with the problem because we have passed it back to the Government of the United Kingdom.

They are now very vulnerable to ridicule from any State, anywhere, at any time.

The government of Britain is exposed.

# CHAPTER 39

## "All that is necessary for evil to triumph is for good men to do nothing" By Edmond Burke

This seems an appropriate quotation to use for what follows.

As you are aware, we have, because we are sure criminal acts have taken place, had contact with the police. We have offered to cooperate; we have travelled hundreds of miles in order to save them travelling time. We have given masses of the relevant information they needed to do their job. In fact, one young officer who supposedly worked on the case for a very short time told us they had never been presented with so much detail; nevertheless we know that means nothing, because the Devon and Cornwall Constabulary have failed miserably in their work and duty. Whether that was as a result of their gross incompetence, their hatred of real work, maybe it was because they feared being sued (as Detective Inspector David Taylor told us) or as a result of Masonic conspiracy and corruption I will not say here.

All the officers that are named were in some way involved with the case and they, and possibly we, know each and every one of their respective motives.

The end result is that persons have been able to break the law without any repercussion; they have not been brought to book.

The police have in fact aided and abetted criminal acts; and been paid handsomely by the tax payers for their toils, or lack of them.

Corrupt freemasonry in the police has played its part.

Some of those involved in this saga are listed here alphabetically:

Mr. Nigel Arnold
Chief Constable, Devon & Cornwall Constabulary
Middlemoor, Devon, EX2 7HQ

Chief Inspector Brendan Brookshaw
Staff Officer to the Chief Constable, Devon & Cornwall Constabulary
Middlemoor, Devon, EX2 7HQ

Inspector Brent Davison
HQ, Middlemoor, Devon, EX2 7HQ

Madhu Dodia
New Scotland Yard
London, SW1H 0BG

Mr. M. Fuller, Chief Constable
Kent County Constabulary
Maidstone, Kent, ME15 9BZ

Chief Inspector S D Lander
Middlemoor, Devon, EX2 7HQ

Detective Superintendent Stuart Newberry
Middlemoor, Devon, EX2 7HQ

Mr. Stephen Otter
Chief Constable, Devon & Cornwall Constabulary
Middlemoor, Devon, EX2 7HQ

Detective Chief Inspector K. Perkin
South & West Devon BCU Headquarters
Paignton, Devon, TQ3 2YF

Sir Paul Stephenson
Metropolitan Police Commissioner
London, SW1H 0BG

Detective Inspector David Taylor
Totnes, Devon, TQ9 5JY

Detective Chief Inspector Tilke
Paignton, Devon, TQ3 2YF

Detective Constable Youngman
Paignton, Devon, TQ3 2YF

The following can be added to the list as they work in the associated "Independent Police Complaints Commission," with special mention of Mr. Mark Withers, who had the affront to lie to a parliamentary minister, namely the Right Honourable Jonathan Shaw. Does this boldness warrant bonus points? You will also note that Inspector Brent Davison is a police officer based at Devon & Cornwall Constabulary Headquarters, yet he represented the IPCC (what definition of Independent do these people use?)

Inspector Brent Davison,
IPCC, HQ, Middlemoor, Devon, EX2 7HQ

Mr. Jonathan Peers
IPCC Casework Manager
London, WC1V 6BH

Mr. Marc Withers
IPCC, Casework Manager
St Mellons, Cardiff, CF3 5EA

So we can finish here by quoting:

**"All that is necessary for evil to triumph is for "good" men to do nothing"**

Or

**"All that is necessary for evil to triumph is for "evil" men to do nothing"**
(The outcome is the same)
Amen

# CHAPTER 40

# MOST RECENT EVENTS

As you know, we have been trying since 2002 to get Alan's Will executed as he wished.

What may not be clear is that when Alan told me of his wishes he made everything very simple and clear. He wished that his two grandsons were to be the ultimate beneficiaries; they were to be the two boys who he wished the fruits of his life's work and toils to finally benefit.

I also recall that he felt a little uncomfortable when he told me that I would inherit nothing and he wished me to be an executor and trustee: The fact is, as I told him at the time, whatever he had was his to do with as he wished; certainly I had expected nothing, and I was completely comfortable with that situation then, just as I am now.

For me what was important was that he entrusted me with the task to fulfil his wishes.

So far the task of executing his Will has cost me thousands of hours in writing and research, piecing together the facts: Many hours, driving hundreds of miles, not to mention my money I have had to use.

What I did not know was that his wife had other, less honourable intentions.

Perhaps it was because she feared she would lose everything if my brother divorced her; Our investigations indicates that a divorce was imminent, and it is certain he would have tried to deprive her of as much of his wealth as he could (rightly or wrongly). He had after all, built the wealth with very little, if any, help from his wife; and she would have known all of this.

Perhaps that is why Alan took out a substantial loan a few days before his demise. He may well have been concealing money from her in preparation for the divorce, and had been creating an image that he was in debt.

If his wife was aware of this, it may well have provided sufficient motive for Alan's convenient demise.

Nevertheless:

    1. I do know that his Will was not executed as Alan wished.

    2. Alan would never have signed any legal documents with errors; and he had good reason.

    3. The Will presented to the Probate Office at Bristol by his widow had very many errors, and without doubt a forgery (the use of cut and paste technique with a computer, I would suggest).

    4. The Will is a forgery as is Alan's signature.

    5. I am confident that I can name the person who forged the signature, and provide evidence to indicate the culprit.

    6. Alan would not have included any member of his wife's family as beneficiaries because he hated them all with a passion; he told me more than once just that, and that they were all alcoholics, as was his wife: Yet his wife's niece, Samantha Jones is named on the Will (but her name does not appear on the Wishes – this document was not lodged with the Bristol Probate Office and it is as it should be in all respects).

# CHAPTER 41

# WENDY YVONNE HINDLEY; a case of PERJURY?

Wendy Hindley has deliberately lied to Her Majesty's Court Service Probate Office when she declared that the other two named executors of her late husband's Last Will and Testament had shown no interest in executing their duty. Wendy was fully aware that several requests had been made for information via her lawyer, Eastleys, Manor Road, Paignton, Devon. Requests made directly by the two executors and by their lawyer.

It was in fact her friend, Barbara Ryell of Penkridge, Stafford, who first told us that the executors have a right to that information; the full disclosure.

You should note that when an executor signs the Probate Documents they become **equally responsible** for the contents of those papers; it matters not if they know or understand the contents.

As the situation stands today, I would respectfully suggest that Wendy Joyce Hindley has committed perjury by swearing under oath in Her Majesty's Court Service Probate Office in Bristol that the other two named executors showed no interest in executing their duty.

We have the documentary evidence that this is exactly what she has done:

Will the Court now act?

Fat chance, they have done nothing and will continue to do the same, as you will now see.

# CHAPTER 42

# CHANGES TO THE INHERITANCE LAW

We have mentioned before that the inheritance laws in the UK permit executors to ignore the contents of any Last Will and Testament; the executors can do exactly as they wish.

You may have seen advertising and promotions to encourage you to write your Will, possibly with the aid of a lawyer.

But the truth is it could be a complete waste of time and effort.

The Law needs to be changed, and changed NOW.

We are campaigning and will continue until we succeed.

As the law stands, it is a blatant abuse of your human rights.

If somebody was trusted with your money, your house, all your belonging while you were alive and they abused that trust; perhaps they took your money for themselves or they gave your home to somebody without your consent, how would you feel? What would you do? After all, they would have committed a criminal act and could be penalised, fined, or even imprisoned. BUT if that same person who you trusted to execute your wishes did exactly the same thing with your belongings after your last breath; they would normally escape any retribution and the state would turn a blind eye, as in our case and many, many others, it will be permitted by the establishment!

What does this really mean to you?

If you or a lawyer compiles a Will, it would normally state on that document that 'YOU ARE OF SOUND MIND'; you may even wish to swear it; yet in the law you can be treated as if you are insane, for once you are dead, your wishes can be totally ignored: Your wishes for the usage of the fruits of your life's work will be decided by your executors. Your rights over your belongings end with your last breath!

You can do nothing about it as you are in no position to return and rectify the 'ERROR': You are dead!

As you know in this case, Alan Hindley is reported to have died in several places on the same day. This we all know is not normal, but it is a fact: Even having such a remarkable death, or deaths, he is not in a position to return to life and correct those abusers actions. He cannot reclaim what is his and redistribute it as he would wish; and the same would apply to you after your demise.

Once you are dead you cannot take any action against those, who would be criminals if you still had life; these abusers of their 'duty', certainly would be criminals if you were alive.

Think about other ramifications:

If you retained any rights over your goods and chattels once you die and the executors of your WILL, possibly any lawyer who may aid the executors with the Will's execution, would then be vulnerable if they strayed from your requirements. But they are not!

They have Carte Blanc to do exactly as they please!

As the law stands today, it has nothing to do with natural Justice; this is immoral.

We; that includes you, me, in fact all of us; we should require the obscene laws to be changed immediately.

Join our campaign and demand this change of your Member of Parliament while you have breath. Demand the change now!

None of us know when we will kick the bucket so act while you have the chance.

How can you help make these changes?

Firstly, SPREAD THE WORD, the more people that are aware of this atrocity the more pressure can be applied to the 'powers that be' for the change that is so desperately required.

Secondly, WRITE to your MP and DEMAND CHANGE; protect your goods and chattels while you still can!

Thirdly, USE YOUR RIGHTS to demand for change by writing to:

Ministry of Justice
102 Petty France
London SW1H 9AJ

# CHAPTER 43

# LEGITIMATE METHODS FOR BYPASSING A WILL IN THE UK
as our case shows.

**IT'S SIMPLE!**
First, go to a lawyer, for example, **Eastleys, The Manor Office, Victoria Street, Paignton, Devon TQ4 5DQ.**, who will, for a small fee, accept your word under oath and allow you to execute a will (anybody's will) in whatever way you wish, even ignoring the deceased's intentions. They will then lodge the will and probate with whichever probate office they choose and see that all assets of the deceased are given to you to dispose of exactly as you wish; this is part of their normal service. I doubt you will have to pay extra for them to turn a blind eye to your actions.

If you need a second opinion, or more detailed information contact: **Mrs. Wendy Hindley, Shorton Cottage, 47 Shorton Road, Paignton, Devon TQ3 1RF**, as she has used and perfected this, and other techniques, to mal-administer at least one Last Will and Testament, and been given every assistance by: Eastleys, the British Police, the British Courts, and even the Ministry of Justice, probably the UK Government.

You are at liberty to use this technique as a legal precedent. .

If you want written confirmation, then below is the contents of a letter received from HMCS, Her Majesty's Court Service, which confirms that the technique is totally acceptable by the British Court and cannot be challenged.

'Re: the estate of Alan Edward Hindley deceased
Thank you for your letter of 31 December, received 5 January.

*"I have now obtained the original file, and note that the Grant of Probate was extracted by a firm of Solicitors rather than as a personal application. Where the application is made via a Solicitor, the executor(s) acting swear an oath before the Solicitor that notice has been given to any executors who are reserving power. No signed power reserved form is filed in such instances.*

*I regret I cannot be of any further assistance, and apologise that I may have given you the impression that such a document may exist, but I was under the impression from what you said that this had been a personal application by Wendy Hindley rather than a Solicitor's application. I would mention that the fee is charged for the search itself and is therefore not refundable.*

*Yours sincerely"*

The above was dated 12 January 2011 from HMCS, Bristol District Probate Registry, The Civil 'Justice' Centre, 2 Redcliff Street, Bristol BS1 6GR

# CHAPTER 44

# LEGAL LOOPHOLE IN THE UK JUSTICE SYSTEM

On Friday 28$^{th}$ January 2011, I had met with DI Karl Thomas of the Kent Police to discuss our case. The session was very constructive and lasted approximately an hour. At the end of that time he showed great enthusiasm and determination to sort this fiasco out, he gave the impression that he would do whatever was needed. The following day I received the email published below, which confirms his willingness to work:

*Dear Mrs Goodsell,*

*I have sent off the paperwork relating to the formal complaint into the actions of PC LEEMING. As soon as I get a formal reference number I will let you know.*

*As agreed I will look into the matter of perjury upon my return to Medway on the 7th of February.*

*It was lovely to meet you yesterday and I look forward to working with you to try and get you some answers.*

*Yours*
*Karl*


*DI 12218 Karl Thomas*
*Medway Crime Group*
*Kent Police*
*01634 792410*

On the 14th February, some two weeks later I received my next email from DI Karl Thomas, which shows a customary 'U-turn which we have always seen:

Dear Mrs Goodsell,

*I hope this email finds you fit and well. As promised I have looked into the matter concerning the probate of your late father. This was initially investigated by Kent Police under Crime Report DY/12112/10.*

***Newly presented evidence:-***

*DY/12112/10 was instigated by an allegation by yourself that a document had been forged concerning the probate of your late father. This matter was investigated at length by DC Leeming and no forged signature could be found. On the 14th of December I asked you via email to identify the document. On the 29th of January you presented me with a letter from The Bristol District Probate Registry stating that no forged document was in existence, and that the Grant of Probate was extracted by a firm of solicitors with the executor swearing on oath that "notice had been given to any executor who are reserving power".*

*As you believe that you were not given notice, you now allege perjury.*

***Evaluation:-***

*At the core of this allegation is the assertion that no notice was given to yourself regarding this will. I limit my enquiry to this assertion.*

*The matter of notice was considered by Devon and Cornwall police under OP RICHMOND. DC Leeming spoke to DI Kay who confirms that the matter of will and probate was investigated at the time. Due to your concerns at the time it was also reviewed by their major crime department.*

*I note from DC Leemings notes that documentation has been received from EASTLEY SOLICITORS, that correspondence was entered into with your solicitor and this would appear to have discharged their duty to notify you. If this is true then the oath was sworn in good faith and would not be perjury.*

*On a personal note I am sorry that I have not been able to identify a criminal line of enquiry that has not already been considered. I know you feel passionately about this and will be disappointed with my evaluation.*

*Regarding your complaint about the conduct of DC Leeming I have passed this to DS Spicer who will consider it. This is in line with the agreement we made on the 29th January. His report will be submitted to Kent Police's Professional Standard Department.*

*Yours*
*Karl Thomas*
*Detective Inspector*

*DI 12218 Karl Thomas*
*Medway Crime Group*
*Kent Police*
*01634 792410*

I was astounded because I felt that this policeman was going to honour his word, but as you can see from what he writes it is not the case. As a result I have emailed my reply which you can read below.

*Dear DI Karl Thomas*

*Thank you for your email received yesterday 14$^{th}$ February and I have noted the contents which are appalling and grossly inadequate.*

*I quote your words in your third paragraph of your evaluation: "If this is true then the oath was sworn in good faith and would not be perjury."*

*Had you and other police officers read the evidence that you have been given you would be fully aware that I and my uncle, independently and via our solicitor at the time, Mr Michael French,* requested from Eastleys Solicitors a full disclosure of my father's affairs.

With our initial request, Eastleys replied with an undertaking to do just that, but to date, despite our various requests, we have never received sufficient information to be able to put our signature to the probate papers.

Furthermore, absolutely no notice of Wendy Hindley's or Eastleys' intention to lodge the Probate papers was received before they actually executed the procedure. I would be prepared to swear this statement is true on any Bible, religious book or sacred relic, or should you prefer, I would swear under oath before any solicitor, commissioner of oaths or judge or in any Court: The same would apply to my Uncle; he would happily swear an oath before anybody or anything. I am confident that my original solicitor, Michael French of Michael French and Booth Hearn of Chatham would take an oath that would confirm that what I am saying is the truth. He was questioned several times about notice being given, and each time he said he had received none, and he also said more than once that he had never previously seen the letter that Eastleys sent me in June 2005. Note and note well: Letters seldom get lost in the post and they do not get lost if they are never posted; a simple technique that Wendy Hindley certainly knew about and probably used elsewhere (this little ploy I learnt from my late father, her husband).

The fact is that it was not until **6 June 2005,** that Eastleys solicitors released a copy of a letter of notice of intention to proceed with filling the probate papers: It was then and only then, some **3 years after the event** that I, my uncle and or my solicitor saw that alleged letter.

**Therefore it is obvious that both Wendy Hindley and Eastleys solicitors undoubtedly knowingly committed perjury by giving false information to the British Court.**

Regarding Will and probate that was going to be lodged with the Probate Office: As you are fully aware, as executors, should we have *signed the probate papers we would be held equally responsible for any false information given to the court; therefore, common sense dictated that we could not add our signatures without knowing the facts contained within the declaration were true, if those statements were not true we could be punished in law, possibly we would be charged with perjury. We had no alternative but to request the full disclosure. It also should be stressed that as executors we were within our absolute rights to request this information; we were purely doing our solemn duty.*

*The result so far is that my father's Last Will and Testament has been mal-executed, certainly not executed in a way he wished, and the British Legal System and the British Police have acted as accomplices by a their failure to act, and act honourably. The facts could not be more damning for you and all others involved.*

*You also mention earlier police investigations, it must be stressed that we were never asked, beyond the initial statement, for further information or clarification of facts by the police, and we also know that certain important parties were only interviewed after the police had intended to stop their initial investigations and they were challenged by my uncle. These are clear indications of gross incompetence and tardiness by the Devon and Cornwall Constabulary. With such a complex case it would be only natural for anyone who was actually working to seek some clarification, but none was requested: Is this an indication that none were working? It would appear that way.*

*Also in your e-mail you mention the Kent Police, who recently required that I obtain additional signatures of my late father so they could be examined by a forensic expert. Two or three weeks after that request, when I had obtained those signatures at a cost of about £180.00; I subsequently telephoned to arrange delivery of them to your officer, DC Leeming; he told me that the case had already been closed: Closed even before your police officer DC Leeming received the evidence that he so recently had requested. This is yet another clear example of gross police incompetence.*

Furthermore, your officer DC Leeming, when he requested these signatures, told me that I could obtain these easier than he could. This is absolute rubbish because I'm sure he could have, had he any intentions to work; obtain these signatures from the Land Registry at no cost whatsoever. Therefore, irrespective of any investigation of my formal complaint no.DY/12112/10 I require you to fully reimburse me for these monies by return of post. The Kent Police can have no reason not to accept full responsibility for this.

In conclusion, your letter indicates your ineffectiveness to do what is right and required, namely, understand the evidence you hold and as a result, pursue justice. This is just another typical example of the complete failure of the British Police in their duty to the British public who they are supposed to serve.

I require you to act in the following ways now

1. Pursue the case of perjury

2. Reimburse me fully by return of post

3. Then continue to do what is right for once: Do your job.

I await your confirmation on all these points.
Yours sincerely
Susan Goodsell
CC. www.howsafeisawillintheuk.com

This underlines what we have said in lesson one, that is: If you swear on oath you will be believed by the British Courts and the British Police Service no matter how much you lie. This probably applies to any legal situation you might find yourself in within the United Kingdom.

# CHAPTER 45

# WHO COMMITTED PERJURY? Proof that perjury has definitely taken place and is permitted by the UK Establishment!

As you will now be aware from reading our many updates about the British Police involvement in our case that they have been nothing more than idle, work-shy and 'back coverers' for their incompetent colleagues.

We have received nothing more than we would expect, considering previous dealings we have had with police constabularies in the UK, therefore we decided that in order to 'dot the *i's* and cross the *t's*' it would be necessary to swear an oath that contradicted the oath sworn by Wendy Hindley; it should be noted that this act would mean that there would be no doubt that perjury had been committed, but by whom? Did Peter and I commit perjury or was it Wendy Hindley? One party certainly did.

You are aware of the correspondence I had with Detective Inspector Karl Thomas and by now know what we have come to expect from police officers who become involved, the usual sudden 'about face' so I contacted him just one more time, the email is self explanatory and so is his reply:

'16/02/2011 11:43
*Dear Mr. Thomas*
*Having re-read your last email dated 14$^{th}$ February 2011, I note your third paragraph of your evaluation and consequently I now require you to arrange for me to swear an Oath in front of a judge at Maidstone Crown Court.*
*Yours sincerely*

Susan Goodsell

**His reply was:**

'Dear Mrs. Goodsell,

I am content that a proportionate investigation has been concluded into this matter. I do not intend to continue to correspond with you about the criminal matter.
With regard to your complaint against Dc Leeming, this is being processed by DS Spicer and you will hear from Kent police Professional Standards department in good time.
DI Thomas'

DI 12218 Karl Thomas
Medway Crime Group
Kent Police
01634 792410

The next step was to be a straightforward one; at the beginning of March, this year, 2011, we independently swore our respective oaths – these oaths meant perjury had, without any doubt, been committed. Now, you might have thought that perjury was a grave crime taken very seriously by the Law Courts of the United Kingdom and the British Police Force; well, you were very much mistaken as will become apparent in what is to follow.

I wrote to my local Probate office in Maidstone, which incidentally has the same address as my next letter, which was sent to HMCS, Crown Court, Maidstone, Kent; I enclosed a copy of my sworn and signed Affidavit. I did not stop there; after all, I was born in, and now live in, the Kent Constabulary's enforcement area, so letters with an attached or enclosed Affidavit were also sent to The Chief

Constable, Learmonth, of the Kent Constabulary, DI Karl Thomas and DS Chris Yarwood of the Devon and Cornwall Constabulary.

> '11 March 2011
> HMCS, *Crown Court*
> The Law Courts
> Barker Road
> Maidstone
> Kent
> ME16 8EQ
>
> *Dear Sir, Madam*
>
> *A CASE OF PERJURY*
>
> *As a named executor of my late father's Will, who was bypassed in the execution of my solemn duty by way of an oath being sworn by Wendy Hindley, with the aid of Eastleys lawyers, stating that they had given notice that they would proceed as sole executors; this statement was knowingly false as no notice was ever received by my lawyer or myself at the time.*
>
> *The enclosed Affidavit, as you will be aware, confirms this. I have also enclosed a 'Statement of Truth' from the lawyer, who was acting, at the time, on my behalf.*
>
> *As perjury is a serious crime I would ask you to act or take the appropriate measures.*
> *Yours faithfully*
> *Miss Susan Goodsell*
> *Enc.*'

The following is the content of the email sent to DI Thomas:

Dear Mr. Thomas
Re: Perjury relating to the late Mr. Alan Edward Hindley's Last Will & Testament

I have attached a copy of my Affidavit, sworn, signed and witnessed, which reiterates what I have been saying to you and other police officers; as you are aware I can support it with evidence. You should also be aware that the lawyer dealing with my late father's affairs has also completed a 'Statement of Truth' which mirrors my affidavit and would, if required, be willing to swear to it on oath also.

You now have two sworn oaths which contradict each other therefore, either Wendy Hindley, with the aid of Eastleys lawyers, or myself, have committed perjury. As perjury is a serious crime I would expect you to treat it as such and investigate immediately.

Yours sincerely
Susan Goodsell

Those that actually replied to my correspondence, which it must be said was all but one, certainly made interesting reading and revealed a lot about the state the British justice system is really in; it is interesting to note that it was HMCS Crown Court, Maidstone who failed to reply, their action of inaction reveals so much.

These replies, as you will see for yourself, confirm that to commit perjury in the United Kingdom is not serious enough to induce, at the very least an investigation and certainly not legal action. Each and every one of the recipients confirm by their pen or silence that perjury will be, and is acceptable, within the Crown Courts, the Probate Registry, Britain's Police Force and by their actions and/or inaction over the past few years, the Ministry of Justice.

I'll begin by sharing with you the response of the Chief Constable of Kent. It is interesting to note that by not investigating me for perjury it becomes obvious that they must believe that I am telling the truth. Therefore, Wendy

Hindley must be the one who has perjured herself; hence the instruction to contact the Devon Constabulary.

*Dear Ms. Goodsell,*

*I refer to your letter dated 12$^{th}$ March 2011, to the Chief Constable, which is linked to your complaint dated 20$^{th}$ November 2010, regarding the conduct of officers from Kent Police relating to the investigation of allegations of fraud by false representation. The allegations surround the execution of your late fathers will, following his death in 2002.*

*During the investigation into your complaint it has become clear matters surrounding your fathers will were investigated by Devon and Cornwall Police, Major Investigations Branch, at the time under Operation Richmond. It has been established this investigation was the subject of complaints you made to Devon and Cornwall Police, Professional Standards Department in 2003 and 2005.*

*I note in your letter to the Chief Constable you now wish to make an allegation of perjury and have forwarded an Affidavit detailing the allegation.*

*I am writing to advise you the most appropriate authority to deal with this allegation are Devon and Cornwall Police, who conducted the original investigation and may have already addressed this matter. Should you wish to pursue this matter, you should forward the relevant documentation to Devon and Cornwall Police, Professional Standards Department, Police Headquarters, Middlemoor, Exeter, EX2 7HQ. They will review the matter and forward to the relevant department. I enclose the original Affidavit you forwarded us.*

*In relation to the complaint regarding the conduct of Kent officers, you will be notified in the near future of the outcome of this investigation.*
*Yours sincerely*
*John Coull Detective Chief Inspector'*

It can be taken as read that DI Karl Thomas made it very clear via an email that he wanted no part in this or any further dealings with me. The correspondence received from the Probate Office, as serious as it is, which it certainly is, when you consider the implications, and makes one question the reason for their existence – Yet another rip off for the UK tax payers, gave me a chuckle; they are obviously expecting, or are they wanting, yet more correspondence from me? I suppose it lifts their boredom, other than rubber stamp papers as they pass through their offices, they're good for little else. Well, that's my opinion and with what I have experienced, I have no other reason to think any differently.

> 'Dear Madam,
> ***RE ALAN EDWARD HINDLEY – Deceased***
> *Thank you for your letter dated 11th March 2011.*
> *The Probate Registry is non contentious and cannot advise you on this matter. You may wish to seek legal advice as to how you should proceed.*
> *We look forward to further correspondence.*
> *Yours faithfully*
> *Miss H. Drummond'*

The reply received from DS Yarwood of the Devon & Cornwall Constabulary had been eagerly awaited for this reply, as it would be needed before this account of our latest fight could be shared with you; his reply proved to be invaluable and the new information given to us is not only confirming how it is possible, and do-able, to commit the 'perfect crime' in the United Kingdom without any fear of punishment or real action by the British Police or United Kingdom Justice System. But there is something else; first read the reply received from Yarwood of the Devon and Cornwall Police:

*'Subject:* Reference your case

*Dear Mr. Hindley and Mrs. Goodsell,*

*I have reviewed the further evidence submitted by yourselves in respect of the alleged altering of the Will of Alan Edward Hindley, and alleged Perjury.*

*I have submitted the statement from Mr. Michael Ansell (MA) for consideration by our Scenes of Crimes Managers, and discussed the document with them.*

*I have discussed the investigation conducted into the death of Mr. Alan Hindley with a number of officers involved in the case. Also the issues they examined, and the conclusions they reached.*

*I have possession of the Affidavits you have both kindly supplied in support of an allegation that Wendy Hindley lied to the Court thus committing Perjury.*

*Firstly, I must explain that the 'level' or 'balance' of proof in Criminal Case's is much higher than in a civil proceeding. The effect of this is to allow the tendering of evidence including hearsay evidence, or opinion, into a Civil Case where it may be excluded or ignored in a Criminal Proceeding. The evidence of expert witnesses can be included in either process; however the aforementioned level of proof still applies.*

*Secondly, witness evidence is also the subject of scrutiny by the courts who take account of the proximity i.e. independence of the witness from the proceedings, whether the evidence is corroborated, either by documentary or physical evidence.*

*Evidence is assessed in applying the 'Full Code Evidential Test'. This is a set of checks and measures originating from Crown Prosecution Service Guidelines on Charging. There are two stages, the 'evidential stage', (applied first) and the 'public interest' stage (applied second). I mention this because it goes some way to explain the decision making process both for the Police, and the Crown.* This code in its entirety is available on the internet should you wish to examine the detail. Of the two tests it is the 'evidential test' which is most applicable as the offences you have alleged against Mrs. Wendy Hart (previously Mrs. Wendy Hindley) would in all likeliness be in the 'public interest' to prosecute, should there be sufficient evidence to prosecute.

It is in this area that your case has run into difficulty in respect of the criminal law (4.5 and 4.6 refers Full Code Test Evidential Stage). Prosecutors must be satisfied that there is sufficient evidence to provide a realistic prospect of conviction against each subject on each charge. They must consider what the defence case may be, and how it is likely to affect the prospects of a conviction. A case which does not pass the evidential stage MUST not proceed, no matter how serious or sensitive it may be. What this means is there is no room for running a prosecution in a Criminal Court on anything other than the strongest evidence.

A jury may only convict if it is sure the defendant is guilty. The standard applied here is 'beyond all reasonable doubt'.

In respect of the alleged Fraud Act offence against Mrs. Hindley in the forging of signatures on the Will of Mr. Hindley; The original enquiry has already investigated the allegation, and was in possession of the report from Mr. Michael Ansell, a copy of which you have forwarded to me. Their conclusion was 'The level of evidence that the Police Service relies upon to forward a prosecution case would not have been reached if it were tended on behalf of the Crown. The number of signatures and samples (controlled or otherwise) that have been used to provide expert evidence are minimal, and cannot be relied upon to categorically state that there have been any alterations or forgeries within the document. This view has been supported both by staff within Force Forensic Departments (Senior BCU Scenes of Crime Managers) and a Senior Prosecutor.' I have also consulted a senior Scenes of Crime manager, re submitting the report you sent me, and he concurs with this view. There have also been enquiries with Eastleys *lawyers, and an independent witness who was present at the signing of the Will. They both corroborate the genuine nature of the will. Eastleys then state that security arrangements relating to Wills were maintained throughout the material times and there could be no 'third party' involvement in alterations of documents which were under their control. They stated that there had been no incidents of insecurity either within the Probate office or Eastleys since the will was submitted. Mr. D. A. Jones (lawyer) was also interviewed, being a primary signatory to the Will, and confirmed that he was entirely sure that the will has not been tampered with.*

*Both of these independent witnesses seriously undermine the credibility of Mr. Ansells report, which cannot be relied upon anyway for the above reasons.*

*I have the affidavits' you have both kindly supplied. I have consulted with Mr. Bailey of Stigant lawyers in Chatham also. I also have read some of the material published on the internet by your selves. I also note your comments, Mr. Hindley, on the honesty of the contents. I do not dispute anyone's honesty or integrity, nor your right to freely report matters accurately, and truthfully. Unfortunately the affidavits' do not provide new evidence sufficient to instigate criminal proceedings for perjury, to reopen the case, or instigate a new enquiry. This is for the reasons above, independent witnesses to the trueness, and integrity of the Will and the management of it. A full investigation has been carried out by an investigative team and concluded that no criminal offences have been committed. The Senior Crown Prosecutor in the case stated that all lines of enquiry were exhausted and the evidence points to their having been 'no tampering with the disputed will.'*

*These may, however, be of assistance in a Civil Action against Eastleys for the mishandling of the process when dealing with the estate. I am not a practitioner of Civil Law and recommend that you consult a Civil Lawyer if you have not already done so, in order to present your case and assess the chances of success with a civil proceeding. If you decide to take Civil Action, the police can be called as witnesses to assist, as can other material witnesses who have formed part of the original criminal investigation. The standard of proof in this arena is on the 'balance of probabilities' i.e. 60/40 and the Courts have more freedom to hear opinion and hearsay when reaching judgements. It is for the resolution of these very issues of fairness, and entitlement to financial compensation, that the civil process exists.*

*I understand that this is not the outcome you wished for, and that you will be disappointed with the result. I have looked at this from an independent viewpoint as someone unconnected with the original incident, or subsequent investigation. It is clear that the original investigative team were in possession of the report of Mr. Ansell, and have made extensive enquiries into the veracity of both the signatures and the witnesses involved. They have consulted with Senior members of the Crown Prosecution Service who have concluded that there is insufficient evidence to prosecute, and that as far as the Criminal law is concerned, we would be unsuccessful should we attempt to prosecute Eastleys, or Mrs. Hindley, for a criminal offence.*

*I am happy to discuss this with you further. I will be in the office on Tuesday the 3rd of May 2011 from 0800hrs.*
*Yours'*

Now you too have learned that Wendy Hindley has actually married the gardener, co-conspirator and lover, David Hart. If ever there was cause and motive for a conspiracy to murder, it could not be more obvious.

The CONCLUSION is simple; we have proved that you can lie under oath, and on an Affidavit with absolute impunity: You can lie through your teeth without fear of any reprimand. If you want to commit any crime, just lie in your statement, no matter what form and you will walk free. This case proves it and sets the precedent.

One of us committed perjury and the British justice system has allowed it to go unchecked.

# CHAPTER 46

## RESUME RECEIVED FROM MP

The following letter has been sent to my MP, Jonathan Shaw in reply to his letter, which also contained a copy of the resume of his involvement with the issues I have raised with him.

*30 April 2011*
*Rt. Hon Jonathan Shaw MP*
*411 High Street,*
*Chatham,*
*Kent, ME4 4NU*

*Dear Mr. Shaw*

*I am in receipt of your letter dated 31$^{st}$ January, and the copy of your action log and note the contents.*

*Please note that the action log is incorrect. For example, there is no mention of my letter to you dated 01/08/2008 (copy enclosed) which advises you that our story is being published on the website: howsafeisawillintheuk.com (as this letter will be). In your 'Case Outline', bullet point June 2009 reads: 'JS confirmed that he had not heard from her since January 2007...' This is not the case.*

*As you have not cooperated by forwarding my letters to your various ministerial colleagues requesting a meeting with them, I have written to them independently. You are fully aware that this case is very complex and requires action from several Ministries.*

*To date I have had only one government department which has had the courtesy to reply; and that is Mr. James Ross on behalf of Baroness Scotland of the Attorney General's Office; a copy of that letter is enclosed. In this letter Mr. Ross informs me that it is for you to act to instigate a change in the laws relating to the executorships of the last will and testament.*

*As you are fully aware the law as it stands makes a mockery of any person's will, even when written by a lawyer, because any executor(s) can, if they wish, partially or completely, ignore the contents of a will (it is written into the legislation). Executor(s) can, and do, dishonour the deceased and their desires for the disposal of their worldly belongings: Our case is not an isolated one, there are many.*

*Also, for your consideration, I would bring to your attention that the legal profession promotes their services in compiling wills under the pretence of validity of their wills, but they know it is a false claim; they are in reality promoting their work under false pretences; and, what is worse, they are fully aware that this is the case. A last will and testament, whether written by a lawyer or anybody else, is actually worthless in English law.*

*The law needs to be changed and action to change this ridiculous law must be taken now, and I would also respectfully suggest the law should be made to act in retrospect.*

*I await you confirmation that you have taken the appropriate action.*

*Yours sincerely*
*Enc*

## A copy of the letter sent to Jonathan Shaw on the 1st August 2008

*01/08/2008*
*Mr. J. Shaw MP*
*411 High Street*
*Chatham*
*Kent ME4 4NU*

*Dear Mr. Shaw*

*Re: Mr. A. E. Hindley*

*Just a short note by way of courtesy to keep you informed.*

*Following the failure of the law and legal system etc. we have started to make public all the events that followed the death of my father. Naturally this will take a little more time to complete and later to transfer to a media with wider readership.*

*People have a right to know the reality of their society, even if it is not good news. The ordinary man in the street should know if justice exists for him or not.*

*It is anticipated that before long everything will be in place, meanwhile the start of the story can be found at www.myspace.com by typing saphireanimal@aol.com into the 'Browse friends' bar.*

*Yours sincerely*

We are in the process of analyzing Jonathan Shaw's resume received with the above letter dated 4th February; this resume is incomplete and inaccurate. As soon as we have finished the task, both the resume and our comments will be added to the web site.

### Jonathan Shaw's Log analysed

Before I give you a copy of my MP's log of his involvement in this case I do wish to make something quite clear. When you read the log of Jonathan Shaw's involvement in the case you may well feel that I have had many meetings with him; this is not so, there has been only two. My first meeting was on Thursday 10th November 2005 which lasted 5 minutes. Then on Friday 15th December 2009 there was a second and final meeting lasting some 12 minutes.

These are just some of the points that need highlighting:

**October 2005** "Bob Marshall-Andrews QC MP, Peter's MP, says there is nothing further he can do at this stage." Reading this one would assume that he had previously acted in some way, but that is not the case; he has done nothing constructive whatsoever; he had only responded to an appeal for help by writing to say he could do nothing.

**Thursday 10th November 2005** During this initial short session Jonathan Shaw told us, (Peter was present on this occasion), that our only course of action was a Judicial Review: Although, what this is, what it involves and how you obtain this, or what it may cost, has never been disclosed by any party. Also Jonathan Shaw told us that his secretary (wife) had spoken with a Mr. Withers at the Independent Police Complaint Commission at St. Mellons, Wales who told her that we had seen Mr. Withers. This was an outright lie and Jonathan Shaw's face showed that he was furious at being given false information; his face literally turned crimson. He said he would contact Mr. Withers himself about the matter (we heard nothing more).

In frustration of the situation Peter made it quite clear that if we did not get satisfaction we would release the facts to the public; Jonathan Shaw advised us that that was a matter for the family to decide. My response was simply a confirmation of Peter's statement, as we had nothing to hide. At this Mr. Shaw's face reddened and the meeting was abruptly ended.

**May 2006** We learn in the log that Jonathan Shaw, on hearing of the forensic experts opinion that the signature on the will is most likely to be a forgery; Jonathan telephoned the lawyer, Michael French, to seek information about how this new evidence could be used: Michael French was reported to be investigating possibilities, but nothing happened, the silence has been deafening. This same evidence of forgery was given to the Devon and Cornwall Police, but they dismissed it. They wrote saying that two witnesses had given statements that the signature was authentic and proper; but did not say who those two witnesses were: The most likely would have been Wendy

Hindley, the deceased's widow, who would have played her part in the forgery, and Kay, Wendy Hindley's friend, who worked in the lawyer's office probate department, and who would have willingly complied with Wendy's wishes. It is most unlikely that the police would have traced the lawyer who drafted the will, and now practices law in the Caribbean, to get his statement. They have proved themselves seriously lacking in all other aspects involving their work so why should we suspect that on this occasion anything would be different.

**February/March 2006** My complaint was made as instructed by Jonathan Shaw (my letter follows). I received a reply much like that of the IPCC – nothing is actually done.

*13/06/05*
*HMCS Customer Service Unit*
*5th Floor*
*Clive House*
*70 Petty France*
*London SW1H 9HD*

*Dear Sir, Madam*

*I wish to make a formal complaint.*

*I have followed procedures set out in Baroness Catherine Ashton's letter dated 17th May 2006 and have been most dissatisfied with the service received from all parties relating to HMCS. I have enclosed correspondence, in date order, which relates to my complaint, totaling 62 pages; they make interesting reading.*

*We first telephoned and wrote to Bristol on 22nd November 2005 regarding the release of my father's will to Michael Ansell, forensic expert. He signed the necessary paperwork on 11th February 06 to have it released to him, note your clause that permits this course of* action had not been deleted from your form. This matter was raised in the correspondence dated 14th March 06, but to date it has not been acknowledged or justified by Bristol Probate Office. Bristol Probate Office also chose to ignore correspondence dated 31st March sent to Mrs. Peacock, jointly signed by Peter Hindley and myself; these are not the only letters ignored!

The probate office has been most obstructive and has made it almost impossible for me, as a named executor and trustee of my late Father's will and estate, to carry out my legal duty. Should I have been elderly or uneducated in these matters then an injustice would have been perpetrated. The report from the forensic expert proves this.

Furthermore, not only have they been obstructive to the extreme they also charged for their appalling and totally inadequate service. Surely as tax payers we are being asked to pay twice?

I was somewhat puzzled to note that payment for the release of the will was paid directly to a Miss H Drummond's personal account; as I understood it, we would be paying Her Majesty's Court Services. I can only ascertain from this action that our payment was not recorded by the courts, therefore bypassing payment of taxes to the state. How can this be justified?

Yours faithfully

***January 2010*** At the second and last meeting with Jonathan Shaw I made it crystal clear, and he fully understood, that I have far more to publish - evidence and information.

# CHAPTER 47

## *Formal Complaint to the Kent Police*

The following letters are self explanatory as far as showing how far we have exhausted all avenues during our investigations with the usual negative response from the British Police Force.

Mr. E. Harris
Service Delivery Unit
Professional Standards Department
Kent Police
18 April 2011
Dear Mr. Harris

I am in receipt of your e-mail dated 13 April 2011 and note the contents in which you ask a question regarding Ms. Susan Goodsell; the answer you hold is in your file.

Unquestionably my formal complaint is separate and independent of any other you may have and to aid you I will clarify the following points: The Kent Police have repeatedly failed to reply or respond within the time limits you specify and publish on your web site.

Your Detective Leeming requested from Susan Goodsell that she should obtain numerous new examples of her late father (Alan Edward Hindley, deceased) as 'New Evidence,' Your officer said that Ms. Goodsell could obtain those signatures easier than he; I respectfully suggest that was an absolute lie.

Two weeks later when Ms. Goodsell phoned that same officer to arrange delivery of the signatures that he requested as 'New Evidence' she was told that the case was closed.

Your officer refused to accept the signatures he had asked for as 'New Evidence.'

In fact ,I paid the fees to obtain those signatures to help Ms. Goodsell, but I am on a limited income and the only regular money I receive is my UK Invalidity Benefit, which amounts to less than £100.00 per week. Obviously I am not in a financial position to squander money at the behest of an idle British Policeman.

I require from you complete reimbursement of the monies (approximately £200.00).

By your officer's actions one must assume he had no intention of using those signatures that he requested, and that he closed the case as he closed the door behind Ms. Goodsell when she left his office: He probably thought that she would never be able to obtain what she did; he smugly thought he had set an impossible task.

You cannot underestimate how appalled I am about the actions (more correctly, inactions) of the Kent Constabulary.

As a public relations exercise it could not be worse. In fact, if you fail to offer an unqualified apology, openly severely reprimand all officers who have been directly and indirectly involved in this case, and reimburse me fully.

Failure to do the later will naturally indicate that the Kent Constabulary do not believe in justice or natural justice; in reality you will be putting a value on the ethics of your organisation of £200.00.

The British Police boast that they are the best police force in the world: Would such a statement be true under the circumstances mentioned above?

The British Police say they are there to serve; But who do they serve, not the public in this case.

I await news of your actions and your cheque.

Yours sincerely.

Two weeks later having had no response from The Kent Police I sent the following e-mail to Mr. E. Harris:

4 May 2011
Mr. E. Harris
Service Delivery Unit
Professional Standards Department

Kent Police

## **Re. Formal Complaint**

Dear Mr. Harris

Further to my e-mail dated 18 April 2011, I have received no acknowledgement from you, and now require you to give me the reference number of my Official Complaint, and the name and number of the officer who will be dealing with my case.

I look forward to receiving your reply by return.

Yours sincerely

Peter Hindley

http://www.howsafeisawillintheuk.com

I know that the Kent Police choose whether to act when a British Subject makes a formal complaint against them; now I wait to see whether they do the same again in this case.

# CHAPTER 48

# PERFECT INCOMPETENCE

As discussed earlier the police choose which formal complaint against them they investigate. As you read carefully you will see that they have chosen to do nothing, which they are so good at and, Mr. E. Harris of the Kent Police Force has created for me, a sister! It's all clever stuff!

*Dear Mr. Hindley,*
*I refer to your letter dated the 18th April 2011, and can advise you that after due consideration your complaints will not be recorded under the provisions of section 12 of the Police Reform Act 2002. The reason for this decision is that your complaints are about the outcome of a previous complaint investigation undertaken at the request of your sister.....*
*You do have a right to appeal against this decision to The Independent Police Complaints Commission, as outlined in the in the following link,*
*http://www.ipcc.gov.uk/Pages/info_leaflets.aspx, - decision not to record.....*
*This appeal must be made direct to The Independent Police Complaints Commission within 28 days of your receipt of this email.*
*Yours sincerely,*
*Eddie Harris*
*PSD Advisor*
*Service Delivery Unit*
*Professional Standards Department*
*Kent Police*

MY REPLY FOLLOWS:
*Dear Mr. Harris*

*I am in receipt of your e-mail and note that you have given me a sister. My parents would be very surprised if they were alive, as am I; and personally I would appreciate you giving me her details so that we can meet for the first time.*

*Thank you in anticipation.*
*Yours sincerely*

Needless to say, Mr. Harris did not appreciate my reply, and that is unfortunate. Subsequently I wrote to Chief Inspector Learmonth on 7th May 2011 at the Police headquarters adding this example of incompetence to my formal complaint which is unacceptable for them to nullify.

# CHAPTER 49

# BLUEPRINT FOR MURDER?

So you have recently discovered that Wendy Hindley is now Wendy Hart and has actually married the gardener, David Hart.

Our account could not read more like a Catherine Cookson novel if we had designed it so; it has arrived at this episode as predicted so much earlier: The main differences is that this story uncovers murder, fraud, corruption, inefficiency and conspiracy in England; but do not forget this is neither a romantic novel nor is it a crime thriller; this is an actual account of what has happened. Everything has been recorded accurately and everything has actually happened.

What is unnerving is the knowledge that this is not an isolated case, we have been given other accounts by our readers, and I gathered many more stories while interviewing people for the Metropolitan Police of London; but they are for use on another day.

Note well: This is not the end of this saga for there is more work to be done, and it is already in hand.

Today, with the latest information, gives us the opportunity to highlight some of the facts; it may help you to understand more of the complicated plot.

The final part of the puzzle is the marriage of Wendy Hart (formerly Wendy Hindley) to the gardener, David Hart. It is absolutely certain that these two were having an affair at the time of the untimely (or for them, very fortuitous and timely,) demise of Wendy's husband, Alan Hindley.

I would suggest that it was Alan's discovery of this affair that induced him to change his Will and start divorce proceedings in the days shortly before his death. But let us change the format here and list some of the crucial facts and anomalies surrounding the death of Alan Hindley.

• The marriage between Alan and Wendy Hindley was not a good one and they had slept in separate bedrooms for a considerable time.

• Alan was serious about a divorce, and Wendy would be fully aware that he would do everything he could to protect all he had worked for in his life, (Wendy had contributed precious little to their wealth) and had cost Alan many thousands of pounds with her loose tongue when she was drunk. He would have concealed all he could from her, just as he had with the Inland Revenue (they discovered nothing, so what chance would an alcoholic with little business sense have?). She would, if the divorce happened, lose so much, and she knew she could end her time with virtually nothing, even homeless.

• Alan did not trust Wendy with business matters and he did not disclose the full extent of his wealth to her.

• Alan Hindley was absolutely furious with Wendy during the weekend before his death: His daughter, Susan, had never known such fury from her father before, although I had seen similar.

• He was seen leaving a lawyer's office by his friend during the week following that weekend, and before his death a few days later: He told his friend that he had been changing his will.

• Alan had a mistress, Joan Tabram of Brixham, Devon. And by her admission, the affair was continuing at the time of Alan's death.

• Ellie Waugh of Brixham, a friend of Joan Tabram, has said she has seen the new will and knew exactly what it contained.

- Alan and Joan had a flat which they used for their 'rendezvous'.
- According to Joan Tabram, Alan kept a selection of his Building Society and bank account statements away from the marital home.
- We know from Joan Tabram that Alan's building society books showed enough money to build the 6 detached houses in the grounds of Shorton Cottage, and buy his much yearned for Rolls Royce, yet just days before he died he had arranged a substantial loan: This loaned money was more likely a rouse to prove he had nothing for Wendy at the time of his imminent divorce.
- Wendy was in fact an alcoholic, and if you needed proof you simply had to watch her hands tremble in the morning and there were bottles of vodka etc. distributed throughout the house in the most unlikely places.
- So how do we know the affair between David Hart and Wendy Hindley was current at the time of Alan's death? Well it was David who had to have his favourite lunchtime snack when he was working in the grounds of Shorton Cottage (Alan was constantly complaining about the food Wendy was preparing for him, and I have personally experienced that and can confirm that it was dire,) but of course she did not need to eat much as the majority of her nutrition was about 40% proof and came out of a bottle.
- Another indication was, during the week after Alan's death, Wendy was very concerned that one particular neighbour would call, via the kitchen door at the back of the house, and she made it her priority to stop this happening; obviously she would not like to be discovered in flagrante delicto.
- Strange at the time was the fact that it was David Hart, the 'casual gardener' who was doing all the

arrangements for the funeral; he was not a particularly close friend of the deceased. He continued to manage the affairs from that time on.

- On the day before my brother's funeral, David Hart told me that he had found his soul mate, I thought it strange the next day when I repeated this to his, then current wife, Jacqui, and her and David's reaction: Being naive I assumed it was Jacqui who was the 'soul mate' not my brother's widow. Incidentall,y David Hart had not been married to Jacqui for more than a few years, and she was not his first wife, possibly not his second or third or fourth (I had been told, but did not bother to remember, the lifestyle of this bankrupt was of little interest to me): It will be interesting to see how long Wendy remains Mrs. Hart.
- During the week following Alan's demise the place of his death changed from 'his chair in the study' to 'the chair in his bedroom' then again to 'the floor of his bedroom', then at the same place, but this time in 'Wendy's arms'; but somehow he managed to get himself onto his bed after he died which puzzled Wendy. If only that was where the versions stopped, but much later the Devon and Cornwall Police were told that he died on the main stair case. I know Alan Hindley was a person who did not conform easily to anything and was a very independent thinker, but this is really taking matters too far.
- Wendy, by her various accounts of Alan's demise, has shown herself to be a liar, but like most liars they do not always have a sufficiently good memory of what they have said; if you are going to lie you need the memory of an elephant, not the folded skin of one.
- It should be noted that with all the versions of his death in his bedroom Wendy said she was in the main kitchen when she heard him cry out; two factors do not ring true; firstly, if you are having a massive heart attack you

cannot cry out, secondly even if he had, it would not have been heard in that kitchen, the layout of the house and the thickness of the walls would have absorbed the sound, even if the television or radio were not on, and they invariably were as Wendy would turn one of them on as she entered the kitchen (an automatic reaction witnessed by many).

• For those who have seen 'Sunset Boulevard' you will know the scene when the delusional Norma Desmond descends the staircase and announces to all the she is ready for her close-up: Well Wendy did just that, she descended the main staircase (presumably she had partaken some more falling down water concealed in the bedside cabinet) and announced to all, "I'm carrying on Alan's work and doing everything for the boys". At the time I thought she meant Alan's two grandsons, but now I know she was doing it for the 'boys' in David Hart's trousers.

Now before we proceed further with the summary of events let us take time to look at the errors in the Will presented by Wendy Hart (previously Hindley).

• Wendy Hart chose to execute this Will as sole executer therefore by- passing myself and Alan Hindley's daughter, Susan. Wendy has lied to the Probate Office when she stated that we were not interested in honouring our duty as named executors. She failed to give information which, as executors we were entitled, and furthermore, she has absolutely ignored the Will and Wishes of her late husband. All, as you know, have been absolutely acceptable to the English Police and United Kingdom Government agencies; hence you now know it is taken as read that you can lie to English police and the Courts without fear of retribution.

• The presented Will is, I am sure, a forgery: Alan Hindley bought 50 Cecil Road, Paignton, Devon, and the lawyers who dealt with the conveyancing omitted to include the easements for services such as gas, water and electricity, although all three were in place when the property was purchased. The result of this lawyer's oversight was a legal fight for negligence which lasted many years, and an out of Court settlement, which paid for Shorton Cottage. More importantly here is the fact that Alan would scrutinise any document and accept and sign only that which was correct: If you glance at the presented Will you will see numerous errors and if you start to study it you will unearth more than twenty; Alan would never sign such a faulty document· Personally I know full well how meticulous he was with the printed word as he helped me with many letters at the time of my divorce.

- As you are aware the signature on the Will was, I am sure one made by David Hart; there are rare characteristics which appear on David's own signature; we did get a forensic expert to analyse the signature on the Will and he reported that he was 95% sure Alan Hindley's signature was a slow copy. As you now know, 95% sure, is insufficient for the Police to take any action (those with criminal intent might find this fact informative; those law abiding folk may find the implications of this fact less than reassuring). More recently the Kent Police refused to accept the new evidence they requested, namely 20 new example's of Alan Hindley's signature.

- The Devon and Cornwall only take the word of independent witnesses, or so they say; but they class the statement of Kaye, a secretary in the probate department of Eastleys lawyers, as independent and choose to ignore the fact that Kaye is a close friend of Wendy Hart's. Now let us consider another aspect of this voyage of discovery: What happened in respect of the authorities at and after the demise, I am loath to use the word murder which is probably more accurate.

- We are told that David Hart was telephoned by Wendy at the time of death (when dealing with the words of a liar one can never be certain); she did not call the doctor or any emergency service which would obviously be the normal action if the circumstances were in fact normal.
- David Hart says he arrived and 'worked on Alan for 15 minutes;' that sounds almost feasible as a possibility until you learn from his own mouth that he is trained in first aid, and he told me that after just 12 minutes all is lost: He was supposed to have travelled to the place of death and then worked to revive Alan for 15 minutes; a total time lapse of at least 20-25 minutes and not a very plausible story. Are we therefore to assume he was present in Shorton Cottage at the time of death? This would be a more realistic scenario to comply with the 15 minutes story. He, Wendy Hart and/or Joan Tabram would know the truth.
- We are told by the current Harts that an ambulance was called, but Alan's body was not taken from the house by them, instead it was removed that night by the undertakers and rested in their premises until the following Monday: This is not a permitted procedure.
- The Police were not informed of Alan's death, although their records were amended at a later date to the contrary. We have written evidence to prove that the Devon Police altered their records to suit their agenda on other occasions.
- A doctor could not be found in Torbay to give the second signature to the death certificate until the eve of the cremation.

- The coroner's report gives Alan's height as 5' 8" when all my life, I and other members of the family have known him to be 5'10 1/2". Perhaps they had an elastic tape measure or another corpse. With so many irregularities nothing can be discounted.
- Thinking of Alan's corpse, Wendy could not have been more eager to have it destroyed, and challenged the undertakers representative persistently regarding the delay of a week; she wanted rid of the body within one or two days.

Now let us turn to Alan's Mistress, Joan Tabram, who no doubt had a desire to be the mistress of the house; could it be the same ambition for David Hart? He has now elevated himself from a bankrupt to the Master of the House.

Although I do feel that Joan has not walked away from all this without a profit: Certainly she has not always been honest with us: She lied about being at the funeral.

So what are we looking at here?

The perfect crime!

# EPILOGUE

This book begins with many examples of paranormal experiences; they are there to give the foundation of what was to follow. We have deliberately omitted the many experiences we had along the way, perhaps that's for another day. There was no point in recording every time an unsolicited document arrived when it was needed or when information was given at the crucial moment. Some people may think that it was purely coincidence, but we have a problem with that scenario.

Obviously we had to do our research and seek the information we needed, which was not easy when the scene of Alan's death was more than 200 miles from our homes, and in later years the distance was far greater for me when I left England. Nevertheless, we gathered so much information during our attempt to have the Last Will and Testament of Alan Edward Hindley executed as he wished.

In fact, it was when we were told, for we did not ask, that Wendy Hindley had finally married the gardener, and her long time lover, it triggered the final editing of this book; this gave us confirmation of what we believed to be true, possibly the final piece of the embryonic puzzle.

In the checking and rechecking of the facts we have given you, we have been rediscovering some of our original notes on what we thought was really happening in Devon; it came as quite a shock to have our early thoughts confirmed by all the discoveries we have made during the 9 years that we have worked.

The task and duty Alan had given us as executors has taken us on a journey of discovery. It is true that we have not been able to Honour Alan and his wishes; we have been prevented from doing that by so many: But that does not mean that we have given up, or that we are alone; there are others ready to continue the job.

We had no idea when we started that we would be travelling in so many directions and unearthing what we have; or for that matter writing this true account.

Our hope is that those in authority will be rectifying the abhorrent things we have exposed and that nobody else has to endure a similar experience to ours. Perhaps I am going into the world of fantasy here as we have seen that the movers and shakers only act to protect themselves. But we can hope.

We have recently learned that our first lawyer, Michael French, has had the Law Society sanction his license to practice on two separate occasions, which has severely affected his business, maybe terminally. Both cases involved his handling of the estate of different clients; and I must add, are not related to our case. It is true, he did not do all he could; he has confirmed that recently to Susan. Had he acted correctly we may not have had to go through what we have. I am sure he did not do what he should have in our case.

Would his downfall, and that of Jonathan Shaw, Member of Parliament, be purely coincidence (which I do not believe in)? Both have proved themselves deficient and possibly receiving their just desserts.

I am reminded of my words to the gardener, David Hart, when he first telephoned me on the night of Alan's death; "Oh God! It's started; it is going to be like a pack of cards." Are these two, who have not done what they could to rectify matters, the first two cards to tumble?

It is quite likely.

This may well be the start.

# WHAT TO DO TO CALL FOR CHANGE

Let me explain; it is simple, Government Ministers and Ministries react to the number of letters received on any subject; the more they receive the quicker they work, so please write now; if you write to the following it will get these people working.

It does not matter where on the planet you live; whether it is in London or an isolated cottage in Wales, your letters will count.

If you are one of our many friends and followers throughout the world, it does not matter whether you are in the United States of America, Brunei Darussalam, Canada, Australia, Iran, Russia, China, Japan, India or a tiny island in the Pacific Ocean, your input is just as important. So please help us now. Write.

You can simply copy the following letter and post it to as many of the people listed as you wish or send it by e-mail. Each letter will contribute to our cause.

*Your Address*
*Name*
*Address*

*Dear ..............*

**United Kingdom Inheritance Laws**

*I/We wish and require you to act now to rectify the gross errors and shortcomings that have been exposed in the inheritance laws of the United Kingdom.*
*You are fully aware of the case published worldwide on www.howsafeisawillintheuk.com which highlights many serious problems which require your attention and action today. You are fully*

*aware that this is not an isolated case and is an absolute disgrace for Great Britain and its people.*

*You are required to act to change all the relevant laws and regulations now, and all the changes to be retrospective in order to exhibit United Kingdom's acceptance of natural justice.*

*Yours sincerely*

*Send your letters and e-mails to:*

- *Your MP (Member of Parliament)*
- *The Prime Minister, 10 Downing Street, London SW1A*
- *The Deputy Prime Minister, 10 Downing Street, London SW1*
- *Ministry of Justice, Justice Secretary, , Ministry for Justice, 102 Petty France, London SW1H 9AJ*
- *Civil Servant, Mr. Paul Hughes at the Ministry of Justice 102 Petty France, London SW1H 9AJ*
- *The Home Secretary, , Home Office, 2 Marsham Street, London SW1P 4DF*
- *HRH Queen Elizabeth II, Buckingham Palace, London*
- *Your national and local newspapers*
- *Your radio stations*
- *Your television stations*
- *Any Head of State*
- *And friends*

## Meet the Authors

About Peter Hindley:
Peter Hindley is a coach to dance competitors and is a jury member for international dance competitions. He left England in 2007 for a new life in France and has been recording events since his brother's unconventional death in 2002.

About Susan Goodsell:
Susan Goodsell, co-author and Peter's niece, lives in England with her partner and their two now grown-up sons. She spent many years in London before returning to Kent in 1997. The year her father died she began teaching English in a secondary school; now after finishing work, she returns home to begin another shift, as a detective and writer.